"This vivid, Christ-centered
real discipleship will come a

J. I. PACKER

Best-selling author, *Knowing God* and numerous other books

"*The Lost Commandment* resurrects a critical and foundational truth that is key to God's people experiencing and transferring his powerful presence to his church. The 'Lost Commandment' is the key to authentic Christianity."

—TONY EVANS
Senior Pastor, Oak Cliff Bible Fellowship, Dallas, TX
President, The Urban Alternative

"*The Lost Commandment* is a clear and powerful challenge to love others the way Jesus loves us. Individually or in small group discussions, Dave Greber's book will guide you on an exciting, life-changing journey."

—GARRY POOLE
Speaker and author, *Seeker Small Groups*

"*The Lost Commandment* provides a compelling vision for transforming the church and reaching the world by learning how to delight in the sacrificial, reconciling love of Christ and letting it flow through us into the lives of every person we meet. A book that every Christian should read, study, and joyfully live out in daily life."

—KEN SANDE
President, Peacemaker Ministries

"In *Knowing God*, J. I. Packer distinguished knowing about God from knowing God personally; thousands were blessed by his words. In *The Lost Commandment*, Dave Greber distinguishes the Golden Rule from the 'new commandment' Jesus gave his followers; thousands will be blessed by his words. *The Lost Commandment* is a great book—valuable for new Christians, yet more than a refresher course for veterans in the faith."

—KENNETH G. ELZINGA
Robert C. Taylor Professor of Economics, University of Virginia

"In this book, Dave Greber provides some fresh, original thinking about Jesus' 'Lost Commandment.' You cannot read this and remain the same."

—R. Dallas Greene
Senior Pastor, Grace Community Church, Frederick, MD

"In this well-written, practical book, the heart and calling of Jesus is put on clear display."

—Jeff Bogue
Lead Pastor, Grace Church, Greater Akron, OH

"*The Lost Commandment* has impacted my thinking and my preaching and my life. My prayers for others and with others have changed. It has even changed how I view and work with people who are difficult to love!"

—Michael Brubaker
Pastor, Grace Community Church, Frederick, MD

"My small group loved studying this convicting, insightful, practical, and thought-provoking book. *The Lost Commandment* helped us deepen our walk with Christ by showing us how to live out Jesus' command to love one another as he has loved us."

—Monte Festog
Small group leader

THE LOST COMMANDMENT

Have We Missed What Jesus Really Wants?

DAVE GREBER

Kregel
Publications

The Lost Commandment: Have We Missed What Jesus Really Wants?

© 2009 by Dave Greber

Published by Kregel Publications, a division of Kregel, Inc., P.O. Box 2607, Grand Rapids, MI 49501.

The Greek font used in this book is SymbolGreekU and is available from www.linguistsoftware.com/lgku.htm, +1-425-755-1130.

Excerpt from *Pay It Forward* granted courtesy of Warner Bros. Entertainment Inc.

The author is represented by MacGregor Literary, 2373 NW 185th Ave., Suite 165, Hillsboro, OR 97124.

This book is printed on acid-free paper.

Library of Congress Cataloging-in-Publication Data
Greber, Dave.
The lost commandment : have we missed what Jesus really wants? / Dave Greber.
    p.   cm.
Includes bibliographical references.
1. Love—Religious aspects—Christianity. 2. God—Love. 3. Jesus Christ—Teachings. I. Title.
BV4639.G74   2009   231'.6—dc22   2009011548

ISBN 978-0-8254-2935-4

Printed in the United States of America

09 10 11 12 13 / 5 4 3 2 1

CONTENTS

Acknowledgments   7
Introduction   9

PART 1—Joy: The Surprise of Christ's Love

   1. Find Complete Joy   15
   2. More Costly Than Gold   29

PART 2—Relationship: The Invitation of Christ's Love

   3. RSVP   47
   4. Enjoy Your New Self   57
   5. Shadow the Real VIP   67

PART 3—Mission: The Determination of Christ's Love

   6. No Mission Impossible   77
   7. Leave No One Behind   92

PART 4—Humility: The Heart of Christ's Love

   8. No One Died and Made Us King!   105
   9. The Last Come First   116

PART 5—Obedience: The Power of Christ's Love

  10. Love Letters from God   127
  11. Ask and It's Yours   142
  12. Show Them How It's Done!   149

PART 6—Forgiveness: The Strength of Christ's Love

  13. Let It Go   157
  14. Get It Together   172
  15. Shuttle Diplomacy   190

PART 7 — Service: The Soul of Christ's Love

    16. Feet and Hands   201

    17. Dollars and Sense   210

    18. Who's Next in Line?   217

Conclusion   227

Appendix A: Scriptures That Echo the Lost Commandment   231

Appendix B: How to Create a Reading Plan   241

Notes   251

ACKNOWLEDGMENTS

I could not have responded to God's call to write this book without the love that he expressed to me through people around me. I dedicate this book to my wife, Lynne, my first and most faithful supporter and encourager, who from the first day really believed that God could accomplish his work through me. I love you, Lynne.

Thank you to my daughters, Lauren and Elizabeth, and my parents, Manny and Marie Greber, who read drafts of my work for several years, and offered wise comments and lots of encouragement.

Thank you to those outside my family who provided me with encouragement and support. Marlene Bagnull agreed to edit some of my early work even though her schedule was already overburdened. More importantly, Marlene has consistently prayed for me, and encouraged me to pursue a writing ministry, as she has many other authors through *Write His Answer Ministries*.

At one of Marlene Bagnull's wonderful writing conferences, I met my agent, Chip MacGregor—a godly author, agent, and friend. God used Chip to open doors that I could not open. Thank you, Chip, for your friendship, and for loving God enough to look for books that will make a difference for Christ.

Thank you to Kregel Publications for their publishing ministry, and especially to Dennis Hillman, Steve Barclift, and Cat Hoort. Your kindness and professionalism are inspiring.

Thank you to my pastors for their love and support. Michael Brubaker met with me for lunch throughout the writing process, to act as a sounding board and encourager. Dr. R. Dallas Greene allowed me to borrow books from his study, and has been a consistent encourager.

Thank you to my small group members: Bob and Fran Coss, Monte and Rosemarie Festog, Bob and Chris Laferriere, Faranda Thomas, and Cole and Gina VanDervort. We studied this book together for more than a year, and your feedback made it a better book.

Thank you to my assistants, Parvene Roelkey and Chris Dattilio, for months of help on this project beyond the call of duty.

Thank you to my writers' group, and particularly to Kendra Parsons and Lyle Carlson.

And thank you also to my many other friends who offered comments and support, including Pastor Randy Neubauer, and especially Ken Elzinga, David Troller, and Kurt Prister, each of whom I have known for more than thirty years. I am grateful to God for all of you.

INTRODUCTION

D o to others as you would have them do to you." That's what my pastor preached, quoting the Golden Rule from Luke 6:31. It was an ordinary Sunday, and I settled in for a good sermon on a very familiar theme. As I listened, I looked through the four gospels to read what Jesus said about love.

And then my eyes landed on twenty words that changed my life: Jesus said, "A new command I give you: Love one another. As I have loved you, so you must love one another" (John 13:34).

I'd been a Christian for twenty-five years. How could I have missed this commandment? But when I talked to my Christian friends about it, they too seemed to have missed it. Every person I asked about Jesus' new commandment answered me with a blank stare.

No problem, I thought. Somewhere there must be shelves of books about the new commandment. After all, it was among Jesus' last words at the Last Supper. He even repeated it (John 15:12, 17). And it's been two thousand years since the new commandment was given. It's not so new anymore.

So I went looking. I asked my most devout Christian friends whether they knew of any books on the new commandment. I went to Christian bookstores. I searched the Internet. I went to a seminary library. I found almost nothing—and nothing at all of book-length—on what I now consider to be the "Lost Commandment."

I continued to study John 13–16. As I did—as I realized the significance of the Lost Commandment and in particular the surprising link between obedience to the Lost Commandment and joy—my life changed. Jesus said, in effect, "Do you want *me* to take joy in you? Do *you* want to experience complete joy? Then do this: love others as I have loved you!" (John 15:10–12, author's paraphrase).

Practicing obedience to the Lost Commandment brings our faith alive—a faith that results in an amazing, joy-filled life. We discover God's purpose for our lives. We experience Jesus' presence and become more like him as we love others the way he loves us. The Lost Commandment also changes our prayer lives. It enables us to better understand God's will on a day-to-day, moment-by-moment basis. Our relationships improve as we love others the way Jesus loves us. And those who don't know Jesus sense his presence in our lives and want to know more about him. No other verse—including the Golden Rule—better summarizes how God expects Christians to treat other people.

Jesus wants us to experience the complete joy of knowing his will. He doesn't want us to live our lives wondering, "What *would* Jesus do?" Instead, he wants us to know the answer to "What *did* Jesus do?" And then he wants us to do likewise in the power of the Holy Spirit.

This book is a practical guide to loving others in obedience to the Lost Commandment. Two premises guide the way this book is organized and written. The first is that we must focus on the Lost Commandment itself in order to follow it. Jesus said that our obedience to *this* commandment brings joy to him and complete joy to us. And in chapter 1, I describe some of the ways we experience this joy, which thrives even in the midst of pain and adversity.

The Lost Commandment is different from the Golden Rule. That's why Jesus called it "new." No doubt, the world would be a much better place if everyone did follow the Golden Rule. But true as this statement is, it misses the point: Jesus commanded us to go into the world teaching others *everything* that he had commanded us (Matt. 28:20). In chapter 2, then, I explain how the Golden Rule is different from the Lost Commandment, and why I believe Jesus intended to replace the Golden Rule with the Lost Commandment.

The second premise of this book is that everything that Jesus has done for humankind throughout history, as revealed in the Bible or experienced in our individual lives, is both an expression of his love for us and an example of how we are expected to love others. Therefore, to obey the Lost Commandment, we have to become students of Jesus' love for us so that we can better love others in this same way. Part of what brings us joy as we obey the Lost Commandment is, in fact, having a better understanding of the depth and breadth of Christ's love for us.

Whether you agree with the first premise of this book or not, the second premise stands on its own. It is not controversial, and represents the majority of the teaching of this book (chapters 1, 3–18). As followers of Jesus, we are called to demonstrate his presence in our lives by the way that we love others (John 13:35). His life is our life example (John 13:15; 1 Cor. 11:1; 1 Tim. 1:16; 1 Peter 2:21).

As we study Jesus' love for us, particularly as revealed in the New Testament, we discover that it has seven major elements that follow a logical sequence and yield practical principles for our lives with God and others. Parts 1 through 7 of this book express these elements as themes.

Part 1: The primary purpose of our lives is to bring *joy* to Jesus, and to our Father God, by practicing obedience to the Lost Commandment. We also experience complete joy when we follow Jesus' loving example in our lives.

Part 2: To follow Jesus, we must have a close, personal *relationship* with God, whose love for us can heal the pain in our lives, as we follow in Jesus' loving footsteps.

Part 3: Our relationship with God requires us to accept Christ's *mission* to transform our lives, and to bring others into a close, personal relationship with God. We do our part primarily by paying Jesus' love forward to others with the help of the Holy Spirit.

Part 4: Our mission, like Christ's, is an expression of *humility* toward God and others.

Part 5: As we follow Jesus' example, our humble dependence on God enables us to tap into God's power through *obedience* to his commands, the most important of which is to love others as Jesus has loved us. The Holy Spirit gives us the power and understanding that we need to obey God as we speak with God, study his Word, and learn from others who follow Jesus.

Part 6: Our humble obedience to Christ leads us to forgive and serve others. God's *forgiveness* makes it possible for us to become reconciled to him. He commands us to forgive others as he has forgiven us, and he empowers us to reconcile with them. He also helps us to act as peacemakers who help others find peace with each other.

Part 7: As Christ lived his life on earth in *service* to us, so he calls us to serve others as though we were serving Jesus himself. We are called to give time and money to those most in need, according to the priorities God gives to each of us.

This book provides more, though, than an overview and a framework for understanding Jesus' love. It also contains insights and illustrations that demonstrate how to allow Jesus' love to flow to others through our lives. Whether you don't know Jesus, you've just met him, or you've known him for years, this book will help you experience the complete joy that comes from loving others as he has loved us.

I pray that the Holy Spirit will use this book to help you find the only love that brings complete joy, and that leads not merely to life, but to abundant life.

PART 1

JOY

The Surprise of Christ's Love

Chapter 1

FIND COMPLETE JOY

A new command I give you: Love one another. As I have loved you,
so you must love one another. . . . If you obey my commands, you
will remain in my love, just as I have obeyed my Father's commands
and remain in his love. I have told you this so that my joy may be in
you and that your joy may be complete. My command is this: Love
each other as I have loved you.

—JOHN 13:34; 15:10–12

As a kid, I had a knack for losing things. Losing watches was my specialty. I'd put my watch somewhere "safe," and then I'd forget where I put it. The watch might be missing for weeks, or even months. Eventually, I found it in an obvious place. I learned a long time ago that something can be in plain sight and still be lost.

After twenty-five years as a Christian, I noticed a commandment in the New Testament that had been lost to *me* even though it was in plain sight. The verse had been in the gospel of John all along. But it hadn't transformed my mind, changed my heart, or renewed my life because I wasn't aware of its significance.

THE LOST COMMANDMENT

According to Jesus Christ, the greatest Old Testament commandment concerning how people are to treat each other is this: "Love your neighbor as yourself" (Matt. 22:39–40; Lev. 19:18), or to put it another way, "Do to others as you would have them do to you" (Luke 6:31). This commandment is popularly known as the "Golden Rule."

But Jesus, just hours before he was arrested and crucified, profoundly redefined how God expects people to treat each other: "A new command I give you: Love one another. *As I have loved you*, so you must love one another" (John 13:34, emphasis added). And as if to make sure we'd remember it, Jesus repeated this new commandment twice (John 15:12, 17). Based on what I've read and seen, though, I fear that many of us have lost this commandment in plain sight, or have failed to appreciate its tremendous importance. That's why I call John 13:34 the "Lost Commandment."

If we lose sight of the Lost Commandment, we take our eyes off of the road to true joy. Look at the surprising connection that Jesus made between obedience to the Lost Commandment and joy. He said, "If you obey my commands, you will remain in my love, just as I have obeyed my Father's commands and remain in his love. *I have told you this so that my joy may be in you and that your joy may be complete.* My command is this: Love each other *as I have loved you*" (John 15:10–12, emphasis added). If, then, we love each other merely according to the Golden Rule—*as we want to be loved*—rather than according to the Lost Commandment, we've missed Jesus' path to joy.

OUR SEARCH FOR JOY

What would we give to find complete joy for the rest of our lives?

Everyone wants to find complete joy, but in my experience few people possess it. I'm not talking about the joy that comes on predictable occasions—like on the day we're married, or when our children are born, or when we get promoted in our jobs. Predictable joy isn't complete; it's fleeting and depends on circumstances.

I'm talking about joy that comes when nothing special is happening, or even when everything seems to be going wrong. Like when we're grocery shopping, or when our lives are such a mess that we don't want to get out of bed. I'm talking about joy that transcends circumstances, overcomes adversity, and stands the test of time. That's complete joy!

When I was in high school and college, I thought I'd find joy in my relationships with friends and girlfriends. Sure, I enjoyed myself at a few parties and made some friends, but all of the parties and most of the friendships didn't last. One of the loneliest years of my life was, in fact, my last year in college, when I was surrounded by people my own age but didn't feel connected to many of them. Parties and superficial friendships didn't bring me joy that lasts—they left me feeling empty.

Many of us are still looking for joy in casual friendships or recreation. We live for the weekend. We long for retirement. We hope for satisfaction in leisure activities. In the end, we often realize that our lives are empty.

After I got out of graduate school and started working, I thought I'd find joy in professional success. My first job as an attorney was great—at first—but then night after night I had to call my wife, Lynne, to tell her I wouldn't be home for dinner. We'd been married only two years.

One evening as I worked late—again—I gazed at the sunset through my office window. As darkness fell, I could see my reflection in the window. In that moment, I came face-to-face with myself, sitting at my desk in my office, and felt as though I was looking into my future. Would I spend the rest of my life, working day and night while my family waited for me at home? Was this the life that God wanted me to have? I felt dread—not joy.

If we do what the world says to do to find joy, we often come to realize that we'll never find joy that way. "I'm missing something," we say to ourselves, "but I'm not sure what." But if we do what Jesus says we should do to experience joy, we find complete joy in our work, in our play, and even in our suffering.

In our suffering? Yes, even in our suffering!

Consider a typical morning in the life of my friend Ed. He lies in bed after another sleepless night. His legs are swollen and every fiber of his body hurts. Seven years. Seven years of surgeries, chemotherapy treatments, transfusions, prescriptions, and consultations, and yet Ed's body is still racked with pain. Everything hurts. Chemotherapy has destroyed the myelin sheaths that are supposed to insulate Ed's nerves. Now he lives with a constant burning sensation throughout his body.

Yet, thanking Jesus for another day, Ed eases his legs over the side of the bed and gets up to have breakfast with his wife and sons.

Joy fills his heart. *God is so good to me,* he thinks. Ed's love for Jesus and others is greater than Ed's pain and brings him complete and lasting joy.

How can someone like Ed find that kind of joy while we can't find it in recreation or professional success? Although we may not have noticed it, the answer is right in front of us: we will experience complete joy by God's grace when we obey the Lost Commandment.

To experience the complete joy that Jesus promises, we have to first understand how he loves us, and then love others in that same way.

HOW JESUS LOVES US

Jesus loves us the way that God loves Jesus (John 15:9)—with all of his heart, soul, mind, and strength. In addition to joy, we can see six other important elements of Jesus' love for us. As you read about them, ask God to help you examine your own heart and life.

Relationship with God

The Bible reveals that when Jesus walked among us, he considered his faith—his relationship with his Father God—to be the most important priority in his life. He devoted his life to his Father's business. And his Father's business was to love us! Loving God is linked to loving others because God asks us to show our love for him *by loving others as he has loved us.*

Jesus knew exactly who he was and who he was not in relationship to God: He knew that he was his Father's beloved Son and the Messiah, but he also knew that without his Father he could do *nothing* (John 5:19, 30; 8:28).

Jesus' relationship with his Father was evident in his actions. He shadowed and imitated his Father, doing what he saw his Father doing (John 5:17, 19–20).

Do we have a close, personal relationship with God through his Son, Jesus Christ? Are we consistently aware of Jesus' love for us? As an expression of our love for God, do we consciously try to love others in the same way that Jesus loves us?

Mission

Jesus was a man on a rescue mission—and he knew it. He knew that God sent him to earth for a purpose—to make it possible for us to know God and experience his love. Jesus was determined to reach and rescue those who were lost, separated from God by their sin. He came to bridge this gap through his death on the cross. Have we accepted God's mission to bring the love of Jesus to those who don't know him?

Humility

Although Jesus was God in human form, he was willing to put aside his equality with God. He became a humble servant not only to God but also to other human beings, including us (Phil. 2:5–8). Do we think like servants of Jesus? Are we known for our humility toward God and others?

Obedience

Jesus expressed his love for God by loving others in obedience to God's direction. His power to love came from God. He knew that the Scriptures were God's Word, accurate in all their teachings. He prayed constantly to receive guidance and help. Finally, Jesus didn't just *tell* us how to love others; he *showed* us how to love others by the way he loves us. Do we consistently spend time reading the Bible and praying for understanding of how God wants us to love others? Do our actions and words reflect obedience to God's Word by modeling Christ's love for others and teaching others by example?

Forgiveness

If it weren't for Jesus' forgiveness, his love for us would last only as long as it takes us to commit our first sin against him—not very long. Jesus loves us so much that he died to pay the price for our sins, knowing that even after becoming his followers, we would continue to sin. Do we forgive others the way Jesus forgives us? Do we promote forgiveness by being reconcilers and peacemakers the way he is?

Service

When he walked among us, Jesus was a servant to his core. He devoted his time and his resources to loving us in obedience to God's priorities for his life. Do we act like servants of Jesus? Do we serve others—particularly the poor, the ill, and the lonely—as though we were serving Jesus himself?

HAVE WE LOST THE LOST COMMANDMENT?

Do we love others as Jesus loves us? If we ask the Holy Spirit, he will tell us. The Bible gives us two important and practical tests to confirm whether we heard his answer correctly. First, are we experiencing complete joy in our lives (John 15:11)? One study has shown that "the more deeply committed to Christianity a person is, the more likely they are to experience greater self-confidence, peace, and fulfillment."[1] Second, do people generally know that we are Christians because we love them the way that Jesus loves us (John 13:35)? If the answers to these questions are yes, then we're probably obeying the Lost Commandment.

Why, however, am I concerned that many of us may have lost the Lost Commandment? In part because most of us have been taught, and are teaching others, that we're supposed to love others according to the Golden Rule rather than according to the Lost Commandment. We can easily find books or sermons that characterize the Golden Rule as the essence of what it means to follow Christ, but, in my experience, it's almost impossible to find a book or sermon that focuses on the Lost Commandment.

What concerns me most, though, is not just the general lack of complete joy that I perceive among Christians, or what's being written or taught. It's what many of us as Christians think that suggests to me that a lot of us have lost the Lost Commandment. Consider how Christians responded to some survey questions:

We know that Jesus loves us so much that he brought us God's good news of love, all the way from heaven. He then commanded us to carry his message to all nations (Matt. 28:19–20). But only 47 percent of Christians say that the statement, "I believe it is important to share my faith with my neighbor because Christ has commanded me to do so," applies completely to them.[2]

Jesus loves us so much that he paid the penalty for our sin by dying on the cross for us so that God would forgive our sins. Jesus commanded us to forgive others (Matt. 6:14–15). But only 55 percent of Christians say that the statement, "God's grace enables me to forgive people who have hurt me," applies completely to them.[3]

Jesus gives us everything that we have and then asks us to care for the poor and suffering as though we were caring for him (Matt. 25:31–46). But only 44 percent of Christians say that the statement, "God calls me to be involved in the lives of the poor and suffering," completely applies to them.[4]

Numerous opinion surveys, in fact, suggest that Christians are often not even *aware* that Jesus commands us to love others the way he has loved us. This wouldn't be the case if the message of the Lost Commandment were ringing loud and clear in the Christian church.

So what about that second test? Do people generally know us as Christians by our love (John 13:35)? Apparently not. A 2002 survey by The Barna Group indicates that, whatever our intentions as Christians may be, few non-Christian adults have positive views of Christians.[5] Only a small percentage of non-Christians "strongly believe that the labels 'respect, love, hope, and trust' describe Christianity."[6]

I can't fully explain why many of us have lost sight of the Lost Commandment any more than I can explain why I can't find my watch sometimes. But today is a new day, and in Christ all of us have the opportunity to understand and follow the Lost Commandment. As we do so, we bring joy to Jesus, and we ourselves experience his complete joy.

HOW WE CAN EXPERIENCE COMPLETE JOY

As I began consciously to obey the Lost Commandment, I experienced joy in ways that I had never before experienced it. Here are some of the ways, beginning with the most surprising one.

The Mysterious Joy That Comes During Hardship

Our joy would not be complete if it left us when times got tough. Christ's love, though, transforms even the worst of circumstances into something beautiful. In his love, we can consider it pure joy even when we face trials of many kinds, because we know that God will use the trials for our benefit and his glory (James 1:2–4). The Bible tells us that the joy of the Lord is our strength (Neh. 8:10). Christ endured the cross because of the joy set before him of fulfilling his Father's will (Heb. 12:2).

How is this possible? "With man this is impossible, but with God all things are possible" (Matt. 19:26). I have found that the strangest and most wonderful joy of all comes in the middle of hardship. In looking back on my life after my finding the Lost Commandment, I can testify from experience that this is true. Let me tell a story to illustrate.

A man once injured me, severely—and on purpose. I had to be hospitalized and have surgery. When I was first injured, I was angry and resentful. But then, as I sat in the hospital thinking about the man who hurt me, I began to think about Jesus and how I had hurt him by sinning throughout my life. I knew that Jesus had forgiven me. And I also knew that because Jesus had forgiven me, I had to forgive the man who hurt me. I decided to forgive him in obedience to Christ.

A few weeks later, I planned to meet with the man privately. Honestly, I can't say that I was looking forward to meeting him. But I prayed that Christ would strengthen me and help me to forgive him. I also prayed that God would prepare the man's heart for what I was going to say to him because I intended to share the gospel with him. I still wasn't experiencing any joy, and I didn't expect to.

When I met the man, though, something very strange happened. As I was sitting and talking to him, explaining that I was forgiving him because Jesus had forgiven me, I suddenly felt overwhelmed by emotion. I felt Jesus' incredible love—not only for me, but also for the man who hurt me. I wasn't thinking about how the man had wronged me. I wasn't thinking about how badly I'd been injured. I was experiencing the pure joy of Christ's love for me and the pure joy of expressing that same love to this man who so desperately needed Jesus. I wasn't angry. I was filled with joy. I'll tell you more of this story in a later chapter.

Now when I obey the Lost Commandment, I come through difficult circumstances with joy and peace. The only explanation is that what I've experienced is the complete joy that Jesus promised in John 15:11.

The Joy of Understanding God's Word

Now when I read Scripture with the Lost Commandment in mind, I realize that most of the teaching of the New Testament can be summarized by the Lost Commandment. In applying God's Word to my life, I no longer have to ask myself, "How would I want others to treat me?" or "What would Jesus do?" I know how God wants me to treat others because I see in the New Testament how Jesus has treated me.

The Joy of Being Aware of Jesus' Love

To obey the Lost Commandment, I have to think all the time about how Jesus loves me. Jesus loves me—and you—with an incredible, overwhelming love. The more I think about Jesus' love for me, the more I notice and experience his love and joy. I have begun to realize by experience that he lives in me, that he walks next to me, and that he works through me.

The Joy of Giving Joy to God

Like most Christians, I have long wanted to live my life in a way that gives joy to God. I just didn't know how to accomplish this in practical terms. Now I know: by obeying the Lost Commandment.

The Joy of Becoming More Like Jesus

For years, I've wanted to become more Christlike. The Lost Commandment taught me that to become more like Christ, I need to love others the way Jesus loves me. The Bible and Christ teach me how, and my life has become the classroom, with the Holy Spirit as my assigned tutor and mentor. Although I'll never stop learning how to be more Christlike, the Lost Commandment has given me a far better understanding of the steps that I should take with the help of the Holy Spirit.

The Joy of Empathizing with Jesus

I know Jesus better by following the Lost Commandment because in loving others as Jesus loves me, I experience some of the same situations and feelings that Jesus did. I feel closer to him emotionally, which brings me joy.

The Joy of Loving and Being Loved by Others

When I follow the Lost Commandment, I experience joy in loving others even if they don't express love for me in return. But I've been amazed at the responses I get from others when I love them as Jesus loves me. Even very tense situations have been diffused with words of prayer and love. Jesus said that all men would know that we are his disciples if we follow the Lost Commandment (John 13:35). And it's fun to watch people try to figure out why in the world I'm treating them so well as I wait for an opportunity to point them toward Jesus for their answer.

The Joy of Future Rewards from God

On one hand, I know that just being in the presence of God in heaven is going to bring me more joy than I can imagine. Jesus was able to endure the cross in part because he anticipated the joy of being in his Father's presence again (Heb. 12:2). Being in God's presence is its own reward, and I don't need or deserve anything more.

On the other hand, God, in his incredible grace, has chosen to tell me that he will reward and repay me for my good deeds, once I reach heaven.[7] He doesn't have to. He just wants to. The way to maximize my reward in heaven is to obey the Lost Commandment.

ADDITIONAL INCENTIVES FOR OBEYING THE LOST COMMANDMENT

By obeying the Lost Commandment, we "remain in" Jesus' love in the same way that branches are connected to a vine that carries the power of life. In Christ, our union with God brings complete joy to God, Jesus, and us. This union bears fruit that glorifies God. We remain in the center of God's purpose for our lives, experiencing peace and a sense of significance that only God can give us. We experience complete joy through this abundant life in Christ.

While joy is our positive incentive to obey the Lost Commandment, avoiding God's rebuke is also an incentive. If we fail to love others as Christ has loved us, God responds as though we have failed to love him. He considers our lack of love for others as proof that we aren't grateful to him for giving Jesus to die for our sins.

God's Response to Our Neglect of the Poor, the Sick, and the Lonely

One of the scariest stories in the Bible is the one that Jesus told to describe the final judgment of God in which he separates the sheep from the goats (Matt. 25:31–46). The sheep in the story are the people who love others by feeding the hungry and thirsty, clothing the naked, and visiting the lonely and the imprisoned. The goats are the people who do not. Both groups of people are surprised to learn that the Lord treats these acts of love as if given directly to him, or as being withheld directly from him. Jesus said that God will say to the goats,

> "Depart from me, you who are cursed, into the eternal fire prepared for the devil and his angels. For *I* was hungry and you gave me nothing to eat, *I* was thirsty and you gave me nothing to drink, *I* was a stranger and you did not invite me in, *I* needed clothes and you did not clothe me, *I* was sick and in prison and you did not look after *me*." . . . [The goats] will answer, "Lord, when did we see you hungry or thirsty or a stranger or needing clothes or sick or in prison, and did not help you?" . . . [God] will reply, "I tell you the truth, *whatever you did not do for one of the least of these, you did not do for me*." (Matt. 25:41–45, emphasis added)

God considers the failure to love others as he has loved us as a failure to love him. The apostle John said, "If anyone has material possessions and sees his brother in need but has no pity him, how can the love of God be in him?" (1 John 3:17). God gives us our material possessions, and he expects us to share them with others as he commands.

God's Response to Our Refusal to Forgive Others

Jesus told a parable to show us that God expects us to forgive others because he has forgiven us (Matt. 18:22–34). A master (God) forgave a large debt (the penalty of our sin) owed by his servant (us). Later, the forgiven servant refused to forgive the debt of a fellow servant. The master then said to the unforgiving servant, "You wicked servant, . . . I canceled all that debt of yours because you begged me to. Shouldn't you have had mercy on your fellow servant *just as I had on you?*" (Matt. 18:32–33, emphasis added).

The master expected the forgiven servant to demonstrate his gratitude by forgiving his fellow servant's debt. When the forgiven servant failed to respond to the master's mercy by forgiving others, the master was offended and rebuked the unforgiving servant.

God's Grace Through Our Faith, Not Our Works

Neither the context of the Bible as a whole, nor the Lost Commandment, nor the Scriptures I've just referred to suggest that God loves us because of what we do. God loves us no matter what we do. He loved us while we were disobedient and before we loved him (Rom. 5:8). But God is also holy and just, so he must punish sin.

To punish sin yet save us, God gave his only Son, Jesus, to die for us so that we would not have to pay the price for our sin. Whoever believes in Jesus and follows him as Lord will have an eternal, abundant, amazingly joyous life with God (John 3:16–17; 10:10; 15:11). Christians are saved from God's judgment by their faith in Christ, not by what they do or don't do (Eph. 2:8–9).

Faith in Christ, however, should be accompanied by fruit in the form of changes in us that show in our love for others. We are obligated to give our entire lives to God, including our best efforts, in faith, because we were "bought at a price" through Christ's death for us (1 Cor. 6:20; 7:23).

The only thing that really counts in our lives is faith expressing itself through love (Gal. 5:6). God expects us to take the love that we receive *from* Jesus and give it *to* others *through* the power of the Holy Spirit. When we give Jesus' love to others, God accepts our love as though it were given directly to him. "For from him and through him and to him are all things. To him be the glory forever! Amen" (Rom. 11:36).

YOU CAN FIND COMPLETE JOY

Is it really possible to love others as Jesus loves us? Jesus is perfect and we, after all, definitely aren't. The answer, though, is yes. And the rest of this book talks about the process of doing that. We *can* love others in the way Jesus loves us. He wants us to obey the Lost Commandment, and he says it's possible if we rely on him and the Holy Spirit (John 14:12). When we ask Jesus for help, he is pleased to give us the wisdom and the power that we need to obey him.

The joy of Christ's love will change our lives and the lives of those around us if we obey the Lost Commandment. Follow in Jesus' footsteps, and he will show you how.

SUMMARY

The Lost Commandment is that we should love others as Jesus has loved us (John 13:34). If we obey the Lost Commandment, we will be known for our love (John 13:35) and will experience complete joy (John 15:11). Jesus' love for us has seven principal elements: joy, relationship with God, mission focus, humility, obedience, forgiveness, and service. But it seems that many of us have lost the Lost Commandment: our lives lack the joy that God intended; surveys suggest that Christians do not generally feel obligated to love others the way that Jesus has loved us; surveys indicate that Christians are not generally known for our love of others. If we follow the Lost Commandment, however, we can experience the complete joy that Jesus promised—a joy that comes not only in predictable situations, but also even during hardship. We can also anticipate a joyful entrance into heaven, rather than the rebuke that will come from God if we don't follow the Lost Commandment.

APPLICATION

1. What important fruit have you noticed in yourself that has accompanied your faith in Christ?

2. List three ways in which your love for others could be more like Jesus' love for you. Now list three tangible steps that you will take to begin to love others as Jesus loves you.

3. With God's help, resolve to learn to love others as Jesus has loved you.

Chapter 2

MORE COSTLY THAN GOLD

Whoever has my commands and obeys them, he is the one who loves me.

—JOHN 14:21

My wife's name is Lynne. God has blessed us with twenty-five years (and counting) of marriage. Soon after we got married, I figured out that Lynne loves to wake up to a good cup of coffee. Coffee is a joy to Lynne, so one way I show my love for her is by making coffee for her in the morning.

If I put Lynne's wishes ahead of my own, that gets her attention. I rode a motorcycle before we got married, and Lynne was afraid that I'd die on that motorcycle. I liked to ride, but I decided to give it up, not because Lynne made me but because I love her. I didn't want her to worry about me. When I agreed not to ride anymore, Lynne smiled at me and said, "You really love me, don't you!"

God has also blessed me with opportunities to show my daughters how much I love them. My oldest daughter, Lauren, used to enjoy a style of music that I disliked, but I still took her to several loud concerts by her favorite bands. The amplifiers were cranked up enough to blow the ears right off my head, but I wanted to know why Lauren enjoyed the music because I love Lauren. More importantly, I wanted Lauren to know that whatever music she enjoys, and whatever she does in life, I'll always love her unconditionally. I might hate her music. I might hate what she does. But I'll never stop loving *her*. In other words, I want Lauren to know that I love her the way Jesus loves me—unconditionally.

A few years ago, Lauren and I had planned to take a girl-friend of hers to a concert almost two hundred miles away from our home. Lauren wanted to arrive at the concert early so we could stand right in front of the stage—right in the middle of the mosh pit where excited fans would bang into each other and pass each other hand-over-hand toward the stage. You parents can imagine how much fun this must be.

The week before the concert, my jaw was broken. A surgeon put it back together with a titanium plate and wired my teeth shut. Lauren was concerned about me, but she still desperately wanted to go to the concert. I easily could have declined. My accident provided a perfect excuse.

But I didn't. Instead, I borrowed a full-face motorcycle helmet, received permission from the concert promoters to wear the helmet into the concert, and stood with my daughter and her friend in the mosh pit, front row, center. I became a human sardine for my daughter. I stood with her in the middle of a mass of sweating, ricocheting teenagers, and probably experienced hearing loss listening to music that I couldn't stand, all because I love her. I admit that going to the concert with a wired jaw wasn't cautious or conservative. But I love my daughter, and I wanted her to *know* that I love her.

So one way I show love to my wife and daughters is by learning how I can do what matters to them. I wish that I'd treated Jesus this same way more often than I have. Too often, I haven't tried to learn how I can do what matters to Jesus.

Our obedience to the Lost Commandment begins with loving Jesus enough to understand what the Lost Commandment requires of us. If we don't even know Jesus' commandments, then we obviously don't grasp them and we can't obey them (John 14:21). If we don't care enough to know what Jesus expects of us, we can't truthfully say that we love him.

To bring joy to Jesus and to experience complete joy, we have to love others with Jesus' special, amazing love. His love is not like any other love. It's not a love that we understand by looking inside ourselves to our own preferences or that we can find in our world's culture. What kind of love, then, are we talking about?

CHRIST'S LOVE IS MORE COSTLY THAN GOLD

The word *love* means different things to different people, but we tend to use the word without explaining what we mean. Our first thought about what *love* means is often the romantic kind of love. But we know there are other types of love as well, such as devoted and sacrificial love, and brotherly love.

God knows that love has a variety of meanings to us. That's why he explained what he meant when he commanded us to love others. According to Jesus, the greatest Old Testament law concerning how people are to treat each other is the Golden Rule (Matt. 22:36–39).

But when Jesus proclaimed the Lost Commandment, he profoundly redefined how God expects people to treat each other.[1] The Lost Commandment requires more from us than the Golden Rule:

- The Golden Rule defines only how to treat others in human terms. The Lost Commandment defines treatment of others in terms of divine love.
- The Golden Rule commands us to treat others the way we would want to be treated. The Lost Commandment commands us to love others as Jesus has already loved us.
- We can understand the Golden Rule without having anything to do with Jesus. To understand the Lost Commandment, we need to have experienced Jesus' love.

These distinctions make a difference in how God expects us to love others. If a friend asks me to walk a mile with him, I might do it if I follow the Golden Rule. If I follow the Lost Commandment, however, I'll do it, and then I'll walk an extra mile with him (Matt. 5:41). The fact is, Jesus loves us more deeply than we expect to be loved by others.

How do we love our neighbors *as* ourselves if we don't even *like* ourselves? Under the Golden Rule, a low sense of self-worth can translate into a low standard of love for others. But the Lost Commandment is based on the value that God places on each of us, as measured by the price that God paid to save our eternal lives—the sacrifice of his Son on the cross.

By obeying the Lost Commandment, we more than fulfill our obligations under the Golden Rule. The converse of this statement, however, is not true: by obeying the Golden Rule, we don't necessarily fulfill our obligations under the Lost Commandment. The Lost Commandment is a higher, more costly standard of love than the Golden Rule.

THE LOST COMMANDMENT REPLACES THE GOLDEN RULE

If Jesus were to walk among us today and someone were to ask, "What is the greatest commandment?" he would probably answer with the words of the Lost Commandment and not with the words of the Golden Rule. Here are eight reasons why I believe that the Lost Commandment replaces the Golden Rule.

"New" Command Means Replacement Command

Jesus called the Lost Commandment a "new" command. What Jesus meant by the word *new* was *replacement*. The "new" command replaced the "old" command. How do we know this?

We can start by looking up the word *new* in a good Bible dictionary. As we know, a dictionary gives us the common meanings of words. The word that is translated as *new* in this case is *kainēn* (καινήν), a form of the Greek word *kainos* (καινός). One of the senses of this word is "what is old has become obsolete, and should be replaced by what is new. In such a case the new is, as a rule, superior to the old."[2]

As we read the New Testament, we find other passages in which the word *new* is clearly used in this way. The apostle Paul used this same word when he declared that, "If anyone is in Christ, he is a new creation; the old has gone, the new has come!" (2 Cor. 5:17). In other words, the new creation replaces the old creation.

But how do we know that this is what Jesus meant when he used the word *new* at the Last Supper? In this case, God's Word tells us what Jesus meant. Jesus used a form of the very same word (*kainēn*) just before he proclaimed the Lost Commandment—probably only a matter of minutes earlier—when he said, "This cup is the new covenant in my blood" (Luke 22:20; 1 Cor. 11:25). As God explains to us through the writer of the book of Hebrews, "By calling this covenant 'new,' he has made the first one obsolete . . ." (Heb. 8:13). The "new" covenant, by definition, renders the "old" obsolete. When Jesus then called his commandment of love for others "new" only minutes later, he also made the previous commandment of love for others—the Golden Rule—obsolete.

The context in which Jesus gave us the Lost Commandment, which I'm about to discuss, makes this even clearer.

The Lost Commandment Was Christ's Last Word on Love

When a person draws up a new last will and testament, it automatically replaces all previous wills. Jesus spoke his new last will and testament the night before he died when he proclaimed the Lost Commandment during the Last Supper.

Picture this scene. Just before the Passover Feast, Jesus gathers his disciples for supper. He knows the time has come for him to leave this world and to return to God (John 13:1, 3). Shortly after the meal, he will be betrayed by Judas Iscariot and will be delivered into the hands of Roman soldiers, who will arrest him and crucify him.

After Judas leaves to get the men who will seize Jesus, Jesus tells his disciples that he will be with them only a little longer (John 13:31–33). This statement fills the disciples with grief, even though Jesus tells them not to be troubled (John 14:1; 16:6–7).

Immediately after announcing his departure, Jesus proclaims the Lost Commandment (John 13:34). He speaks to the disciples as they finish dinner, announces that they have to leave (John 14:31), and then continues to speak as they walk. He is then arrested.

It all happened so fast. We can only imagine how shocked and afraid the disciples must have been as this scene unfolded.

In his last words to his disciples, Jesus explained how obedience to the Lost Commandment maintains the flow of love from God, to Jesus, to us, to others. Here's a summary of what he said:

- Jesus loves us the way God loves Jesus (John 15:9).
- If we love and have faith in Jesus and God, we will obey Jesus' commands (John 14:15, 21, 23–24; 15:14).

- Jesus commands us to love others as he loves us (John 13:34; 15:12, 17).
- When we love others as Jesus loves us, all people know that we are Christians (John 13:35).

Obedience to the Lost Commandment will bring these blessings:

- God and Jesus will love us, and Jesus will show himself to us (John 14:21).
- Jesus and God will come to us and "make their home with" us (John 14:23).
- The Holy Spirit will live with us and be in us (John 14:15–17).
- We will "remain in" Jesus' love (John 15:10) and then "bear much fruit" (John 15:5) that glorifies God (John 15:8).
- We will receive what we request from God in Jesus' name (John 15:7).
- Jesus will take joy in us (John 15:11).
- Our joy will be complete (John 15:11).

God's love flows down from him, to Jesus, to us, to others, like a cascade of living water in a river of love. Obedience to the Lost Commandment keeps the water moving, acknowledging its source, maintaining its force, and continuing its flow in its intended direction.

If Jesus had wanted us to follow the Golden Rule, he certainly would have said so in his last words. He never mentions it, but instead proclaims the Lost Commandment three times. When something is repeated three times in the Bible, it is usually an indication of emphasis. For example, God is described as "holy, holy, holy" (Isa. 6:3; Rev. 4:8).

The Lost Commandment Is a Better Summary of the New Testament Than the Golden Rule

The core teaching of the New Testament resonates with the teaching of the Lost Commandment, not with the teaching of the Golden Rule. We are told, for example, that our attitude toward others and God should be the same attitude that Christ had, and still has (Phil. 2:5–7). We might call that the Lost Commandment of attitude. We are *not* told that we should have the same attitude toward others that we would want others to have toward us. That would have been the Golden Rule of attitude.

We are told to "forgive as the Lord forgave you" (Col. 3:13)—the Lost Commandment of forgiveness—not to forgive others as we would want others to forgive us (Golden Rule). We are told to serve others as Christ has served us (John 13:14–15)—the Lost Commandment of service—not to serve others as we would want others to serve us (Golden Rule).

The Lost Commandment requires us to love others by helping them, because Jesus helps us. Jesus saves us, serves us, feeds us, teaches us, comforts us, and gives us abundant life. The Golden Rule arguably emphasizes doing no harm to others, rather than affirmatively helping them (Rom. 13:9–10).

Appendix A includes verses from eighteen different books of the New Testament that directly or indirectly connect the love of God or Christ for us with our obligation to love others in this same way. Teachings from other New Testament books are also consistent with the Lost Commandment. We can't come up with a comparable list of Scriptures based on the Golden Rule.

Jesus Said That His Disciples Follow the Lost Commandment

Jesus told his disciples, "Come, follow me" (Matt. 4:19). When we follow him through the pages of the Gospels, we realize something startling: Jesus didn't obey the Golden Rule—he obeyed a higher standard. He didn't decide how to treat others by asking himself how he would want them to treat him. Instead, he loved others as his Father God had loved him (John 15:9) and as his Father commanded him (John 10:17–18; 14:30–31).

Jesus said that "all men" can tell who follows him: those who obey the Lost Commandment are his disciples and the others are not (John 13:35). The mark of a Christian is whether we obey the Lost Commandment, not whether we obey the Golden Rule.

We Must Fulfill Our Highest Calling

The Golden Rule says that we are to treat others "as ourselves," that is, the way we treat ourselves. But the Lost Commandment requires us to treat others better than we treat ourselves. That's a higher calling than the Golden Rule. Jesus said, "If anyone wants to be first, he must be the very last, and the servant of all" (Mark 9:35). If we obey the Lost Commandment, we more than obey the Golden Rule. But if we obey only the Golden Rule by treating others equal to the way we treat ourselves, then we disobey the Lost Commandment. We have to fulfill our highest calling by meeting the higher standard.

The Lost Commandment Is Part of the New Covenant in Christ

The Lost Commandment is part of God's new covenant relationship with his people. Before Christ, God gave the Jewish people certain physical requirements through which they were to demonstrate their love for him. The outward sign of God's covenant, given through Moses, was the physical circumcision of men. The worship of God was to take place at the physical temple built in Zion, in Jerusalem. The Levites, physical descendants of Jacob's son Levi, were designated as priests. Each of these external factors was supposed to be accompanied by deep spiritual faith.

In order to give us a spiritual heart transplant, God chose to remove many of the external trappings of Jewish ceremonial law by fulfilling those laws in Christ. To demonstrate this change, God gave us a new priest, who would intercede for us before God in a new temple, based on a new covenant, under a new law that is written on our hearts.

Christ is our new high priest, now and forever (Heb. 7:20–21). His priesthood is based not on his lineage but on the power of his "indestructible life" (Heb. 7:16). Because Jesus lives forever, his priesthood is permanent (Heb. 7:24).

Christ built us a new, spiritual temple that replaced the physical temple in Jerusalem. At the moment of Christ's death, the thick curtain of the temple in Jerusalem, which represented the separation of holy God from sinful man,[3] was torn in two from top to bottom (Matt. 27:51; Mark 15:38; Luke 23:45). The temple itself was destroyed in A.D. 70 and was not rebuilt physically. Christ's spiritual temple is now in the hearts of those who believe in him.

Each Christian is a temple of the Lord (1 Cor. 3:16), as are all believers in Christ as a group (Eph. 2:19–22).

As our new priest, Christ has given us a new covenant from God (Luke 22:20; Heb. 9:15). The covenant is based not on full compliance with the Law of the Old Testament but on belief in Jesus Christ as Savior and Lord. The new covenant is this: "That if you confess with your mouth, 'Jesus is Lord,' and believe in your heart that God raised him from the dead, you will be saved. For it is with your heart that you believe and are justified, and it is with your mouth that you confess and are saved" (Rom. 10:9–10).

Jesus, our new high priest, was also given a new law, "For when there is a change of the priesthood, there must also be a change of the law" (Heb. 7:12). The Lost Commandment is part of that new law and best summarizes that new law. Under the new law, "The only thing that counts is faith expressing itself through love" (Gal. 5:6).

The Golden Rule is the best summary of how the Old Testament Law and the Prophets say that we should treat others (Matt. 22:36–40). Christians are now called, however, to live according to the new law of the Spirit of life, based on our relationship with Jesus Christ and not on compliance with Jewish ceremonial law (Rom. 8:1–5). The Spirit of life is the Holy Spirit of Christ, alive and living in those who believe that Jesus is their Savior and who follow him as Lord (Rom. 8:9–11).

The law of the Spirit of life is the gospel of God's grace and love, which each of us embodies and expresses as we practice obedience to the Lost Commandment. The gospel sets us free to "serve in the new way of the Spirit, and not in the old way of the written code" that is summarized by the Golden Rule (Rom. 7:8). The Lost Commandment is the new way of the Spirit in which we are called to serve. As we follow the Lost Commandment, we "remain in" Christ's love (John 15:10–12), and he and God live with us and in us (John 14:15–23). The Golden Rule doesn't help us understand, nor is it consistent with, the law of the Spirit of life. It represents the old way of the written code, and doesn't express how or why we are to love others.

The Gospel of John Entirely Omits the Golden Rule

The Golden Rule is omitted entirely from the gospel of John. It appears in three epistles (Rom. 13:9; Gal. 5:14; James 2:8), but not in the epistles written by John.

In all likelihood, John intended this omission. John wrote his gospel for the specific purpose of helping his readers to believe that "Jesus is the Christ, the Son of God" (John 20:31). John was with Jesus from the very beginning of his public ministry, longer than the other gospel writers. Based on all of the gospel accounts, John spent more time with Jesus than the other writers did and was closer to him than they were. John would not have omitted the Golden Rule from his gospel if the Golden Rule was, in fact, the Great Commandment with which Christians were to fulfill the "Great Commission" to make disciples of all nations.

How close was John to Jesus? They were apparently cousins as well as close friends. Jesus' mother and the apostle John's mother (who may have been named Salome) were probably sisters.[4] Like John's brother James, as well as Peter and his brother Andrew, John was one of the earliest followers of Jesus. All four gospels indicate that John was part of Jesus' inner circle. For example, John, James, and Peter were selected to be with Jesus when he was transfigured and Moses and Elijah appeared to him (Luke 9:28–36).

John sat next to Jesus at the Last Supper when the Lost Commandment was given (John 13:23). Jesus chose John, James, and Peter to be close to him in the garden of Gethsemane when he prayed before being arrested (Matt. 26:36–37).

John was present at the crucifixion, along with Jesus' mother. As Jesus was dying, Jesus committed the care of his mother to John (John 19:25–27). In doing so, Jesus passed over not only the other apostles, but his own siblings, including his brother James, who later became a leader of the church at Jerusalem.

After his death, resurrection, and ascension, Jesus sent an angel to John to convey messages to seven Christian churches to reveal the events surrounding his second coming and to describe the end of the world as we know it. John wrote down what he saw and heard in what we now know as the book of Revelation, the last book of the New Testament.

It's apparent, then, that none of Jesus' disciples were closer to Jesus than John was. John therefore had a better opportunity than any other disciple to understand the significance of the Lost Commandment. It's likely that John omitted the Golden Rule from his gospel because he correctly understood that the Lost Commandment replaced the Golden Rule.

The Golden Rule Leads Back to the Lost Commandment

If we apply the Golden Rule properly, we still end up with the Lost Commandment. Here's what I mean. The Golden Rule says, "Do to others as you would have them do to you" (Luke 6:31). Would we prefer to be loved the way Jesus loves us, or some other way? We would obviously prefer to be loved the way Jesus loves us. There's no greater love than Christ's love for us, and we would want others to love us the way Jesus loves us. Therefore, under the Golden Rule, we should love others the way Jesus loves us! For that matter, if we love *ourselves* less than Jesus loves us, we are not within God's will. What right do we have to love ourselves less than Jesus loves us? None.

If we end up in the same place using the Golden Rule, why not continue to teach and follow the Golden Rule like we always have? Because Jesus intended to replace the Golden Rule with the Lost Commandment, and because we don't naturally do the mental gymnastics that lead us from the Golden Rule to the Lost Commandment. When we are told to do to others what we would have them do to us, we naturally think about our future preferences rather than about Jesus' past love for us. We should do what Jesus commands, not what we prefer. We should follow the Lost Commandment.

WHY IS THE GOLDEN RULE IN THE NEW TESTAMENT?

If Jesus intended to replace the Golden Rule with the Lost Commandment, then why is the Golden Rule in the New Testament at all? I think it's because the Golden Rule is part of a three-step progression from the standard of behavior that the Jews of Jesus' time thought was established in the Old Testament, to the Lost

Commandment standard of love proclaimed and modeled by Jesus in the New Testament.

Step One: Do No Harm

At a minimum, loving behavior toward others means not hurting them. Leviticus 19:18 expresses the Golden Rule this way: "Do not seek revenge or bear a grudge against one of your people, but love your neighbor as yourself. I am the LORD." We might say that this is a negative requirement, in the sense that it expresses what we *don't* do, rather than positively expressing what we *do* do.

Although the Law and the Prophets include some positive requirements (e.g., "Honor your father and your mother" [Exod. 20:12]), most of what they require can be summarized by the phrase "do no harm." Do not murder. Do not commit adultery. Do not steal. Do not give false testimony against you neighbor. Do not covet your neighbor's house. (See Exod. 20:13–17.) The apostle Paul said, "Love does no harm to its neighbor. Therefore love is the fulfillment of the law" (Rom. 13:10).

Possibly as a result of a "do no harm" over-emphasis, rabbis before Jesus' time expressed the Golden Rule in its negative form: "Do not do to others what you would not want them to do to you."[5] This negative form of the Golden Rule is also found in Hinduism, Buddhism, and Confucianism.[6] There's nothing uniquely Christian or Jewish about the Golden Rule as expressed in this way.

Step Two: Do Good According to the Law and Prophets

But Jesus corrected the rabbis' expression of the Golden Rule by repeating the positive form found in Leviticus 19:18. By doing this, Jesus repeated both the negative and positive requirements of the Law and the Prophets. He said, "Do to others as you would have them do to you" (Matt. 7:12; Luke 6:31).

Before he replaced the Golden Rule with the Lost Commandment, Jesus taught the Golden Rule as a summary of the teaching of the Law and the Prophets (Matt. 22:39–40; Mark 12:31). When, for instance, certain Jews asked Jesus questions like, "Teacher, what good thing must I do to get eternal life?" Jesus' answers included the Golden Rule (Matt. 19:16–19; Luke 10:25–28). That's because the questions focused on doing good things under the Law, and the Golden Rule is one of the two greatest commandments in the Law (Matt. 22:36–40; Mark 12:28–31). The writers of the New Testament Epistles also quoted the Golden Rule as a summary of the Law (Rom. 13:9; Gal. 5:14; James 2:8).

But just because the Golden Rule is part of an accurate summary of the Law doesn't mean that the teaching of the New Testament about how we are to love others can be summarized by the Golden Rule. It can't. Jesus' teaching about love added to the Old Testament's requirements by commanding a higher standard of outward behavior, and an inward purity of our hearts that is consistent with the spirit of the Law.

Step Three: Love as Jesus Taught and Loved

When it comes to loving others, Jesus raised the Old Testament bar to New Testament heights. The Sermon on the Mount offers several examples. The Ten Commandments say don't murder (Exod. 20:13); Jesus says don't even get mad (Matt. 5:22). The Ten Commandments say don't commit adultery (Exod. 20:14); Jesus says lust is just as bad (Matt. 5:28). The Law demands retribution for injury (Exod. 21:23–25; Lev. 24:19–20; Deut. 19:21); Jesus says turn the other cheek (Matt. 5:39). The Law says love your neighbor (Lev. 19:18); Jesus says love your enemy (Matt. 5:44). The examples are many, but the point is, Jesus didn't embrace the Golden Rule as a summary of *his* teaching. Rather, he took its focus on behavior as a starting point from which to redefine the Golden Rule in terms of the love that we are to have for others.

Jesus didn't proclaim the Lost Commandment to crowds of people, such as those gathered at the Sermon on the Mount, probably because most in the crowd didn't really know him—if they knew him at all. What would the crowds have thought if Jesus had said, "As I have loved you, so you must love one another"? They would have thought, "You don't *love* me. You don't even *know* me." They wouldn't have understood Jesus' commandment. Instead, Jesus waited to proclaim the Lost Commandment until his Last Supper with the apostles, who had personally experienced his love.

Another reason that Jesus apparently waited until the Last Supper is that he wanted to reveal the "full extent of his love" before proclaiming the Lost Commandment (John 13:1). Throughout his life, Jesus demonstrated his love for people. By waiting until the Last Supper to give us the Lost Commandment, Jesus made clear that we are to love others to the full extent that he has loved us.

WHY DID MATTHEW, MARK, AND LUKE OMIT THE LOST COMMANDMENT?

If the Lost Commandment was so important, why didn't the other gospel writers record it? We don't know, but there are plausible explanations. Imagine how the apostles must have felt when Jesus told them that he would be leaving them. Jesus proclaimed the Lost Commandment just after telling the apostles that he would be with them only a little longer (John 13:33). The first question recorded after Jesus proclaimed the Lost Commandment came from Simon Peter: "Lord, where are you going?" (John 13:36). Nothing was asked about the Lost Commandment. Jesus acknowledged that the apostles were filled with grief about his leaving (John 14:1; 16:6). News of Jesus' departure may have been so overwhelming that most of the apostles didn't remember that Jesus had given the Lost Commandment, even though he proclaimed it three times.

In any case, God loves us so much that he made sure that the Lost Commandment was recorded. It sits in plain sight in the gospel of John for each of us to discover in our own time.

JESUS IS THE BEGINNING

We can't begin to understand the Lost Commandment or to love others as Jesus has loved us unless we first know Jesus and have experienced his love. Real life, real joy, begins with a personal relationship with Jesus. In part 2, we'll discuss what we need to do to experience a relationship with Jesus that bears fruit and produces complete joy.

SUMMARY

We express our love for Jesus in part by caring enough to understand what the Lost Commandment requires of us. The Lost Commandment is different from the Golden Rule, which says that we must treat others the way we would want to be treated (Luke 6:31). Through his love for us, Jesus more than fulfilled the Golden Rule, and the Lost Commandment is, therefore, a higher standard of love than the Golden Rule. From Jesus' use of the word *new* (John 13:34), and for seven other reasons, it's obvious that he intended to replace the Golden Rule with the Lost Commandment.

APPLICATION

1. Decide to obey the Lost Commandment. Tell Jesus that you will obey the Lost Commandment with his help and in his strength. Ask him to help you, beginning now.

2. Read the Scriptures in appendix A. Ask the Holy Spirit to show you how these Scriptures apply to your relationships with others.

PART 2

RELATIONSHIP

The Invitation of Christ's Love

Chapter 3

RSVP

Then he said to them all: "If anyone would come after me, he must deny himself and take up his cross daily and follow me. For whoever wants to save his life will lose it, but whoever loses his life for me will save it."

—Luke 9:23–24

Life can change for the better with the right invitation. My life changed the moment Lynne accepted my invitation to be my wife. It changed when I got letters offering to admit me to college and to graduate school. But no invitation has changed my life more than the invitation to follow Jesus Christ as my Savior and Lord. All of us have been sent that invitation, whether we know it or not, whether we have considered it or not, and whether we have accepted it or not. Loving others as Jesus loves us begins with our acceptance of the invitation to follow Jesus. If we believe that Jesus is our Savior and Lord, then we will—and we must—accept his invitation to follow him. Let me explain why it's so important to accept this invitation.

God loves us, and because he loves us, he invites us to a relationship with him that is personal and real. The invitation comes through God's messenger, the Holy Spirit: Follow my Son, Jesus, as your Lord and Savior, and I will give you an amazing life! Not an easy life. But an amazing, abundant life. The invitation also comes through Jesus himself as he speaks to us through the words of the Bible: "Come, follow me" (Luke 9:23). If we accept his invitation, we begin a new life that brings joy and bears fruit.

But *why* should we accept Jesus' invitation? What if we like our lives just the way they are? We hate change! Why should we risk following Jesus when we don't know where he will lead us?

THE BAD NEWS

Understanding Jesus' invitation to follow him begins with grasping and then acknowledging a terrifying fact. Imagine receiving a letter in the mail that reads something like this: "We regret to inform you that you have been diagnosed with a common but fatal condition. Your condition is so grave that for all practical purposes, you are dead now!" That's what it's like when we first understand God's invitation to follow Jesus. Without Jesus, we're dead people walking. That's the terrifying fact.

Why? We all suffer from the condition called sin, and it's always fatal if left untreated. Sin is not doing what God expects us to do. All of us have disobeyed God (Rom. 3:23)—and the older we get, the more quickly we admit it.

Consider, just as an example, the Ten Commandments:

Have we ever put anyone ahead of God (Exod. 20:3)?

Guilty.

Have we ever put anything ahead of God (Exod. 20:4)? Say, our job? Pleasure?

Guilty.

Have we ever misused the name of God (Exod. 20:7)? I'm not talking just about swearing, although most of us are guilty of that. I'm also talking about using the name of God in pointless ways, like using his name as an exclamation or punctuation.

Guilty.

Ever failed to rest on Sunday (Exod. 20:8)? Ever failed to honor our fathers or our mothers (Exod. 20:12)? Ever really wanted something that belongs to someone else (Exod. 20:17)?

Guilty, guilty, guilty!

We get the idea. There's no point in going over the many, many other ways in which we fall short every day of God's plan for us. We're guilty. We have no defense.

But in our defense, we might try to say, "But we've done a lot of good things too! Good and noble things! Doesn't that offset the bad things?" Well, to use a human analogy, that's a little like a mass murderer saying, "I know that I killed ten people, but I was very loving to the people I didn't kill." The good deeds don't cancel out the bad deeds in the eyes of an earthly judge. If you killed ten people, then you deserve punishment under the law. Very severe punishment.

Although God loves us, there will come a day when all of us will face his judgment. Unlike any human judge, God is completely holy. The Bible says that angels surround God day and night and never stop saying, "Holy, holy, holy is the Lord God Almighty, who was, and is, and is to come" (Rev. 4:8). God's holiness is so great that humans can't even look at him. He lives in "unapproachable light" (1 Tim. 6:16).

God is not just holy. He is also completely just. His justice demands that sin be punished. Sin is a stench to God, and what we deserve for sinning is death (Rom. 6:23). Not just physical death— that's not the worst penalty in this case. Spiritual death. Spiritual death is an eternal separation from God that begins immediately and extends into eternity. After our physical bodies pass away, our sin will bring God's judgment on us, and we will be thrown into a "lake of fire" where we will remain forever (Matt. 25:41; Rev. 20:15). Because of our sin, we are literally dead people walking. We are alive physically but dead spiritually because we are separated from God—unless we believe in Jesus as our Savior and Lord.

Hearing this is like getting that letter that I talked about earlier. We were all sent the letter that says, "You suffer from the fatal condition called sin."

How do we react to this news? Each of us reacts differently to some degree. But one common reaction—both to this news and to news of a fatal physical condition—is denial and anger.

NO WAY!

"No way! This letter is somebody's idea of a cruel joke," we might say. "Who sent me this letter?" It's normal to want to question bad news. We all do it. Our questions usually begin with the source. "Who says so?" we huff, with our hands on our hips.

In real life, the source of this bad news is not a mysterious letter in our mailbox. The source is the Bible. Whether we're considering becoming a Christian, or are living as a Christian, we all have to decide how to react to the Bible. Is the Bible just fictional literature with inspiring stories and important lessons? Or is the Bible something much more than that? Is it actually the true Word of God, inspired by his Spirit and miraculously preserved through history? If the Bible is just fictional, then we'd be crazy to make important decisions based solely on its words. But if the Bible is the Word of God, then it's fatal to ignore its commandments and warnings.

Belief that the Bible is the Word of God is a matter of faith. Millions of people over the span of thousands of years have accepted its words as the Word of God and have attempted to live their lives according to its precepts.

Accepting the Bible as God's Word, however, is not *just* a matter of faith and hope. The accuracy of many of its historical accounts has been substantiated by archaeological discoveries and the words of writers from the earliest periods of the Christian Church (see book recommendations in appendix B).

The first step in assessing for ourselves what we believe about the Bible is to read it. That's where I began my journey of faith. I was a third-year student in college and not a Christian at the time. My life didn't seem to have much purpose, and I wanted to know what God expected of me. Instinctively, I began by reading the Bible, not because I was persuaded that it was the infallible Word of God, but because it just seemed like the best place to start. At the time, I was not attending church. No one was leading me through any process. I just began reading the Bible, a little each day. Before reading, I'd pray something like, "God, please help me to understand what I'm reading and how it applies to my life."

What I read was nothing like what I was used to reading. As an English major, I read books by some of the greatest writers and poets of all time. But the Bible is different. Its wisdom is compelling but counterintuitive. The Gospels give different accounts of the same events, but each gospel was written for a different reason, to a different audience, and from a different perspective. The Old Testament types and prophecies interlock with the New Testament accounts of Jesus' life in so many ways that it would have been challenging for a single writer to create all the connections in a single manuscript on a computer. But the Bible wasn't written that way. It was written in separate books by different people separated by hundreds or even thousands of years—all before any human being even thought about assembling the books into the single volume that we now know as the Bible.

I concluded based on my reading that the Bible was inspired by God and that he intended us to treat it as accurate and true. So when the Bible says that all of us suffer from a fatal condition called sin, we all have to decide whether to take this statement seriously. We can treat the Bible as bogus, ignore its warnings, and go about our business. Or we can treat the Bible's statements about sin and its consequences seriously, and look for God's cure. Either way, we're making a critical decision.

As for me, the Bible led me to believe that I had sinned against God and others. I couldn't save myself. I needed a Savior.

OUR ONLY HOPE

What do we do if we accept the message of the Bible that our sinful condition is fatal? Is there any hope for us? Yes. His name is Jesus.

He is our doctor, and he is our only hope for a cure for sin. We can't save ourselves. We need a Savior, a redeemer, a rescuer. God loves us so much that he gave us one: "For God so loved the world that he gave his one and only Son, that whoever believes in him shall not perish but have eternal life. For God did not send his Son into the world to condemn the world, but to save the world through him" (John 3:16–17). And Jesus willingly gave himself for our sins to rescue us, according to God's will (Gal. 1:3–4). Jesus did this for the entire world, knowing that many would reject him, and understanding that even those who accept him would continue to be disobedient at times. His love covers all of our sins.

The more we think about what Jesus did for us, the more we grasp how stunning his love for us really is. He has known us since we were in our mother's wombs (Ps. 139:13). Knowing all of our faults and while we were still choosing to sin, he died for us (Rom. 5:8). He stepped off the throne of heaven, became a human nobody (Phil. 2:7), lived a sinless life, and then allowed himself to be crucified for our sins so that we could have a relationship with him and with God.

During his entire physical life as a human being, Jesus lived knowing that our sin would nail him to the cross. Yet he spent his life showing his love for us and teaching us how to love one another. After all of that, after enduring the torture and the shame of crucifixion, Jesus rose from the grave to the glory of God, and now sits next to God in heaven (Eph. 1:20.) After everything that he endured, and after everything that we have done wrong—and continue to do wrong, and will do wrong—he still loves us. Nothing can separate us from the love of God and from his Son, Jesus (Rom. 8:35).

THE TREATMENT DECISION

What do we have to do to be cured of the sin that's killing us? Is it enough to simply know that Jesus died to save us? No, according to the Bible, that's not enough.

What would we do if we really got a letter that said, "You have a fatal physical disease"?—and if the letter were genuine. For most of us, the answer is simple: we would do whatever it takes to live. Need to have surgery? Done. Need to take medication that makes us feel sick? Bring it on. Have to pay our doctor a lot of money to help us? Whatever it takes!

If we want a cure for our sinful condition, we have to be willing to do whatever it takes to live. We can't earn our cure by what we do. To avoid spiritual death, we can't take more vitamins, quit smoking, eat a special diet, and become well. The cure for our sin is God's G.R.A.C.E. alone. By G.R.A.C.E., I mean **G**od's **R**iches **a**t **C**hrist's **E**xpense. Otherwise, we'd be able to say that we saved ourselves, and that boast would not be acceptable to God (Eph. 2:8–9).

What God says we must do is acknowledge that Jesus died for our sins and was raised from the dead, and accept him as the Lord of the rest of our lives (Rom. 10:9–10). Passively believing that God exists is not enough. After all, even the demons (James 2:19) believe that! We have to accept Jesus' invitation to follow him. From that point forward, we owe God an eternal debt of gratitude that we can never fully repay. We owe him the continuing debt to love him with our entire hearts, souls, minds, and strength, and to love others as Jesus has loved us (John 13:34; Rom. 13:8).

Before we accept the treatment for our fatal condition that God offers through Jesus, Jesus wants us to be aware that the treatment is costly (Luke 14:25–33). We have to be willing to give up everything we have. Everything means everything (Matt. 10:37–39). Our money. Our family. Our future. All of it. It may seem foolish to give up everything, but we can't take it with us to the grave anyway, and what we receive in return is far greater than what we give up. Jesus said, "The kingdom of heaven is like a merchant looking for fine pearls. When he found one of great value, he went away and sold everything he had and bought it" (Matt. 13:45–46).

The treatment also has serious side effects. If Jesus were a human doctor, he might want us to sign a consent form that reads something like this:

> You have been advised that you suffer from a fatal condition called sin. There is only one treatment: you must acknowledge your condition to Jesus and place your entire life in his hands—forever. Although this treatment is 100 percent effective and will save your spiritual life, the following side effects will or may result from the treatment: personality change, mood swings—including occasional bouts of inexplicable joy and euphoria—changes in priorities, changes in desires, loss of appetite for money, radical improvements in vision, compelling impulses to give to the poor and to visit the sick, loss of friends, loss of family relationships, loss of job, unforeseen changes in plans and schedules, persecution, and physical death.

We have a choice. We can decline the treatment. A doctor's recommended treatment is, after all, only his recommendation—not an order—based on his professional training and experience. Doctors don't actually force their patients to undergo treatment.

And neither does God. God doesn't force anyone to follow Jesus. He gave us the freedom to accept or reject him.

But our choices have consequences. If we refuse to follow Jesus, we continue to be separated from God—not by God's choice but by our choice. We become like runaway children whose father looks out the window day and night, hoping that his kids will come home. God calls to us from the door of heaven, saying, "I love you. Follow Jesus home to me. Please come home."

After reading that consent form, are we crazy to accept the treatment that God offers us? Are we foolish to follow Jesus? Where else would we go when Jesus has "the words of eternal life" (John 6:68)? As the late Jim Elliot said, "He is no fool who gives what he cannot keep to gain that which he cannot lose."[1] To put it another way, you're smart to trade your physical life, which you'll lose eventually anyway, for an eternal life with God through Christ. It's foolish not to follow Jesus because he is the way home to God, the truth about what really matters, and the life we were meant to live (John 14:6).

HOW DO WE RSVP?

Jesus waits for our decision. He stands patiently watching us read the consent form as we twirl our pens in our fingers. He has invited us to accept his treatment plan. How will we RSVP? If we don't accept the treatment, we won't be cured. He hopes that we'll sign the form while there's still time, before our physical death settles our choice.

In reality, there is no form to sign to become a Christian. There are no magic words. On a beautiful day in April of 1980, I accepted Jesus' invitation by saying something like this to God and to Jesus:

> Father, I love you. I know that I haven't always done what you wanted me to do. I've sinned against you and other people, and I deserve to die for my sins. But I believe that your Son, Jesus, died on the cross to pay the price for my sins. I believe that you raised Jesus from the dead and that he is in heaven with you now.

Jesus, I give you all that I am, and all that I have, and all that I will be. Come into my life as my Lord and show me how to follow you. Fill me with your Holy Spirit. I love you. Amen.

From the day we accept Jesus' invitation, we have life in Jesus and follow him wherever he leads us. Then, we tell others what we have done, and in obedience to the Bible are baptized (Mark 16:16).[2]

WHAT'S NEXT?

Life in Christ is so much more than the initial decision to follow him. God wants us to be not just free from the consequences of the sickness of sin; he wants us to have an abundant and victorious life in Christ. He wants to help us out of our spiritual hospital bed and into the Christian weight room. We are like athletes on the most powerful team on earth. We are called to become stronger in Christ. We are called to love God and others more deeply every day. And we are called to fulfill the mission that God has given us in Christ until the day that we join him in heaven.

After we become Christians, we are new creations in Christ. As we will discuss in the next chapter, understanding who we are in Christ brings us tremendous healing and strength so that we can begin living an abundant and victorious life, loving others as Jesus loves us.

SUMMARY

The first step in obeying the Lost Commandment is to accept Jesus' invitation to begin a relationship with him. This invitation contains both bad and good news. The bad news is that our disobedience of God has caused us to suffer from a fatal condition called sin. The good news is that Jesus offers us the only known cure for our condition. If we acknowledge that Jesus died to pay the price for our sins, and agree to follow him as our risen Lord, we are cured. Our response to Jesus' invitation is the beginning of a joyful life with him.

APPLICATION

1. Take a few minutes to think about how much God and Jesus love you, and about God's amazing grace.

2. If you aren't sure whether you've accepted Jesus' invitation to follow him, stop what you're doing, find a quiet place, and do it now! Then tell someone what you've done.

3. If God puts people in your path who don't know his Son, Jesus, pray for an opportunity to share Jesus' invitation with them. Then when the opportunity presents itself, share Jesus' love with them.

Chapter 4

ENJOY YOUR NEW SELF

Therefore, if anyone is in Christ, he is a new creation; the old has gone, the new has come!
—2 CORINTHIANS 5:17

Jesus not only saved us *from* death; he saved us *to* life. The best way to begin our life with Jesus, after accepting his invitation to follow him and have a personal relationship with him, is to understand and accept who we are as Christians.

We are deeply loved by God. His love heals our emotional and spiritual wounds. Before we accept Jesus as Savior and Lord, we are like accident victims whose hearts have stopped. Then help arrives. We make the decision to follow Jesus, and our hearts start to beat again. God's love transforms us.

But our bodies have been pounded by our own sins and the sins of others. We may still be bleeding from the cuts of insults that we endured as children. Our legs may be crippled by emotional insecurity caused by rejection from our parents, our spouses, our siblings, or even strangers. Our minds may be battered by the world's view that beauty, brains, and money measure a person's worth. In this condition, we're in no shape to get up and walk, let alone assist the Great Physician with other patients.

To restore our health and our strength, our minds need to be transfused with a large dose of Christ's love. The Bible teaches us that we change our lives by renewing our minds (Rom. 12:2). The Holy Spirit is our teacher and our counselor in this process (John 14:26; 16:7). As our thinking changes, so do our actions as we obey God.

By God's grace and power, our changed thinking and changed actions make us new people in Christ (2 Cor. 5:17). We become spiritually and emotionally healthy and strong. We develop the ability to understand what God wants us to do, because in relationship with him we've come to know him better through his Word and by our experience with him. As we grasp and are changed by Jesus' love, our capacity to love others as Jesus loves us increases.

When we understand the specific ways that Jesus loves us, we become more certain of his love. And we need to be certain. Remember the game that little kids play with the petals of a flower? To figure out whether someone loves him, a boy plucks the petals off, saying, "She loves me. She loves me not. She loves me. She loves me not." The last petal is supposed to provide the answer.

When it comes to our relationship with God, we're tempted to measure his love for us in a similar way. Something good happens to us. He loves us. Something bad happens to us. He loves us not. We get a job. He loves us. We get sick. He loves us not. We're tempted to measure God's love based on how we like our present circumstances. But in this way, we never really know whether God loves us. Our uncertainty casts a shadow of doubt over our hearts that affects everything we do.

God doesn't want us to live like that. He wants us to know beyond a shadow of a doubt that he loves us. He wants us to be able to embrace the truth that in all circumstances, he works for the good of those who love him (Rom. 8:28). God proved his love for us by giving his only son, Jesus, to die for us, in order to save our eternal lives (John 3:16–17). That should settle the question of God's love in our minds—permanently! But here are five more ways to know that God loves us.

WE ARE LOVED UNCONDITIONALLY

What would life be like if God's love for us were based on our actions, rather than on our faith in him? Scary. Very scary. Imagine God plucking the petals off of a flower as he describes what we do. "Dave goes to church. I love him. Dave yells at his kids. I love him not. Dave gives to the poor. I love him. Dave forgets to call his mother. I love him not." If God weren't able to separate how he feels about our sin from how he feels about us, that's what he'd be doing, except there'd be far more reasons to say "I love him not" than reasons to say "I love him."

But that's not how God works. He hates our sin, but he loves us no matter what we do. Because we've accepted Christ as Savior and Lord, we are no longer condemned for our sins (Rom. 8:1). No one and nothing can separate us from God's love (Rom. 8:35–39). In Christ, our relationship with God is based on God's grace, not on our actions (Eph. 2:8). Christ's love sets us free from worrying about God's love for us.

Should we intentionally keep sinning because God will forgive us? No way! Following Jesus as Lord means doing all that we can to avoid sinning (Rom. 6). Christ's love sets us free from the grip of sin, and enables us to follow him. He also sets us free from fear. His perfect, unconditional love blows our fear away (1 John 4:18). No one is ever more on our side than God is.

How does this affect our lives? It makes all the difference. Following Jesus isn't always easy. We're asked to walk a straight and narrow path. God's love, forgiveness, and encouragement through the Holy Spirit make it possible. It's as though by following Christ we're learning to walk on a beam as narrow as our feet, with the Holy Spirit as our coach and encourager. God's love puts the beam flat on the ground, so that if we lose our balance, we won't get hurt. The Holy Spirit teaches us how to keep our balance. If we fall off the beam, the Holy Spirit encourages us to get back on. We also have angels watching us (Heb. 12:1) and cheering us on. "You can do it," they cheer. "Don't be afraid!" We're free to do our best in Christ, and to live a life of joy in him.

Imagine what it would be like if, instead, God took the same beam, suspended it a mile off the ground, and said, "Now walk on it. One slip and you're dead!" Our fear of falling would make it almost impossible for us to keep our balance, let alone walk. What if we also had no coach and encourager? And what if we had to contend with a crowd that was jeering, "You can't do it! You always blow it! You're worthless!"? What chance of success would we have? None. What kind of a life would we lead? Miserable.

As we accept God's unconditional love for us, we can begin to love others unconditionally. What would our world be like if all of us loved others unconditionally? What would our lives be like if others encouraged us and didn't hold grudges? How would our spouses, our children, and our parents feel if, at just the right time, we said, "I love you. I forgive you. I believe in you. You can do it." I'm not sure what it would be like, but I know that Jesus wants us all to find out. He commands us to find out.

WE ARE FAMILY

Our experiences with our human families often influence how we relate to God as our heavenly Father. If our human fathers are unloving, we tend to see our heavenly Father as unloving.

I wish that everyone could grow up in a family like mine. No, it wasn't perfect. We had hard times like everyone else. But one thing was always the same—I always knew that I was loved and could count on my family's support.

My dad's love for me made it easy for me to understand that my heavenly Father is loving. I've never doubted that my dad would take on the entire world to protect me. An early childhood experience proved this to me.

When I was six or seven years old, my friends and I were playing hide and seek in the neighborhood. One of our neighbors had full, bushy hedges, and if I leaned into them, I pretty much disappeared. I was hiding in one of these hedges when a hand grabbed my head and threw me down onto the ground. It was the neighbor. He yelled at me for hurting his hedge. I was so scared that I wet my pants and ran home crying. It was humiliating.

I told my parents what happened, gasping for breath between sobs. Mom hugged and kissed me. Dad said, "Hurry up and change. We're going to see this man." Dad walked so fast to the neighbor's house that I had to run to keep up.

Dad's knock on the neighbor's door echoed through the neighborhood. The man answered. My father loomed in the doorway, larger than life. "This is my son," he said. "Did you put your hands on my son?" The neighbor sputtered something about hedges, but

Dad didn't let him finish. "Don't ever touch my son again," he said firmly. "Do you understand me? Don't you *ever* touch my son again." The neighbor took a step back from the door and looked as though he might cry. Then we turned and walked home. It had started off as a terrible day, but it became one of the greatest days of my life. My dad was large and in charge. I was his son, and he loved me.

It's unfortunate that not everyone has a dad or family like mine. Not all of our human fathers love us and protect us as they should. Parents sometimes divorce or are absent physically or emotionally. They sometimes spend more time yelling at their kids than speaking with them. Home is not always a place of safety and belonging—it's often painful.

But in Christ, we've been adopted as sons and daughters into God's royal family. We call the King of the universe "Daddy" (Rom. 8:15–17; Eph. 1:5; Gal. 4:6–7). Isn't that amazing? That makes us princes and princesses. We are nobility. Because we are God's children, we're also heirs of God, and co-heirs with Christ who will share in Christ's glory (Rom. 8:17).

In Christ, we have not only a loving heavenly Father, we also have millions of brothers and sisters. We may be the only child in our earthly family, or be estranged from our siblings, but in Christ, we have lots of family. Our physical families may fall apart, but our spiritual family remains intact.

Our membership in God's royal family, however, comes with great responsibility. Because spiritual family is so important to him, God wants us to help him adopt more children in Christ. He wants us to carry his invitation to follow Jesus to those who are around us, and to those who are on the other side of the world.

God also wants us each to make the church a place of love and belonging, particularly for those who are disconnected from their physical families. We are called to look after orphans and widows in their distress (James 1:27). For our loving purposes, an orphan can be someone whose parents have died, or who is physically or emotionally separated from his or her parents. A widow can be someone whose spouse is dead, or who is divorced. We are to love all of them, and welcome them in the name of the Lord.

WE ARE UNIQUELY VALUABLE

God made each one of us as original, unique works of his art. Before he formed us in our mothers' wombs, he knew us (Ps. 139:13). Before we were born, he prepared good works for us to do (Eph. 2:10). Our uniqueness makes us uniquely valuable to God, and he prizes our individuality.

Because we are unique, the love that we have to offer others has special characteristics. Understanding how God made us and how he has allowed our lives to unfold gives us insight into the particular ways in which we are called to love others and to serve him. Understanding ourselves helps us to love others as Christ loves us.

We don't usually think about what makes us unique from God's perspective, and how it relates to God's calling on our lives. Author Jay McSwain has developed a ministry that helps us discover how God made us. He has developed an assessment process called "PLACE." PLACE helps Christians discover our place in ministry by helping us understand how our personalities, spiritual gifts, abilities, passions, and life experiences can be used within the church to love and help others. *PLACE* is an acronym that describes this assessment process:

> The **P** in PLACE is for personality discovery.
> The **L** represents learning spiritual gifts.
> The **A** stands for abilities awareness.
> The **C** is for connecting passion with ministry.
> The **E** represents experiences of life.[1]

When we better understand how God has lovingly made us and shaped us, we not only feel his love, but also better understand how to love others as Jesus loves us.

WE ARE A WORK IN PROGRESS

We are all works of God's art in progress. As we follow Jesus and love others as Jesus loves us, God uses our life experiences to shape us into his intended masterpieces. In his love and grace, God often uses our mistakes to shape us. I was reminded of this fact while writing this book. Our family took my oldest daughter to college for the first time while I was doing research for the book. Lauren is a very intelligent, self-sufficient young woman, but living away from home at college was a new experience. We were also putting her on a tight budget, not only out of necessity but to teach her to be a good steward of money. The budget, more than the new environment, concerned Lauren.

On the last day of her move-in weekend at college, Lauren got upset about her budget. She wasn't sure whether she would have enough money to provide for her needs. I didn't want her to worry. I wondered how I could love her in this situation as Jesus loves me.

My thinking started off on the right foot. I thought of how God has provided for our family through the years. I thought of how Jesus taught his disciples not to worry about money. Jesus pointed out that God provides for birds without their having to do anything and that God would certainly provide for the disciples as well (Matt. 6:25–34). So far, so good, right?

And then came the stumble, when I opened my mouth. "Lauren, haven't your mother and I always been there for you? Haven't we always provided for your needs? In your whole life, have you lacked for anything?" As I said these things, I knew that I was stumbling. My first clue was that I felt indignant that Lauren was worried about her finances. I took it as a lack of trust in me. I was focusing on me. My second clue was that Lauren got more upset, and then got angry, as I spoke to her. She wasn't feeling the love of Jesus the way I intended.

I stopped talking for a few minutes, and asked God what I had done wrong. As I felt him respond, I felt embarrassed. *Wow,* I thought. *You're really the guy who's going to write a book about Jesus' love? You've got a lot to learn.*

What I sensed God saying was this. "Dave, the first mistake you made was not asking me what to say and how to say it. I was trying to help you, but you weren't listening. Your second mistake was that you made it about you, and not about me. It's not about you. It's about me. You're driving home in an hour, and eventually you'll come Home to me for good. I'm the one who is staying with Lauren to look out for her. But don't give up. Give it another try. This time, reassure her the way Jesus reassures you."

As I thought about it, the way that Jesus reassured the disciples was to point them back to God's love for them. Jesus said, "Look at the birds of the air; they do not sow or reap or store away in barns, and yet your heavenly Father feeds them. Are you not much more valuable than they?" (Matt. 6:26). Even Jesus didn't make it about himself. He made it about his heavenly Father.

So I gave it another try, and said something like this to Lauren: "Lauren, I'm sorry about what I said about mom and me always providing for you. Please forgive me. That's not what you need to know. What you need to know is that it's always been God who has provided for you. He has done that through mom and me in the past, but he will do it through others in the future. We won't always be with you at college, but God will always be here for you. He loves you and will never let you down."

God showed his love for me by helping me do a better job of parenting. He gave me a second chance to teach Lauren about his love. Because I got it wrong the first time and saw the consequences, I will not forget what he taught me. Ironically, God taught me the same lesson that I was trying to teach Lauren—that he provides us with what we need. Lauren needed reassurance that her financial needs would be met. I needed a practical lesson on how to love Lauren as Jesus loves me. God gave both Lauren and me what we needed at the same time.

WE HAVE MISSIONS TO ACCOMPLISH

God loves us so much that he gives each of us missions to accomplish and work to do. One of our most important missions is to love others as Jesus loves us. We can do that, of course, no matter where we are or what work we're doing. By showing that kind of love, we pray that others will decide to follow Jesus and have eternal life with God. We're called to baptize new believers in the name of the Father and of the Son and of the Holy Spirit, and to teach them to obey everything that Jesus has commanded us (Matt. 28:19–20).

As we teach new believers to accept their part of this mission and to follow the Lost Commandment, the love of God spreads throughout the earth. Each believer is like a branch that grows from a godly vine. Each branch, fed by the love of God and infused with the Spirit of life in Christ, grows and bears fruit. The fruit grows in our own lives and in the lives of others.

God not only gives us missions to accomplish, but he also gives us specific work to do. It may not be what we typically think of as "missionary" work, but it's work that helps us to accomplish our missions. When God created us, he prepared good works for us to do through Christ (Eph. 2:10). God plans what we should do, shows us what to do, shows us how to do it, and helps us to do it through the Holy Spirit. What more could we ask a loving father to do? God's love for us is perfect.

If God didn't give us important things to do, our lives would feel pointless and hopeless. God doesn't *need* us to do anything, because he can accomplish all things without us. But he chooses to include us in his work because he loves us. He wants us to know him by working with him, and by allowing him to work through us to love others.

What we do has divine purpose and eternal significance. Our lives count for something important in God's eyes. We are important because God made us to be important in him.

ACCEPT GOD'S LOVE FOR YOU

One of the ways that we show our love for God is to accept his love for us. His love is a gift that we shouldn't refuse. If we refuse his gift, we refuse him. If we accept his gift, we accept him, and he heals our emotional and spiritual wounds. As he is healing us, he allows us to help him heal others by giving us opportunities to love others as Jesus loves us. We become both doctors and patients, both healers and healed. And we come to know and deeply love our Great Physician in the process, as we walk next to him through our lives. Knowing him in this way, and spending the rest of our lives—and eternity—with him, is our greatest purpose and joy in life.

Once we have accepted Christ as our Lord and Savior and allowed his love to heal us, we are ready to stand up and walk with him. In the next chapter, I'll discuss how we get to know Jesus by learning to walk with him.

SUMMARY

We can't give what we don't have. To love others as Jesus has loved us, we must first enter into a personal relationship with him. We do that by accepting Jesus' healing and strengthening love for us. In Christ, we enjoy unconditional love from God, membership in a community of faith, unique gifts and talents to use in serving God, grace to improve without fear, and a mission to accomplish made just for us. We are new people in Christ, with rewarding and purposeful lives ahead of us.

APPLICATION

1. Consider some of the many ways that God loves you. Thank God for each of them.

2. Make the decision to accept who you are in Christ—loved and eternally valuable in the eyes of God.

3. Make the decision not to look to others or your circumstances for your self-esteem. Place your trust in Christ alone.

4. When thoughts come to your mind or statements are made to you that contradict God's truth about you, respond to them with the truth, in love.

5. Ask God to show you how others have hurt you over your lifetime. Ask him to heal your emotional wounds with his love for you.

6. Accept the fact that emotional healing begins with your decisions, but is accomplished through Christ's healing process over time.

7. As you are able and have the opportunity, help others to heal by loving them as Jesus has loved you. Helping others heal will often help you heal.

Chapter 5

SHADOW THE REAL VIP

Jesus gave them this answer: "I tell you the truth, the Son can do nothing by himself; he can do only what he sees his Father doing, because whatever the Father does the Son also does."
—JOHN 5:19

I used to love a television show called *The West Wing*.[1] The show was about a fictional American president named Jed Bartlett, and the people who worked for him in the West Wing of the White House. By watching the show, viewers learned about President Bartlett by following him around from morning until night. His thinking, his character, his personality, and his priorities were all revealed by following him around. The more viewers watched the show, the better we could predict what President Bartlett would do in a given situation.

One of my favorite characters on the show was named Charlie Young. Charlie was the president's body man, and he and the president had an interesting relationship. Charlie's job was to follow the president wherever he went, all day long. He woke up the president in the morning. He announced visitors to the president's office before they were permitted to enter. He opened doors for the president and carried his briefcase. Charlie had the opportunity to know the president better than anyone else on the president's staff, because he was always with him. And the president confided in Charlie, asked his opinions, and treated him like the son he never had.

KNOW JESUS BY FOLLOWING IN HIS FOOTSTEPS

Jesus wants us to be his body men and women. He wants us to know him by shadowing him and obeying him, in the same way that he shadowed God and obeyed him when Jesus walked the earth as a man. When he lived on earth as a man, Jesus said that he couldn't do anything by himself. He could do only what he saw his Father doing, because whatever his Father did, Jesus did (John 5:19).

We shadow Jesus by loving others in the same way that we have seen Jesus love us. If we obey Jesus in this way, he says that he'll show himself to us (John 14:21). We get to know Jesus by experience, by following his example from morning until night. As we follow him, we love others more like he loves us, and we actually become more like him.

Obeying the Lost Commandment requires that we do two things. First, we watch and listen to Jesus. Second, we follow him by doing in our lives what he did—and still does—in his life. We see that he humbled himself before God and others, so we humble ourselves before God and others. He obeys God and, with the help of the Holy Spirit, we obey God. He forgives us, so we forgive others in his name. Jesus serves us, and therefore we serve others. Following the Lost Commandment isn't always easy, but it isn't necessarily complicated either.

Let's begin this journey together, first by watching and listening to Jesus, and then by following him.

WATCH AND LISTEN TO JESUS

The only way we get to know someone well is to spend lots of time with that person, and to pay attention to what he or she says and does. My dad and I are very close. We've spent lots of time together over about five decades. I can recognize my dad's walk a mile away. I can pick out his voice in a crowd just by its tone. When I think about my dad, I sometimes find myself walking and talking like him.

Jesus wants us to know him that way. He wants us to be around him enough to know his "walk" so well that we find ourselves "walking" the same way. He wants us to hear his voice so clearly that we find his words coming out of our mouths. He wants us to be so filled with the Spirit of his love that his love overflows into the lives of everyone we meet. Jesus wants us to know him well, because to know him well is to love him beyond description and to love others as he loves us.

If we want to know Jesus well, the best place to start is to walk with him through the New Testament. We know from the Gospels that Jesus did a lot of walking and talking. By his walk and his words, Jesus taught us how to follow in his footsteps.

Walking with Jesus through the Bible is not just a matter of covering ground by passively reading pages. We should engage Jesus in conversation as we go. We talk to him as we read, just as though we were having a conversation with him while walking a dusty road near Jerusalem. We might say, "Lord, please teach me what I should know about you and your love, and show me how to love others as you have loved me."

Then, we watch carefully how Jesus walked through various circumstances. We might ask, "Father, show me through your Holy Spirit any circumstances in my life that are similar to what I'm reading about. Teach me to walk the way Jesus walked, and to love the way Jesus loves." We ask Jesus questions, and then listen for his answers. We pause in silence to let him speak to us through his Holy Spirit.

Other things might, of course, pop into our minds along the way. We, for instance, should want to praise Jesus for who he is, or we might feel guilty about something and need to confess it to him to receive his forgiveness. We might be worried about something and need his assurance. We might have a decision to make and need his guidance. Jesus listens to us, and generously gives us what we need. We know that Jesus loves us not only because the Bible tells us so, but also because he shows his love for us every day. Thank you, Jesus, for loving us.

As we watch and listen to Jesus by reading the Bible, and pay attention to the way he loves us, we learn some things about him as a person:

- *Who Jesus is.* Knowing more about Jesus' love means knowing Jesus better. Jesus is love. We learn more about how Jesus loves us by paying attention to the specific ways in which he loves us.
- *How Jesus feels.* We understand better how Jesus feels as he loves us. We experience his joy and his pain vicariously by walking next to him, and experientially as we love others the same way that he loves us.
- *Why Jesus loves.* Jesus' love for us is an expression of his gratitude to God. God loves Jesus, then Jesus loves us in the same way that God loves him (John 15:9). In Scripture, Jesus doesn't elaborate with words about how God loves him. He just shows us by obeying God's command to love us.

When he took the form of a man, Jesus became as human as we are. He felt joy and pain and longing. God loves us so much, that he made it possible for us to relate to Jesus on a human level.

By walking with Jesus and talking to him, we also learn about how he loves us. By *how*, I mean two things. First, how was he able to love us? Where did he get his strength and wisdom? And second, how did he express his love for us? How did his relationship with God, his mission, his humility, his obedience, his forgiveness, and his service affect how he loves us in practical terms. We can't learn how to love others the way Jesus loves us unless we can figure out how his love for us works on a practical level in our daily lives. Jesus wants to teach us how through our walk with him, through the Bible, through his Holy Spirit, and through experiences in our lives.

In addition to listening to Jesus, and walking with him through the pages of the Bible, is there anything else that we can do to know him and his love? Yes, the most important thing: follow in his footsteps by loving others as he has loved us. We can't really understand Jesus' love by simply watching and listening. We must walk with him by living according to the Lost Commandment.

WALK WITH JESUS AND KNOW HIM

Our first steps in our walk with Jesus are baby steps. Most of us have watched babies learn to walk. Some of us have actually been blessed to watch our own kids take their first steps. Isn't it fun? All of us were so cute—goofy looking, but cute—when we learned to walk.

We started by being able to hold our heads up in our parents' arms. Then we figured out how to roll over in our cribs. Then we learned how to crawl on all fours. One day, we figured out that we could stand up if we pulled ourselves up using pieces of furniture. Our parents took our hands, and we were able to walk while they held us. And then the big moment: we walked on our own, wobbling and smiling. *Plunk.* We fell on our bottoms. But we pulled ourselves up and tried again. Gradually, we learned to walk with confidence. And then run. And some of us might have even learned to vault or pirouette.

Learning to walk is a process. None of us popped out of the womb and immediately performed a pirouette. The process takes time. It takes encouragement. It takes a certain amount of courage from us. And it takes patience. Our parents needed to be patient, and we need to be patient with ourselves, and with our kids.

Learning to walk with Jesus is also a process. We're not instant pastors or elders when we first become Christians. It takes time. It takes encouragement, teaching, and support from God the Father through the Holy Spirit. And it takes patience from both God and ourselves.

The process of learning to walk with Jesus involves more than watching and listening to him, just as the process of learning to walk as a toddler involves more than watching and listening to our parents. What if a parent insisted that the best way to teach his kid to walk was to make his kid watch and listen to walking lessons? The parent's teaching outline might look something like this:

- Read Humpty Dumpty. Discuss importance of balance when encountering heights.
- Demonstration: safe sitting.

- Read Jack and Jill. Discuss adverse effects of slope and speed on balance while walking or running.
- Lecture: "Walking Shoes for All Occasions."
- Demonstration: safe walking.
- Lecture: "Great Walkers of History."
- Lecture and discussion: "Walking in Theory and Practice."
- Lecture: "The Physics and Ergonomics of Walking."

At this rate, the kid would grow old and die before ever taking his first step, and still wouldn't really know how to walk. We'd call this parent crazy, or maybe cruel.

The only real way to learn to walk is to do it. We can watch others doing it. We can listen to coaching on how to do it. But mainly we just have to do it. We have to fall on our bottoms, and bump into furniture, and skin our knees. That's part of the process. If we let the bumps and scrapes scare us, we'll never learn to walk. Those of us who are parents know that.

Learning to walk with Jesus also involves bumps and scrapes, or worse. But the only way to learn to walk like Jesus—or to love like Jesus—is to just do it as best we can, and let God teach us through our mistakes. We follow the Lost Commandment not by simply watching and listening to Jesus. We can't just watch Jesus love us, listen to Bible lessons, and remain in our seats. To follow the Lost Commandment, we've got to stand up, step up, and step out. We've got to walk forward in the love of Christ and in the power of the Holy Spirit.

Jesus said, "If anyone would come after me, he must deny himself and take up his cross daily and follow me" (Luke 9:23). We can't just watch Jesus carry his cross. We have to pick up our own crosses and follow him. Watching Jesus carry his cross for us through the pages of the Bible teaches us intellectually about his love. Experiencing what it's like to carry a cross in our own lives, by loving others as Jesus loves us, teaches us practically and emotionally about Jesus' love.

When we love others sacrificially, we begin to really understand and appreciate Jesus' incredible love for us. Our greater appreciation for Jesus' love fuels a greater love for God and others. We show our gratitude by praising God, and by taking action to love others as Jesus loves us. In this process, by our actions we relate Jesus' love for us to our love for others. By our imitation of his love in our lives, our relationship with Jesus is strengthened.

This imitation is like walking down the road beside Christ. He is dragging his cross for our sake and for the sake of the whole world. We each drag our own much lighter cross for those whom God gives us to love. We look at Jesus, and he looks at us. As we focus our attention on Jesus and his love for us, and consciously imitate his love by loving others, we know and identify with Christ on a much deeper level than we had before. We experience some of his pain and joy. When we are rejected or persecuted because of our faith, we feel some of Jesus' pain. When others become Christians after we give them Jesus' invitation to follow him, we experience some of Jesus' joy. Knowing Jesus in this way makes life worth living, and justifies whatever sacrifice we make in Jesus' name.

WHERE TO?

We are alive in Christ, healed by his love, and commanded to walk out the Lost Commandment. Where do we go from here? We know that we follow Jesus, but what are his marching orders? All of us are given a mission. It's exciting. It's dangerous. It's important. But will we accept it? I'll discuss the mission in the next chapter, and challenge us to accept it.

SUMMARY

The best way to begin learning to love others the way Jesus loves us is to follow Jesus around through the pages of the Bible, watching how he acts. Along the way, we can ask him to give us the understanding and strength that we need to follow his example. We should pay particular attention to the seven principal elements of Jesus' love: joy, relationship with God, mission, humility, obedience, forgiveness, and service. Then we should do what Jesus did, rather than remaining a passive observer.

APPLICATION

1. Recommit your life to following in Jesus' footsteps.

2. Set aside time each day to watch and listen to Jesus by walking with him through the pages of the Bible.

3. Ask the Holy Spirit to open your eyes to Jesus' love for you. Ask him to teach you how to love others in the same way that Jesus loves you.

4. Ask the Holy Spirit to show you specific people who need you to love them as Jesus loves you.

5. As you go about your day, ask the Holy Spirit to give you opportunities to love others as Jesus loves you.

6. When you have a chance to love others as Jesus loves you—and you will—ask the Holy Spirit for help in doing it.

7. Then do it. Just do it. While thinking about how Jesus loves you, and visualizing how he has loved you, love others as he loves you.

PART 3

MISSION

The Determination of Christ's Love

Chapter 6

NO MISSION IMPOSSIBLE

*I tell you the truth, anyone who has faith in me will do what I have
been doing. He will do even greater things than these, because I am
going to the Father.*

—JOHN 14:12

I used to love a television show called *Mission Impossible*.[1] The
show was about members of a top secret United States government organization called the Impossible Missions Force (IMF).
At the beginning of each episode, Mr. Phelps, the leader of IMF,
received a tape-recorded message from "the secretary" of an undis-
closed government agency, and an envelope with instructions out-
lining a mission.

Each mission was very dangerous, top secret, and complicated.
Each required intricate planning and infiltration into hostile for-
eign territory. The missions were so dangerous and so complicated
that they were considered impossible. That's why "the secretary"
always gave Mr. Phelps an option: he could accept or decline the
mission. The tape-recorded message would always end with the
words, "As always, should you or any member of your IMF be
caught or killed, the secretary will disavow any knowledge of your
actions. This tape will self-destruct in five seconds." And then
came the dramatic, suspense-filled theme song.

Most of us would have listened to that tape and said, "No
way!" But not Mr. Phelps. He always accepted the mission. And
he always accomplished the mission using amazing planning and
timing, and a fantastic array of disguises and high-tech gadgets.
But he didn't do it alone. Other members of the IMF were given

assignments that used their unique skills and experience. All of them risked their lives, week after week, to save the world.

OUR MISSION IS MANDATORY

Although some of us may not have realized it, all of us who have accepted Jesus as Lord and Savior are called to be a part of a mission. We don't all have the same roles within the mission. Each of us has a personality, gifts, abilities, passions, and experiences that make us uniquely suited for different roles within the mission. Each of us operates within our circumstances—our homes, our workplace, our church—to accomplish our part of the mission.

God gives us freedom to refuse to participate in the mission, but he doesn't give us the right to refuse the mission without consequences. Jesus is Lord of the mission. To refuse the mission is to refuse his lordship in our lives.

When it comes to our mission, becoming a Christian is a little like joining the army. When we make the decision to follow Jesus as our Lord and Savior, it's like going to the recruiting office and signing the induction papers. After we're inducted into the army, the army has the right to send us on missions. If we refuse, we're guilty of violating a direct order, and are subject to military discipline. If we run away, we are AWOL: absent without leave. When we're caught, we can expect very serious consequences.

Having a mission gives our lives purpose, focus, and a sense of urgent determination. We're on a mission from God! How much more exciting or meaningful could our lives be? What else could possibly be more important in our lives? Jesus lived his life with a sense of purpose driven by his mission. We are called to do the same.

HOW JESUS' MISSION AFFECTED HIS LIFE

Jesus lived a purpose-driven life. His purpose was to fulfill his mission given to him by God. Simply put, Jesus' mission was to love God by loving us as God commanded. To fulfill his mission, Jesus humbled himself, proclaimed the Kingdom of God, forgave, and served as God commanded until the day that Jesus finished his mission by dying on the cross for us. Jesus never took his eyes off the cross.

Jesus' mission compelled him to do what he wouldn't otherwise have done if he had followed the human part of his nature. As a boy, Jesus' mission compelled him to stay in the temple courts in Jerusalem, even after his parents left town (Luke 2:41–49). Jesus' mission led him into the desert to be tempted by the Devil (Matt. 4:1). When it came time to go to the cross, Jesus didn't want to go. Who would? But Jesus kept his mission in his mind and heart. He prayed, "My Father, if it is not possible for this cup to be taken away unless I drink it, may your will be done" (Matt. 26:42). Jesus' mission directed and focused his entire life on God's purpose for his life.

WHAT IS OUR MISSION?

Our mission is more amazing, more dangerous, and in some ways appears more impossible than any mission we'd see on an episode of *Mission Impossible*. Our mission is to change ourselves and our world with God's help, by following the Lost Commandment. We are to rock our world with the love of Christ. And we begin with the hardest part of the mission. We begin by working with the Holy Spirit to change ourselves—our attitudes and thoughts—as required by the Lost Commandment. We then continue Jesus' mission through our words and actions by loving others the way he loves us.

HOW IS THE MISSION POSSIBLE?

Our mission seems overwhelming. How is it remotely possible? A famous comedian once did a routine that parodied the discussion between God and Noah when God first asked Noah to build an ark. You'd expect Noah to respond to God's request with awe and reverence. And that's pretty much how the Bible says Noah responded. But in this comic routine, when God asked Noah to build a huge ark, Noah responded, "Riiiight." Right—meaning "You must be kidding!"

That's how we may want to respond to our mission from Jesus: Riiiight! We may have wrestled with personal struggles for our entire lives and feel powerless to change. We may look at a world full of pain, and hate, and hunger, and feel powerless to help. We may look at Christ's perfection and our sinfulness, and be tempted to quit before we even start. But we must not. Christ has given us a mission: we must love others as he loves us. In faith, we must obey. In faith, we must stand up, step up, and step out.

We Have Who It Takes to Accomplish Our Mission

Our mission is completely impossible if we try to accomplish it ourselves. If we try to accomplish it ourselves, God will probably let us fail. He wants us to realize our weakness and our need for him, so that he can have a loving relationship with us. When we try to do things on our own, we quickly forget about God. But when we realize our weakness, when we confess our sins and humble ourselves before God, when we offer our lives to him as our spiritual act of worship (Rom. 12:1), then watch out—because big things are about to happen.

When we're weak in this way, we can understand what Christ meant when he said, "My burden is light" (Matt. 11:30). He helps us carry our burdens and sends others to help us as well. Even Christ couldn't do anything apart from God (John 5:19), and we can't do anything apart from Christ (John 15:5). Understanding our weakness is how we begin to find our strength in Jesus.

When we are weak in this way, then we are strong in the Lord (2 Cor. 12:10). We can do all things through Christ, who strengthens us (Phil. 4:13). Jesus said, "I tell you the truth, anyone who has faith in me will do what I have been doing. He will do even greater things than these, because I am going to the Father" (John 14:12). Yes, we heard right. Jesus said that we would do even greater things than he did.

It's not that we have *what* it takes to accomplish the mission, but that we have *who* it takes to accomplish the mission. We have the Holy Spirit living inside of us. Through the Holy Spirit, we have access to the power and resources of heaven. Jesus said, "You may ask me for anything in my name, and I will do it" (John 14:14).

In my name doesn't just mean including Jesus' name in the prayer. It means that if we ask for something that is consistent with Jesus' character, Jesus will give it to us. Anything we need to accomplish the mission that Jesus gave to us is consistent with Jesus' character.

Our Mission Is Dangerous, But We Don't Need to Be Afraid

The fact that our mission is possible, doesn't mean it isn't dangerous. We may lose everything that we have, or even lose our lives, to accomplish our mission in Christ. That's part of the deal. That's what we signed up for when we asked Jesus to be the Lord of our lives.

Even though our mission is dangerous, our victory is certain and our reward is secure. We have to lose our lives by giving our whole lives to Jesus, even if it means physically dying for him. If we lose our lives for the sake of Christ, figuratively or even literally, we will truly be alive in him. But if we hold our lives back from him, we will lose true life (Matt. 10:39). Jesus told us that we would be persecuted (John 15:20), but that ours would be the kingdom of heaven (Matt. 5:10). He said we will have trouble in this world, but in him we will have peace (John 16:33). We may lose our family relationships or our possessions by following him, but he has promised that we will receive a hundred times as much as we lose, and that we will inherit eternal life (Matt. 19:29). We have to accept the risk of Jesus' lordship over our lives in order to receive the benefits of following him.

Once we accept and embrace the danger of following Jesus, his perfect love casts out our fear. Then we can begin to see life as an adventure in him, without worrying so much about the future. We're walking through life with the Holy Spirit of God within us and the almighty Lord of the universe walking next to us. Our eternal future is secure in the love of Christ, so we really have nothing to fear.

Unlike the mysterious "secretary" in *Mission Impossible*, Jesus will never disavow knowledge of us. He will never leave us or forsake us (Heb. 13:5), and nothing can separate us from his love (Rom. 8:35–39). "So we say with confidence, 'The Lord is my helper; I will not be afraid. What can man do to me?'" (Heb. 13:6; see also Ps. 118:6–7).

81

SO WHAT'S THE PLAN TO ACCOMPLISH THE MISSION?

Now that we know we have who it takes to accomplish our mission, what's the plan? Each of us is responsible for carrying out our part of our common mission within our own lives and circumstances, according to our personalities, spiritual gifts, abilities, God-given passions, and experiences. God gives each one of us our own unique opportunities to love others as Jesus loves us. Each one of us follows the Lost Commandment in unique ways in the context of our own lives.

Each of our lives in Christ is unique, and we each carry out a variation of the Lost Commandment. We Christians together are a little like a snow fall. Each snowflake is unique, but when all the snowflakes come to rest on the ground, we don't see individual snowflakes; we see one beautiful blanket of snow. Likewise, when individual Christians follow the Lost Commandment, the world should not so much see us, as they should see the One whom we have in common: Jesus.

So rather than talk about the different ways in which each of us loves others according to the Lost Commandment, let's talk about what our love in Christ has in common. We all follow the Lost Commandment by allowing the power of the Holy Spirit to change our attitudes, our actions, and our words to reflect the love that Jesus has shown to us. As the love of Christ is reflected through our lives into the lives of those around us, the love of Christ transforms our world, one situation, one conversation, and one relationship at a time. Here's how it works in our lives and in our world.

Change Happens in Ourselves

The first step toward accomplishing our mission is for each of us to accept our mission. God will use our obedience to the Lost Commandment to change us, if we will build four behaviors into our lives, with his help: determination, Christ consciousness, planning and accountability, and present focus.

Determination. The word *mission* conveys a sense of determination and urgency. We can't be casual and be on a mission. We've got to get serious. We've got to get focused. We can't mess around. Our mission requires that we get determined to know and follow Jesus.

The apostle Paul compared our mission to the training of a serious runner. If we're going to run the race of our lives with Christ, we need to run in such a way as to get the prize of praise from him (1 Cor. 9:24). We need to go into strict training (1 Cor. 9:25) with the specific purpose of knowing Jesus and his love, so that we can love others as he has loved us. We have to live our lives with a sense of purpose, and not just let life happen to us.

Our determination should also be demonstrated by our reactions to setbacks and adversity. We can't be whiners or quitters. Sure, we're going to get hurt following the Lost Commandment. Sure, it's okay to say "Ouch," or to cry in pain, or to commiserate with others. That's not being a whiner. That's being human.

But we can't let ourselves be surprised by adversity, or be indignant that we're experiencing it. Jesus told us that we're going to experience adversity (John 15:20). We need to embrace adversity as an opportunity to develop perseverance, maturity, and a more complete understanding of Christ's love for us (James 1:2–4). After some crying and commiseration, there comes a time when we have to say to ourselves, in the words of a former assistant of mine, "Buck up, you whining crybaby!" And then we have to pick ourselves up, dust ourselves off, and get back in the race.

We also need to be determined to obey Christ. We need to follow in his footsteps by sticking close to God as Jesus' loving disciples. We are God's humble, obedient, and forgiving servants, just as Jesus is.

Christ consciousness. To successfully accomplish our mission, we need to keep our minds and hearts connected to Christ. He is the vine, and we are the branches. If we stay connected to Christ by "remaining in" him, our lives will be fruitful (John 15:5). We remain in him by being aware of his presence, by meditating on his Word, by speaking with him, and by obeying his commands.

Notice that Jesus says that we are branches connected to his vine. We always remain connected to him through the Holy Spirit.

We're not like bees who visit him like a flower and then fly away. As branches, we don't dock to the vine of Jesus on Sundays and Wednesdays, and then disconnect and blow away during the rest of the week. We stay connected.

Our objective, therefore, should be to take every one of our thoughts captive, making them obedient to Christ (2 Cor. 10:5) so that the Holy Spirit can change us through the renewing of our minds (Rom. 12:2). We should develop a consistent, constant state of Christ consciousness.

How does this work in real life? There's no specific formula, but it might look something like this. When we wake up and, after thanking God for another day, we might pray something like, "Here I am Lord. Send me wherever you want me. I mean wherever. Teach me about your Son Jesus' love today, and show me how I should love others in that same way." We might then get up, go to a quiet place, and read the Bible. We might read, memorize, and meditate on God's Word, and pray, "Lord, please show me through these words who you are, and what you want me to do." During the day, we should be in an ongoing conversation with Jesus. We should ask him to teach us about himself, and we should listen and watch intently for his answer. We should proactively look for people to love as Jesus loves us. And before we go to sleep, we might pray something like, "Thank you for loving me, Lord. Forgive me for the times when I didn't love you or others as I should have. Tomorrow, help me to love you and others more the way you love me." And the next day, we get up and do it again. And again. For as long as we live.

Planning and accountability. There's an old saying: "Fail to plan, plan to fail." Whatever God tells us to do, we should plan to do. If we know that we should spend more time studying the Bible and praying, we should open our calendars, pick times to do that, and write it down. We should have our calendars next to our Bibles when we spend time in prayer before God. If we sense that there's something that God wants us to do, or someone God wants us to call, we should write it on our calendar. And then, of course, we should do it.

We should also share our plans with accountability partners and ask them to hold us accountable to our plan. Our spouses can be an accountability partner, but it also helps to have others alongside. I meet with a group of men once a week. Each of us has areas of our lives that we believe God wants us to change. We try to encourage each other to be specific about what God is saying we should do, and then we ask each other whether we've done what he said. Accountability groups work only if we're honest about our struggles, so the group should commit itself to strict confidentiality and honesty.

Present focus. Having a present focus means living life to the fullest in Christ in the present. We still remember the past, and we learn positive lessons from the past, but we don't allow our past mistakes to drag down our attitudes toward the present and the future. If the past indicates that we have something to change, then we work toward constructive change. Other than that, we leave our mistakes in the past, rejoice in the forgiveness of Christ, and embrace our new life in him.

Regrets about the past that do not lead to positive change don't come from God (2 Cor. 7:10). We need to consciously put our mistakes behind us by asking God and others for their forgiveness, by doing what we can to make things right, and then by moving away from our mistakes mentally and emotionally.

Having a present focus doesn't mean that we don't plan for the future. It just means that we focus on the implementation of the plan one day at a time. We shouldn't worry, for example, about where our food and clothes will come from, because we know that God will provide them for us (Matt. 6:28–32). Jesus said that we should make God's kingdom and God's righteousness our first priority, and then take each day as it comes. He said, "Each day has enough trouble of its own" (Matt. 6:34).

If we concern ourselves with more than one day at a time, we can become overwhelmed and distracted from our mission. In fact, if we're in particularly difficult circumstances, such as when we have significant physical or emotional pain, we should shorten our present focus. We might have to focus on an hour at a time, or a minute at a time, or a breath at a time. We increase our ability to endure adversity and develop perseverance when we apply this principle.

When we build these behaviors into our lives, not only do we change—the world around us begins to change. Here's how.

Change Happens in Our World

When we begin to look at each situation, each conversation, and each relationship as an opportunity to love others as Jesus has loved us, amazing things begin to happen around us. We begin to see the world around us changing in response to the love of Jesus. Seeing that change also changes us as we experience Jesus' love in the lives of others. We come to know Jesus through a deeper experience of his presence and love.

Having said this, it's important to remind ourselves of why we follow the Lost Commandment and to limit our expectations concerning how specific individuals will respond to our love. We love others as Jesus has loved us as a response to Jesus' love for us, and not as a means toward our personal end of fixing those around us. As both the Bible and my mom have taught me, we need to spend most of our energy on changing ourselves, rather than trying to change those around us. Otherwise, we'll take our eyes off of our first priority and get discouraged.

The Lost Commandment helps us to understand this principle and adjust our expectations. Under the Golden Rule, we have a natural expectation that others will repay our love with their love. If we, after all, are doing to others what we would have them do to us, isn't it reasonable to expect others to reciprocate our love? We've given love, and we want to be paid back in love. If others don't love us as we have loved them, then isn't it natural under the Golden Rule to feel resentment that we didn't get our due?

But the Lost Commandment doesn't lead us to expect to be paid back, because it's based on the principle of paying forward. Why should we expect to be paid back when Jesus has paid us in advance, and in full? His love is the inexhaustible down payment on the love that we are to have for others. We can never repay Jesus in full for what he did for us on the cross, and for what he does in our lives every day. We owe Jesus a continuing debt of love.

As a partial repayment, Jesus asks us to pay his love forward to others by loving others as he loves us. Our hope should be that others will repay our love by giving their lives to Jesus, and by paying his love forward to others. When we free ourselves from our expectations of being loved by all others in return for our love, we're free to experience the joy of watching Jesus' love multiply in this way.

How great an impact can our lives have for Christ when we obey the Lost Commandment? A huge impact.

Pay Jesus' Love Forward

I'm always amazed at the effect that my mood and actions have on those around me. On any given day, life can be hectic in my household and in my workplace. I'm sure all of us experience this. If I respond to my circumstances with impatience and crankiness, impatience and crankiness multiplies all around me. Not only do I get crankiness in return, but others around me pay my crankiness forward to others. Suddenly I'm surrounded by crankiness.

On the other hand, if I respond to my circumstances with patience, love, and grace, the same multiplication takes place, but in a positive direction. If I respond to the crankiness of others with love and patience, I can almost see their stress melting away from them. Then I see them pay my love and patience forward into the lives of others. And suddenly, I'm surrounded by love and patience. It's amazing how reliably and quickly the pay-it-forward principle can work.

Loving others in small ways is like throwing a pebble into a pond. The ripple effects extend far beyond where the pebble first fell. But when we love others as Jesus has loved us, it's like throwing a boulder into the pond. The ripple effect is large and can spread all the way to the edge of the pond. God wants the love of Jesus to reach the very edges of the earth, to all creation. If all of us follow the Lost Commandment, this will be accomplished quickly, to the glory of God.

I just love the movies. One movie that demonstrates well the power of the pay-it-forward principle, though in a secular context, is *Pay It Forward*.[2] In this movie, seventh-grade student Trevor McKinney receives an unusual assignment in social studies class: think of an idea to change our world—and put it into action! On his way home from school, Trevor takes a detour through a construction site, where he sees a group of homeless people. That's when Trevor comes up with his plan to change the world. He decides to take home with him a homeless drug addict named Gerry.

Trevor gives Gerry food, a place to sleep, a shower, some money, and friendship. Rather than accept anything in return as "pay back," Trevor explains to Gerry that he wants Gerry to "pay it forward." Gerry must perform three generous acts of assistance to three different people, and refuse to take anything in return. Instead, Gerry must explain to each of the three people that they also have to pay it forward on the same terms.

Trevor later explains his plan to his social studies class, using this diagram:

Me

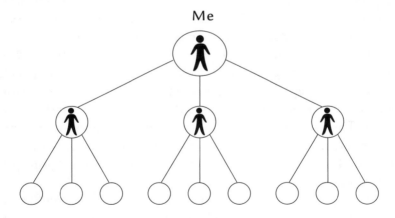

He says, "That's me and that's three people. And I'm going to help them. But it has to be something really big, something they can't do by themselves. So I do it for them. And they do it for three other people. That's nine. And they do it for three more. And that's twenty-seven."[3] And so on. What motivated Trevor to come up with a plan? He thinks the world stinks, and needs to change.

To honor his commitment to pay it forward, Gerry then fixes Trevor's mother's truck. He develops a new sense of hope that he can get clean from drugs, he gets a job and an apartment. Although he later slips back into drug use, he goes on to save the life of a woman who's about to jump off of a bridge into a river.

As he's saving the woman, Gerry says, "I owe someone a favor." "Not me," the woman responds. But Gerry continues: "You know a minute ago all I could think about was getting my next fix. And I saw you and I changed my thinking. . . . Do me a favor: save my life."[4] The woman abandons her plan to kill herself. Her self-worth is restored by the love that Gerry shows her, and by her new mission to save someone else. And Gerry's life is saved when he realizes that his life is important.

When later asked why more people don't pay love forward, Trevor says, "I think some people are too scared or something, to think things can be different. . . . I guess it's hard for some people who are so used to things the way they are, even if they're bad, to change. And they kind of give up. When they do, everybody kind of loses."[5]

Trevor couldn't be more right. That same fear of change inhibits our obedience to the Lost Commandment. But imagine the power of the pay-it-forward principle, if what we're paying forward is the love of Jesus, and if we don't limit the number of payments to three. What if each of us devotes the rest of our lives to paying forward the love of Jesus? The pond of our world would be filled with waves of Jesus' love, until the very edges of the earth overflow with the love of Christ. May each one of us commit to changing the world with Christ's love.

WILL WE ACCEPT THE MISSION?

Okay . . . now we're like Mr. Phelps in *Mission Impossible*. We've just heard what's involved in the mission. Will we accept? Will we change ourselves and our world by our obeying the Lost Commandment? Please take a minute to close your eyes and consider this question in prayer before the Lord. And then give him your answer.

In the coming chapters, we'll be more specific about what's involved in our mission, first by discussing whom we should love as Jesus loves us, and then by discussing how to love them.

SUMMARY

When we give our lives to Jesus as our Lord, we accept a mission that may seem impossible: to follow the Lost Commandment, which will change us and the world. But in Christ, all things are possible. We begin by allowing Christ to change us through his Holy Spirit. We accomplish our mission with Jesus' help by marshalling our determination, focusing our attention on Christ, planning our steps with his help, making ourselves accountable to others, and taking one day and one situation at a time. As we are changed by the love of Jesus, we are better able to pay his love forward to others and see change in the world. If we devote our lives to loving others as Jesus loves us and to teaching others to do the same, the entire world will be transformed by the love of Christ.

APPLICATION

1. Consider the specific and practical implications in your life when you accept Jesus' mission possible.

2. Discuss any concerns that you may have about the mission with Jesus, your pastor, and your family.

3. Make a serious decision to accept the mission, no matter what it may cost you.

4. Develop a sense of determination about accomplishing the mission with Jesus' help.

5. Develop a constant awareness of Christ in your life, in part by praying and reading the Bible, and in part by continuously focusing your mind on him.

6. Pray that God will show you, through his Holy Spirit, what steps you should take to accomplish the mission.

7. Take out your calendar and plan to do what God is telling you to do.

8. Share your plans with your spouse and Christian friends, and ask them to hold you accountable.

9. Be alert throughout the day to opportunities to love others as Jesus has loved you.

10. Learn from the past, plan for the future, live in the moment.

Chapter 7

LEAVE NO ONE BEHIND

Again Jesus said, "Peace be with you! As the Father has sent me, I am sending you."

—JOHN 20:21

An Orange County, Florida, man looked out his window one Monday morning to see his neighbor's house on fire. He could see the neighbor's truck parked next to the house. So he dashed across the street, ran into the burning building, and rescued his neighbor, who was asleep in a back room.

Although the rescuer didn't lose his life, he reenacted the divine rescue mission that saved all of us who believe in Jesus Christ. In a sense, God looked down from heaven and saw our houses on fire with sin. Many had died and were lost in hell's fire, but many of us were still asleep and oblivious to the danger. We needed—and still need—a rescuer. God loves us so much that he sent his Son, Jesus, into the world to save us (John 3:16–17).

Without Jesus, all of us are like sheep who have gone astray (Isa. 53:6), and there's nothing more clueless or defenseless than sheep gone astray. Jesus said, "I am the good shepherd . . . and I lay down my life for the sheep. . . . This command I received from my Father" (John 10:14–18). And now Jesus commands us to do the same. The Lost Commandment says to love others as Jesus has loved us, and Jesus loved us when we didn't know him. So part of the Lost Commandment is loving those who don't know him. Jesus said, "My command is this: Love each other as I have loved you. Greater love has no one than this, that he lay down his life for his friends. You are my friends if you do what I command" (John 15:12–14).

HOW JESUS LOVES THE LOST

How did Jesus lay down his life for us? He obviously died on the cross to rescue us from the penalty of our sin. But that's not all he did. He laid down his life every day by loving those who didn't know him. He loved both *on* purpose and *with* purpose. By *on* purpose, I mean that he made it his mission to love us while we were still lost sheep (Rom. 5:8). By *with* purpose, I mean that he wanted us to be changed by his love in specific ways. He wanted us to come into his fold by believing in him, and then he wanted us to follow him in his mission. And today, Jesus still wants to turn found sheep into shepherds who will commit *their* lives to loving lost sheep *on* purpose and *with* purpose.

If we take a close look at the way Jesus loves the lost, we see that in addition to his love having seven principal elements, his love also has four important characteristics: his love is committed, capable, compassionate, and courageous. If we're going to love others the way Jesus has loved us, our love for the lost should also have these characteristics.

Jesus' Love Is Committed

When I was a third-year student in college, I was a lost sheep. No one seemed to know that I was lost except God and me. My grades were good. My health was good. My family loved me. But I still felt empty and sad. I began to ask, "Is this all there is to life?"

I also began to want to know more about God and my relationship to him. What did he expect of me? Did he care about my plans and my life? To find answers, I wanted to talk to someone whose life demonstrated a real and personal relationship with God. But because I wasn't going to church at the time and didn't have many Christian friends, I wasn't sure where to turn.

As I considered who to approach, the first person who came to mind was not a pastor or a peer, but my economics professor, Ken Elzinga. Ken was—and still is—a wildly popular teaching professor, and a nationally-recognized expert in antitrust economics. During my very first semester at the University of Virginia, I took an introductory class in economics from him. The class had two sections of about six hundred students. When Thanksgiving came, Ken made a general announcement to both sections of the class. He said, "I know that many of you students won't be able to go home for Thanksgiving, so I invite every one of you to have Thanksgiving dinner at my house." This wasn't a single grand gesture. He's made this announcement every year, for the last forty years or so.

As a third-year student, in the spring of 1979, I was again studying under Ken, but this time in a smaller class on antitrust law. In the previous semester, Ken's wife, Barbara, had died of cancer. Rather than keep his pain to himself, as most people would, Ken explained to the class that his loss might cause him to feel the need to visit friends out of town, and that he might miss class occasionally—as though he needed our permission to take leave. I thought that Ken's expression of grief and humility was an unusual act of love and respect for his students. He was sharing his life with us to demonstrate that he cared about us. I wouldn't have been surprised, given Ken's popularity and fame, if he were arrogant. I was very surprised by his kindness and humility.

One day, during Ken's office hours, and after discussing antitrust law for a few minutes, I took what felt like a risk by asking him honest questions about Christianity. Ken answered these questions gently and thoughtfully from his personal experience and study. That day began a series of discussions that led me to Jesus, my Good Shepherd. At one point, Ken bought a book for me, wrote a letter of encouragement to me, and then personally delivered the book and the letter to my room.

There's nothing accidental about Ken's love for his students. Like Jesus, Ken has a passionate commitment to pursue lost sheep and turn them into shepherds. That commitment might be expressed like this: leave no one behind. Pursue every opportunity that God provides to love the lost the way Jesus has loved us. Look out the windows of our houses. Look for fire in our neighbor's houses. Be prepared to run into those burning houses to save our neighbors.

Jesus told us that his life's purpose was to fulfill his Father's will by pursuing lost sheep. He said, "For I have come down from heaven not to do my will but to do the will of him who sent me. And this is the will of him who sent me, that I shall lose none of all that he has given me, but raise them up at the last day" (John 6:38–39).

In the spirit of the Lost Commandment, Jesus has now passed this mission to us. As God sent Jesus to the lost sheep of the world, so Jesus has sent us (John 20:21). He has commissioned us to go out into the "open country" (Luke 15:4) of the world, to all creation (Matt. 28:19; Mark 16:15; Luke 24:47), to bring his lost sheep into his fold, and then to help him transform these sheep into shepherds who share his mission. Nothing is more important to Jesus than the fulfillment of this mission.

We don't necessarily have to travel far to find lost sheep. For many of us, all we have to do is look across the dinner table of our homes, across the streets of our neighborhoods, or across the halls of our offices. Lost sheep are running loose everywhere. But we have to learn to look.

Part of learning to look involves developing a deep awareness of how important this entire mission is to Jesus. We are tempted to separate our love for Jesus from our love for others. But after his resurrection, Jesus had a conversation with Peter that emphasized that these two loves are inseparable. Three times Jesus asked Peter whether he loved—truly loved—Jesus. Each time Peter said yes, Jesus responded, first by saying, "Feed my lambs," then by saying, "Take care of my sheep," and finally by saying, "Feed my sheep" (John 21:15–17). Peter was hurt because Jesus asked him the same question three times (John 21:17). But it wasn't Jesus' intention to hurt Peter. Jesus was emphasizing the connection between our love for him and our love for others. Jesus wants us to commit to finding and caring for his sheep out of love for him.

Once we're committed to the mission for the lost, what must we do to fulfill our commission to go out to the lost? Three things: be capable, be compassionate, and be courageous.

Jesus' Love Is Capable

When I asked Ken questions in his office, he was capable of answering them because he was both prepared and willing to talk to me about Jesus. If I had asked Ken what it meant to him to be a Christian, and he had fumbled for an answer or evaded my question, it wouldn't have helped me find Jesus. I probably would have concluded that Jesus didn't really exist, that he didn't mean much to Ken, or that I didn't mean much to Jesus. Part of following Jesus as Lord is to "always be prepared to give an answer to everyone who asks you to give the reason for the hope that you have. But do this with gentleness and respect" (1 Peter 3:15).

To be prepared, we don't have to have Jesus' knowledge of Scripture. That would be impossible. All of us can be stumped if asked enough questions about the Bible. But no one can refute our testimony about what Jesus actually did for us in our lives. Some memorization of Scripture is helpful, though, if only a few key passages that describe how Jesus, in his love for us, saved us from our sin. Many have found these Scriptures, which are nicknamed "the Romans Road," to be helpful in describing God's plan of salvation: Romans 3:23, 6:23, 5:8, and 10:9–10.

We also don't have to be eloquent speakers. For most of us, that's not how God made us. But we do need to be capable of explaining in our own words, with gentleness and respect, what Jesus has done in our lives, and how others can come to know him as well. If we don't explain who Jesus is when given the opportunity, how will others find Christ? How can people believe in Christ if they haven't heard of him (Rom. 10:14–15)? *We* have been sent to tell the world about Jesus. *We* are Christ's ambassadors, as though God were making his appeal through us (2 Cor. 5:20). *We* must show our love for Jesus by committing our lives to a never-ending search for sheep who are astray in the open country, and then by sharing Jesus with them.

Jesus' Love Is Compassionate

One day, Jesus rested from his travels at a town called Sychar, in the region of Samaria. He was tired, so he sat down by a well while his disciples went into town to buy food for lunch. It was about noon.

While Jesus was sitting there, a Samaritan woman came to draw water. She was alone, which probably meant that she had been shunned by the other women in the town. Typically, women would go to draw water together, but not in the middle of the day.

Jesus knew exactly who this woman was. He knew that she had been involved in sexual relationships (five) out of wedlock. He knew that she was not Jewish—she was a Samaritan, and therefore would be considered an enemy by most Jews. And yet Jesus asked this woman for a drink, spoke with her about God, and told her that he was the Messiah. Although Jesus made it clear to the woman that he knew about her sin, he did not shun her or judge her (John 4:4–26). In response, the woman was not only drawn to Jesus, but she ran to get the whole town so that they would come and listen to Jesus too (John 4:39–42).

Jesus responds to sin by showing compassion to sinners. Compassion is a heartfelt response to suffering that prompts a desire to put love into action. It's the opposite of hypocritical pride that casts condemnation on others, and in doing so, abandons them. Jesus wept at the sight of Jerusalem (Luke 19:41) and longed to gather her children together as a hen gathers her chicks under her wings, even though it was a city that had killed prophets and stoned those whom God had sent to it (Matt. 23:37). When Jesus saw a crowd of people, "he had compassion on them, because they were like sheep without a shepherd. So he began teaching them many things" (Mark 6:34). When the teachers of the Law and Pharisees brought to Jesus a woman caught in adultery and said that the law of Moses commanded them to stone her, Jesus said, "If any one of you is without sin, let him be the first to throw a stone at her" (John 8:7). After the woman's accusers had left, Jesus told the woman that he did not condemn her, but that she should leave her life of sin (John 8:11).

It's so easy to find fault in others, and so hard to see sin in our own lives. Jesus wants us to concentrate on letting him change us before he uses us try to change others (Matt. 7:3–5). If we need to confront the sin of others, we should do it with love and compassion, remembering the love and compassion that Jesus has shown to us when dealing with our own sin.

Christians should never forget that we are Christ's ambassadors, as though God were making his appeal through us (2 Cor. 5:20). If we express Jesus' compassionate love to those who are lost in sin, then they may sense Jesus' presence and want to follow him. But if we are cold or critical toward others, we may abandon sheep that have gone astray—sheep that Christ has committed to our care.

We should ask ourselves how we react to the sin of others and to those who don't know Jesus. Begin by meditating on how Jesus loves us even though we don't always act as though we love him. What patience he has. What persistence in pursuing us. How gently he speaks to us. Are we treating others with this same loving compassion? We should be like Jesus to them.

Jesus' Love Is Courageous

About two months after I became a Christian, I took a summer job as a messenger for a law firm. One day, I was talking to the firm's receptionist, and the subject of faith came up. As the conversation continued, the woman looked at me and said, "Are you one of those born-again Christians?" By the look on her face, it was as though she were asking me whether I was a lunatic. That was the first time I realized that some people think that born-again Christians are just plain crazy.

Three years later, in my third year of graduate school, a friend of mine and I decided to start a Christian fellowship for law students. I was a little concerned about how this would be received by the students and professors, because in my first year at the law school one of my professors had said, "We tried to find some Christian law professors to teach here, but we couldn't find any who were smart enough." Undeterred, I made a poster that read, "Bible Study," and tacked it on the bulletin board in the main stairwell leading to the library. I then watched from the top of the stairs as students reacted to the poster. "Bible study?" one student joked. "I haven't been to a Bible study since elementary school."

At times, I've been treated badly because I'm a Christian, but nothing like the persecution that Christ or some of his disciples have experienced. Christ was crucified. Paul and the other apostles were chased from one place to another. Most of them were eventually killed for their faith. Even today in some countries, Christians are in constant danger of losing their lives. And it will always be so, until Christ comes again.

We shouldn't be surprised by persecution. Jesus almost guaranteed that we would experience it. He said, "Remember the words I spoke to you: 'No servant is greater than his master.' If they persecuted me, they will persecute you also. If they obeyed my teaching, they will obey yours also. They will treat you this way because of my name, for they do not know the One who sent me" (John 15:20–21). If we love others the way Jesus loves us, some will love us back and others will hate us, but we will be blessed in any case. Our reward in heaven will be great (Matt. 5:11–12).

Although Jesus said that his followers should be willing to lose their lives for him (Matt. 10:39), for most of us the actual stakes are much smaller. Most of us risk not our lives but embarrassment or rejection. We risk the look of disdain from a receptionist. We risk being ostracized from our friends or being belittled by our teachers. We risk the disapproval of our family or our employer. Knowing of this risk, we are tempted to be ashamed of Jesus.

Jesus addressed this temptation bluntly. He said, "If anyone is ashamed of me and my words in this adulterous and sinful generation, the Son of Man [Jesus] will be ashamed of him when he comes in his Father's glory with the holy angels" (Mark 8:38). Rather than be ashamed, we need to ask that God give us courage to stand firm in the faith. Only by God's grace and power can we join with the apostle Paul in saying, "I am not ashamed of the gospel, because it is the power of God for the salvation of everyone who believes" (Rom. 1:16).

THE JOY OF BEING AN ASSISTANT SHEPHERD

I don't know why, but I didn't tell Ken that I'd committed my life to Christ until about two weeks after I'd done it. I casually mentioned it to him during office hours. Ken responded by praying for me, and I then prayed for him. After we opened our eyes, I noticed that Ken's eyes were filled with tears. They were tears of joy.

I suppose I thought that people coming to Christ was a common occurrence that didn't merit much fanfare. I was wrong. There is rejoicing in the presence of the angels of God over one sinner who repents (Luke 15:10). Jesus, our Good Shepherd, also rejoices when he finds a lost lamb (Matt. 18:12–13). When we love the lost as Jesus loves us, Jesus fills us with his joy over the sheep that we helped find. We find amazing joy in serving as assistant shepherds to the Good Shepherd.

SUMMARY

God sent Jesus into the world on a mission to love and rescue the lost. Jesus has now sent us into the world with this same mission. To fulfill our mission, we need to commit ourselves to it, develop our capability to answer questions that non-Christians typically ask about Jesus, have compassion for those who don't know him, and become courageous enough to tell others how Jesus has loved us. We experience great joy when others accept Jesus' invitation to follow him.

APPLICATION

1. Contemplate your own sin. Make a habit of humbling yourself before God by contemplating your own sin and your need for a Savior. The purpose of this exercise is not to ensnare us in self-condemnation. God uses feelings of guilt to lead people to repentance that leaves no regret, but Satan uses guilt to destroy us (2 Cor. 7:10). We need to discern the difference between these two types of guilt. But when we're unaware or forgetful of the price that Jesus paid to redeem us from our sin, we are tempted to be prideful, judgmental, and unloving toward those who do not know Jesus. He who has been forgiven little, loves little (Luke 7:47).

2. Meditate on the Scriptures describing Jesus' love for the lost. Read Luke 15:3–32 and envision yourself as the shepherd who lost one of his sheep, the widow who lost one of her coins, and the man whose son left home with his inheritance. Hear the Great Commission of Christ to "go" to make disciples of all nations (Matt. 28:19–20), and to care for Christ's sheep (John 21:14–19).

3. Prepare to be a witness to Christ's love.

    a. Write a sentence (try about thirty words) that you can use to tell someone what Christ has done in your life. The sentence should arouse curiosity that would lead someone to ask for more information.

    b. Write a short testimony that describes how you came to realize that you need Jesus as your Savior, how you asked him into your life, and what differences you've seen in your life since then. Assume that you only have sixty seconds to deliver this testimony in your own words. Don't try to memorize what you've written as if it were a script. Use it as preparation, and plan to give it spontaneously without notes.

    c. Write a short prayer that you can pray with someone who is prepared to give his or her life to Christ. Use the Scriptures of the "Romans Road" as guidelines for what should be included in this prayer. Generally, short prayers are best in this case.

4. Pray for an opportunity to show the love of Christ in a tangible way to non-Christians. In my experience, love demonstrated in actions should usually precede love expressed in words.

5. Act when God opens the door. The Holy Spirit provides us with open doors of opportunity to express love to others, and to tell them about Jesus. We need to seize the opportunities when they are presented, because they may not occur again.

PART 4

HUMILITY

The Heart of Christ's Love

Chapter 8

NO ONE DIED AND MADE US KING!

Your attitude should be the same as that of Christ Jesus: Who,
being in very nature God, did not consider equality with God
something to be grasped . . . He humbled himself.
—PHILIPPIANS 2:5–6, 8

Love is not proud (1 Cor. 13:4). It's humble. Jesus was gentle and humble in heart (Matt. 11:29). His humility toward God enabled him to love God, and to obey God's command to love us.

In fact, humility toward God is the heart of Jesus' love for us. Without humility, Jesus would have refused his Father's command to come to earth on the greatest rescue mission of all time. Without humility, Jesus would have been unable to remain obedient to God while living on this earth as the God-man. He certainly wouldn't have been able to obey God's command to die on the cross for us. Without humility, Jesus would not have forgiven each of us for the sin that nailed him to the cross. Without humility, Jesus would have been unable to become a lowly servant to us. Instead, he would have demanded that we serve him. So without humility toward God, other elements of Jesus' love that he expressed for us—such as obedience, forgiveness, and service—would not be possible.

Thinking of the shape of the cross, humility toward God (the vertical part of the cross) leads to humility toward others (the horizontal part of the cross), because God commands us to be humble toward others (Eph. 4:2). The two humilities are joined by Christ. So if we find ourselves being prideful toward others, then we know that we probably also have a pride issue with God.

In order to obey the Lost Commandment, we have to cooperate with the Holy Spirit by developing a heart of humility toward
God. Humility is the most important vital sign of a healthy spiritual heart and mind. It's an attitude that deeply affects every
relationship that we have. If our humility is compromised by the
deadly spiritual poison of pride, our heart begins to die, we can't
see straight, we can't hear well, our speech is impaired, and our
mind begins to hallucinate spiritually. Our heart loses its compassion for others. We become unable to see God's hand in our lives.
We lose our hearing of God's voice through the Holy Spirit. And
our speech becomes filled with the delusions of our own grandeur.

Humility is not something that comes naturally. Our natural, sinful inclination is to think of ourselves more highly than we
should, and to forget about God, except when it comes time to
complain about our circumstances. So the starting point in our
quest for humility is to know that we can choose, with the help
of the Holy Spirit, to be humble. Then we need to know what
humility does and doesn't look like, as well as how we can develop
true humility. We need to observe Jesus' humility toward God, and
then ask the Holy Spirit to help us to be humble as Jesus is humble.

HUMBLE OURSELVES OR BE HUMBLED:
OUR CHOICE

Humility is an attitude that results in actions that acknowledge
God as God. Pride is an attitude that exalts ourselves as god. Rule
One with God—the first commandment—is that we shall have no
other gods before him (Exod. 20:3). So if we try to take God's place
by being prideful, he'll eventually put us in our place. God will
simply not settle for second place in our lives. He opposes the proud
but gives grace to the humble (Prov. 3:34; James 4:6; 1 Peter 5:5).
The choice is ours: humble ourselves or be humbled by God. If we
choose to humble ourselves, God will exalt us, but if we choose to
exalt ourselves, God will humble us (Matt. 23:12).

What did Jesus do? Did he humble himself or did God humble
him? He humbled himself (Phil. 2:8). And the Bible teaches us
that we should have the same attitude as Jesus: we should humble

ourselves (Phil. 2:5). Let's look at how Jesus was humble toward God when Jesus walked the earth as a human being, and how we can also be humble toward him.

JESUS' HUMILITY TOWARD GOD

Jesus was perfectly humble before God. On the inside, his attitude toward God was always loving and submissive. On the outside, his actions demonstrated his loving submission to his Father. He was humble from the inside and out.

Jesus was humble regardless of his circumstances. When things were going great—the times when *we* are tempted to forget and ignore God—he was humble. Picture what it must have been like for Jesus before he was born as a man. He was in heaven! Literally! He was sitting right next to God. They were listening to music—the sound of millions of angels singing praises to them. Life couldn't get any better than this.

And then God may have said something like this to Jesus: "I've got a difficult mission for you, Son." If I were in that position, I would've felt a twinge in my heart when I heard this. I would've thought, *I've got a better idea. Why don't you go do it and I'll stay home and take care of things here!*

But that's not what Jesus did. Jesus, "who, being in very nature God, did not consider equality with God something to be grasped, but made himself nothing, taking the very nature of a servant, being made in human likeness. And being found in appearance as a man, he humbled himself and became obedient to death—even death on a cross!" (Phil. 2:6–8). Jesus humbled himself in heaven by accepting God's mission to rescue us. He knew that it was a death mission. He did it anyway, out of love for his Father. Therefore, God raised Jesus from the dead and exalted him above all others (Phil. 2:9–11), except God himself.

When Jesus' circumstances were routine—the times when *we* are tempted to lose our focus on God in the monotony of life—Jesus never lost focus. He always remained deeply connected to his Father. Jesus ate, slept, traveled, dealt with the demands of his family and strangers and friends, had enemies, and generally experienced life very much like we do. Yet in all of this routine, Jesus was conscious that his Father was with him, and he continually humbled himself before God.

The acid test of humility, though, is during life's trials. When life doesn't turn out the way we expect, such as when we get sick or are facing disaster, that's when our attitude toward God becomes clear. At times like this, our pride toward God can show up as bitterness, anger, or resentment. We want to get in God's face and shake our fists at him. We want to demand an explanation of why we, of all people, deserve such affliction. We want to give God a piece of our minds. Or we may get so mad at him that we declare that he doesn't exist. Basically, we completely forget who God is and who we are. In our pride, we act as though we are entitled to judge God.

Jesus showed us how to humble ourselves before God in difficult times. Consider what Jesus did in the garden of Gethsemane on the night before he was crucified. He had eaten his last meal with his disciples. He had taught them for the last time, and proclaimed the Lost Commandment. After dinner, it was time for Jesus to prepare himself for his arrest and crucifixion. This probably would have been easier if Jesus hadn't known exactly what was coming. But he knew exactly was coming. Even for Jesus, these were overwhelming circumstances.

So Jesus took Peter, James, and John to the garden of Gethsemane, and asked them to keep watch while he prayed (Mark 14:32, 34). "My soul is overwhelmed with sorrow to the point of death," Jesus told them (Mark 14:34). He then went a little farther into the garden to pray by himself.

At this point, in his moment of deep anguish, Jesus did three things to humble himself before God. In our moments of anguish, we can follow his example.

Jesus Fell to the Ground

Jesus began to humble himself by falling to the ground in front of his heavenly Father (Mark 14:35). He didn't stand before God and shake his fist. He didn't swagger in to see his Father as though Jesus were his Father's equal. No, when in the presence of the holiness of God, Jesus fell to the ground, not only out of anguish, but also to acknowledge God as his sovereign King and Lord. He wasn't just going through the motions. He was acknowledging God as his God—as the *only* true God—with all his heart, soul, mind, and strength.

In the same way, whether in difficult circumstances or in celebration, we are expected to acknowledge God as our only true God. We must bow before God to humble ourselves. Bowing is more a matter of attitude than physical posture. Our mental, emotional, and physical approach to God should reflect that he is our God. Otherwise, our posture is a prideful offense to the King of Kings and the Lord of Lords. Scripture tells us that one day, when Jesus' name is spoken, every knee will bow, in heaven and on earth and under the earth, and every tongue will confess that Jesus Christ is Lord, to the glory of God the Father (Phil. 2:10–11). Let's not wait. Let's bow down now before God and Jesus.

When we bow in the presence of God, his holiness reminds us of our sinfulness. After committing some particular wrong, we might think, *Wow, am I in big trouble!* Kind of like how we felt when our parents used to catch us red-handed doing something we weren't supposed to do. When the prophet Isaiah came into the presence of God, he cried, "Woe to me! . . . I am ruined! For I am a man of unclean lips, and I live among a people of unclean lips, and my eyes have seen the King, the LORD Almighty" (Isa. 6:5).

God loves us, and doesn't want to punish us. But he expects us to tell him what we've done wrong, and ask for his forgiveness. He obviously already knows what we've done. But he wants to see that *we* know what we've done wrong, and he wants us to ask for his forgiveness. Confession is an act of humbling ourselves before God.

In our human nature, we fear that if we admit to doing something wrong, God will punish us. But the Bible assures us that if we confess our sins, God will forgive us and purify us from all unrighteousness (1 John 1:9). God reacts in a similar way when we humble ourselves. He doesn't hold us down. He lifts us up (James 4:10). What a great and loving God we have. His grace is amazing.

After Jesus fell to the ground to acknowledge God as his God, he spoke to God in prayer.

Jesus Prayed, "Abba, Father"

If any human being had the right to talk to God as a peer, it was Jesus. Jesus was God embodied in a man. Jesus was with God in the beginning. I mean the very beginning. The world was made through him (John 1:2–3). He was the very Word of God, who came to live with us as a human being (John 1:1, 14). Jesus was sinless. So we'd expect Jesus to talk to God as an adult would speak to another adult who held a higher position of authority.

But Jesus' humility was much deeper than that. When he talked to God, Jesus prayed, "Abba, Father" (Mark 14:36). These two words describe Jesus' humble, loving relationship with God. *Abba* is an Aramaic word that probably best translates as "daddy," or maybe even "dada." An infant would use this word to refer to his father, and it suggests an innocent, unquestioning love.[1]

In the original text, *Abba* is paired with the Greek words for "father," *ho pateer.* Jews became familiar with Greek through trade with the Greek provinces, and through their use of a Greek translation of the Old Testament. They often intermingled Greek words with their own language.[2] The Greek words for "father" suggest an intellectual understanding of the relationship between father and son.[3] So these three words, taken together, suggest that Jesus lovingly submitted to his Father with both his childlike, humble heart and his mind. He fully depended on God with his entire being.

In Christ, we are God's adopted children (Rom. 8:23). Therefore, the Spirit of God's Son, Jesus, lives in our hearts—the Spirit who calls out "Abba, Father" (Rom. 8:15; Gal. 4:6). Jesus' disciples once asked him, "Who is the greatest in the kingdom of heaven?" (Matt. 18:1). Jesus called a little child and had him stand among them. "And he said: 'I tell you the truth, unless you change and become like little children, you will never enter the kingdom of heaven. Therefore, whoever humbles himself like this child is the greatest in the kingdom of heaven'" (Matt. 18:3–4).

All of us need to first humble ourselves in order to be changed and become like God's children. We need to cultivate a spirit of humility in our hearts that enables us to gaze at God in wide-eyed wonder. We need to trust him in our hearts and minds. God loves us enough to humble us through his discipline when we become prideful (Heb. 12:5–11), but he would much rather we humble ourselves instead.

"Sure," we might say, "Jesus could act this way when he was in pain and anguish. But that's Jesus. Would it really be possible for a normal human to react this way?" Not if we rely on our own strength. But through the power of God poured into us through the Holy Spirit of Christ, who lives in our hearts, all things are possible (Phil. 4:13).

When faced with trying circumstances, we can choose to become bitter, or choose with God's help to become better. Pride claims an entitlement to be free from pain and suffering, and turns our misery into bitterness toward God. But the humility that enables us to pray "Abba, Father" allows the Holy Spirit to create beauty out of our misery. We become more like Jesus in our suffering when we depend on God with humble, childlike innocence.

Here's a modern example of humility in the face of hardship. My friend Ed is a devout Christian with four great kids and a devoted wife. All of them love the Lord. Nine years ago, when Ed's kids were ages five through sixteen, Ed was diagnosed with cancer. He actually had two kinds of cancer at the same time, but doctors caught only one of them at first, so he had to go through cancer treatment twice.

Then Ed developed a condition called neuropathy as a result of the chemotherapy. Do you know what it feels like to hit the "funny bone" in your elbow—that first moment of excruciating pain? That's pretty much how Ed's entire body feels all the time. All day long, Ed has to concentrate on blocking out his pain so that he won't be overwhelmed by it. He also gets cold easily, so he often has to wear a coat, gloves, and heavy slippers. The doctors don't know how to relieve his pain. Recently, Ed's muscles have also grown weak.

As a result of all this pain and weakness, Ed virtually lives in a wheelchair. But he still gets to church almost every Sunday. He still wants to shake your hand, even though it puts him in significant pain. He still cares more about how you're doing than how he's doing. He speaks with gentle compassion, and a quiet assurance of the love and sovereignty of God.

Ed doesn't complain about his circumstances. He praises God even in his pain. Recently, I apologized to Ed about not getting to his house to visit him enough. His response was, "Don't feel bad if you can't come here. God visits with me every day. He has provided me everything that I need."

Ed's suffering—like Jesus' suffering—has a divine purpose that is not immediately apparent to those around him. A humble, childlike faith enables Ed to be at peace without knowing God's purpose for the pain. He knows that our heavenly Father loves him, and would not allow him to suffer for no reason.

So let's go back to the garden of Gethsemane. Jesus had fallen down before his Father, acknowledging God's holy sovereignty. He had addressed God as his "Abba, Father." And then he talked to God. How did humility affect Jesus' prayer?

Jesus Prayed, "Not What I Will, But What You Will"

Jesus didn't want to go to the cross, if there was any way around it. Would you? He knew that God could do anything, so he asked God not to make him go to the cross. But in the same breath, Jesus also prayed, "Yet not what I will, but what you will" (Mark 14:36).

Humility toward God requires us to decide to do what God wants us to do, whether or not we want to do it. How we feel about it is beside the point. When Jesus says, "Come, follow me," he doesn't mean, "Unless you have something that you'd rather do." He doesn't mean later. Through the Holy Spirit, we need to cultivate a spirit of humility in our thinking and in our emotions that enables us to respond to God by saying, "Yes, Lord. Wherever you go, I will follow."

FALSE HUMILITY

We need to understand not only what humility is, but we also need to understand what humility isn't. Here are two examples of false humility.

Self-Professed Powerlessness

God often gives us missions that are more than we think we can accomplish. And they are. They are more than we can accomplish by ourselves. But they are not more than we can accomplish through God's power. Still, in pride, we're tempted to develop a faithless focus on our own inabilities. We forget that when God calls us to do something, he promises to do it with us and through us, if we will let him (John 14:12–14; Phil. 4:13; 1 Peter 4:11). It's not humility to tell God, "I could never do that." It's false humility. It's pride. It's doubt.

Great men of faith have been guilty of this type of false humility at one time or another—even Moses, whom the Bible described as "a very humble man, more humble than anyone else on the face of the earth" (Num. 12:3). God appeared to Moses in a burning bush and told him to go to the Pharaoh of Egypt in order to bring the Israelites out of Egypt. "But Moses said to God, 'Who am I, that I should go to Pharaoh and bring the Israelites out of Egypt?'" (Exod. 3:11).

God was patient with Moses. He explained everything that he was going to do. He assured Moses that he would be with him the whole time. When Moses was concerned that no one would believe him, God enabled Moses to turn his staff into a snake as a demonstration of God's power, so that everyone would believe that the God of Abraham, Isaac, and Jacob had appeared to Moses (Exod. 4:1–5). When Moses was concerned about his ability to speak eloquently (Exod. 4:10), God said, "I will help you speak and will teach you what to say" (Exod. 4:12).

"But Moses said, 'O Lord, please send someone else to do it'" (Exod. 4:13). Moses' concern about his abilities was not the result of humility. He just didn't believe what God was saying, or worse yet, simply didn't want to do what God was asking him to do. This made God angry at Moses (Exod. 4:14). He appointed Aaron, Moses' brother, to speak for Moses (Exod. 4:14–16). But in his grace, God still allowed Moses to lead God's people.

Refusal to Accept Praise

If we follow the Lost Commandment, we'll probably receive praise and thanks from people. What's a truly humble person to do with this praise? Many of us are inclined to refuse to accept any praise or credit for work that we do. We want to say, "It wasn't me! It was God!" After all, Jesus said that apart from him, we can do nothing (John 15:5).

But just because we can do nothing apart from Jesus doesn't mean that we do *nothing*. It doesn't mean that God expects us, out of a false sense of humility, to deny the truth that in fact we did do something. God creates us in Christ Jesus to do good works, which God prepared in advance for *us* to do (Eph. 2:10). He wants us to be praised, but to acknowledge him in receiving our praise.

Many of us have been delighted to work on projects with our children. It's not that we need their help to get the work done—we simply want to be with our kids. We want to teach them things and experience the joy of watching them learn and grow. We hope, though, to receive their affection and thanks as we spend time with them. In the same way, God involves us in his work not because he needs our help, but because he wants a close relationship with us.

If someone sees the project that we've been working on with our kids, and complements it, what do we hope our kids will say? We'd feel sad if our kids said, "I didn't do anything. My dad did it all." That makes it sound like the child was left out of the work, and doesn't reflect well on the dad. But we'd also be disappointed if our kids said, "I did it all without any help from anybody." That would be very ungrateful. It doesn't recognize the parent's contribution. Both statements are false.

What we hope our kids will say—and what I think God hopes we'll say—is something like, "Thanks! My dad and I worked on it together. I couldn't have done it without him." Praise, if received in humility, is a tremendous encouragement to us. The world can be a very hostile and discouraging place. At times, we need to be able to hear "well done" from people, and accept those words as though they were spoken by God himself.

SUMMARY

Jesus' humility toward God enabled him to love God as well as to obey God's command to love us. In order to obey the Lost Commandment, we have to cooperate with the Holy Spirit by developing a heart of humility toward God. In the garden of Gethsemane on the night before he was crucified, Jesus showed by example how to humble ourselves before God. He fell to the ground to acknowledge God's sovereignty, spoke to God out of both affection and respect, and deferred to God's will rather than insisting on getting his own way. In addition to following Jesus' example, we also need to avoid false humility. Self-professed powerlessness and refusal to accept praise are sometimes signs of pride or a rebellious attitude, rather than of humility.

APPLICATION

1. Spend a few minutes in prayer praising God. Then ask him to show you ways in which you have not been humble toward him. Listen for his response. Ask his forgiveness.

2. Ask the Holy Spirit to help you to be truly humble toward God.

3. Meditate on the Scriptures that describe Jesus' time in the garden of Gethsemane (Matt. 26:36–46; Mark 14:32–42). Focus your mind and your heart on bowing down before God, on opening your heart to him as your dad, and on making his will more important than your will.

4. Consider when you have shown false humility. What will you do to avoid making the same mistakes in the future?

Chapter 9

THE LAST COME FIRST

Sitting down, Jesus called the Twelve and said, "If anyone wants to be first, he must be the very last, and the servant of all."
—MARK 9:35

Jesus is humble toward us because he loves us. By humble, I mean that he is modest in his attitude, in his actions, and in his speech. He's not conceited. He's not a show-off. He's not a braggart, or a name dropper, or a complainer. We never hear Jesus say, "I can't believe I'm walking around with smelly fishermen and slimy tax collectors when I could've hung around with those popular, smooth-talking Pharisees." We never hear him say, "You know, I could make the sun stand still in the sky if I wanted to." Jesus' humility is the heart of his gentle, compassionate love for us.

And so, to follow the Lost Commandment, humility must be the heart of our love for each other. Humility helps us to understand who we are in Christ, and who we are not. It creates harmony among us by building godly relationships, enabling forgiveness, and encouraging service to one another (Mark 9:35; 1 Peter 3:8). Pride, on the other hand, creates division by encouraging power struggles, grudges, and demands to be served by others. Pride builds walls that divide us; humility tears down those walls in the name of Jesus.

How do we cultivate humility toward others? From the inside and out. With the help of the Holy Spirit, we begin with an accurate assessment of who we are. We then accept that God, in his love, made us so that we would need each other. Next, we learn what it means to act and speak modestly. We begin to honor others for their value as God's children, and become willing to submit to those God has placed over us. Finally, we learn to accept help from others.

ACCURATE SELF-PERCEPTION

It's hard to be humble if we don't understand who we are in relation to God and others. We talked about our relationship to God through Jesus in previous chapters. As far as where we stand in relationship to others, the Bible teaches us that we are supposed to evaluate ourselves with "sober judgment" (Rom. 12:3). To the extent that we are able, we should try to see ourselves through God's loving and perceptive eyes.

First, our humble self-evaluation should be accurate in two ways. We need to ask the Holy Spirit to help us see both our strengths and our weaknesses, both our righteousness and our unrighteousness. If we accurately perceive our weaknesses and our unrighteousness, it's more difficult to fall into the pit of a prideful attitude. We also become more receptive to the teaching and correction of others, as well as to the prompting of the Holy Spirit. In general, we become more pleasant people to be around.

Second, we need to know why we sometimes succeed in making righteous choices, why we've been blessed with skills and abilities, and why we have opportunities that others don't have. God's grace is the reason why, not our righteousness. That's just a fact. As the apostle Paul wrote, what do we have that we did not receive from God (1 Cor. 4:7)? It's not "sober"—it's just plain crazy—to think that we have more than others because we are better people.

To the extent that we have more than others, we need to thank God for his love for us, and promise to be good stewards of what we've been given. Remember: God chooses to use people considered lowly by society to accomplish his purposes, in order to avoid the boasting of the powerful among us (1 Cor. 1:28–29). That's how much God despises pride.

ATTITUDE OF LOVING INTERDEPENDENCE

Once we see ourselves accurately, as God sees us, we realize that God gave us our weaknesses to encourage us to depend on him and each other. "Just as each of us has one body with many members, and these members do not all have the same function, so in Christ we who are many form one body, and each member belongs to all the others" (Rom. 12:4–5). We might call this "loving interdependence." God encourages us to love one another by making us need one another. The body of Christ—his church—needs all of its members, with their diverse strengths and weaknesses (1 Cor. 12:14–31). We are meant to be a *community* of faith.

Satan, though, will try to attack God's plan. He uses pride to divide us by tempting us to brag about our strengths. He uses pride to blind us to our weaknesses, so that we won't seek relationships with others. Satan wants us all to think that we can live life to the fullest by ourselves. That way we are isolated and vulnerable. If he catches us alone, Satan can more easily trip us.

None of us can have the kind of life God wants us to have if we are deceived into thinking that we don't need others. That's not sober thinking. That's craziness. All of us need to develop the humble mindset that we should love each other interdependently, and not strive for independence.

MODEST BEHAVIOR

If we want to live in humility, in loving, interdependent community, we have to learn how to behave modestly; we can't think or act like show-offs. If we think like show-offs, we'll end up acting like show-offs. Show-offs think of ways to look impressive in front of people. Their minds are not on being righteous before God. In their pride, they want to look good to others. Most of all, they want to look good to themselves.

To avoid thinking like show-offs, we need to spend time quietly before God in prayer and ask the Holy Spirit to judge our true motives. If we pray sincerely, "Test me, O LORD, and try me, examine my heart and my mind" (Ps. 26:2), the Lord will reveal our pride to us. And then we need to ask for his forgiveness and his help to change our ways.

Whether we think like show-offs or not, we have to be careful how we act around others. We want to avoid the appearance of pride, which causes resentment in others. When we pray in public, we have to be careful not to pray big, long, showy prayers. Otherwise, we get caught up in impressing others with our eloquence, and we forget we're talking to God Almighty.

When we give, it's often best to give anonymously (Matt. 6:3–4). Otherwise, we may be tempted to give in order to receive the praise of others, rather than to be obedient to God. In the same way, when we fast or suffer for the sake of the gospel, we should not flaunt our fasting or our suffering (Matt. 6:17–18). Otherwise, we may be tempted to think that we are very pious, righteous people.

Being humble also means associating with people whom the world considers lowly. Jesus was criticized for spending time with tax collectors and sinners (Matt. 9:10–11). He talked to an adulterous woman, who wasn't even a Jew, and revealed to her that he is the Messiah (John 4:7–27). He let another woman, who was probably a prostitute, wash his feet with her tears and dry his feet with her hair (Luke 7:38). This was absolutely outrageous conduct to those around Jesus, as it might be to us today.

What was Jesus' response to the criticism about the people he spent time with? He said, "It is not the healthy who need a doctor, but the sick. . . . I have not come to call the righteous, but sinners" (Matt. 9:12–13). The apostle Paul taught us to follow Jesus' example. He said, "Do not be proud, but be willing to associate with people of low position. Do not be conceited" (Rom. 12:16). We are still surrounded by "sick" people whom society despises but who desperately need the love of Christ.

One more thing. To be humble, we can't be presumptuous about how others feel about us. Better for us to humble ourselves by avoiding presumption than to be humiliated by others when they put us in our place. Jesus talked about this when he went to eat in the house of a prominent Pharisee:

> When he noticed how the guests picked the places of honor at the table, he told them this parable: "When someone invites you to a wedding feast, do not take the place of honor, for a person more distinguished than you may have been invited. If so, the host who invited both of you will come and say to you, 'Give this man your seat.' Then, humiliated, you will have to take the least important place. But when you are

invited, take the lowest place, so that when your host comes, he will say to you, 'Friend, move up to a better place.' Then you will be honored in the presence of all your fellow guests. For everyone who exalts himself will be humbled, and he who humbles himself will be exalted." (Luke 14:7–11)

MODEST SPEECH

Jesus said, "Out of the overflow of the heart the mouth speaks" (Matt. 12:34). Our prideful hearts sometimes cause boasting to shoot out of our mouths like sparks from a fire. If we don't control our tongues, we can set our whole world on fire with our boasting (James 3:5–6). It can happen that we say something prideful, believe it, and then begin to live our lives as prideful people rather than humble people. God opposes the proud (James 4:6), and if God opposes you, your world catches on fire.

When I was a very young boy, my dad had a nice car. So did my friend's dad. One summer day after dinner, my friend and I got into a discussion about which car was better. I don't know who started it, but it got ridiculous. "My dad's car has air conditioning," my friend said. "My dad's car does too," I replied. "My dad's car has power windows," I jabbed. "So what! My dad's does too," my friend countered. We kept this up for a while. Then each of us had to run back into our houses to ask our dad about some other feature of our car that made our car better than our neighbor's car. This happened about forty-five years ago, but I still remember how envious this little contest made me. It didn't do my friendship with my buddy any good, either.

When is speech boastful? Whenever our motive is to elevate ourselves over others, or when what we say tempts people to think more highly of us than they should. Exaggeration is boastful because it makes it seem as though we did something that we didn't do. Bragging is boastful because it implies that we, rather than God, deserve all the credit for whatever it is we're bragging about.

The saying "no brag, just fact" is not biblical, because a brag can be a fact. Even a truthful statement can be a boast if we know that it will cause people to think more of us than is warranted. We should not boast, except in the accomplishment of others, and in the cross (Gal. 6:14).

HONOR AND SUBMISSION TO OTHERS

Humility and love require us to honor one another above ourselves (Rom. 12:10), and to submit to each other out of reverence for Christ (Eph. 5:21). To honor means to appreciate and to esteem. By our actions and our words, we need to show others that they are valuable to us and to God. We should devote more time and energy to appreciating others than we invest in celebrating ourselves.

I have a friend who is now honoring her mother and father above herself in an extraordinary way. Last year, she came to see her ailing parents for what she thought would be a two-week visit. She found her mom and dad unable to care for themselves. They desperately wanted to come home from the hospital rather than be placed in a nursing home. My friend chose to bring her parents back to their home, where she now cares for them twenty-four hours a day. She has put her own life aside for an indefinite period of time in order to honor her parents. Her extraordinary devotion and sacrifice would not be possible without the power of the Holy Spirit within her, and a large dose of humility.

Submitting is different than honoring. The Greek word that is translated as *submit* is primarily a military term that means "rank under."[1] God asks us out of reverence for Christ to submit to the authority of governments, parents, husbands, and others whom he places in rank over us. Obviously, submission is challenging. It requires humility. Ultimately, we are all under the authority of Christ, the Lord of Lords, and submit to his authority. If we focus on Christ and our love for him, submission to each other is an act of reverence for Christ.

ACCEPTING HELP FROM OTHERS

Accepting help from others requires humility. Some people can't even ask for directions because they don't want to admit that they're lost. They want to maintain the illusion of their independence, rather than accept the biblical concept of loving interdependence.

Jesus said, "It is more blessed to give than to receive" (Acts 20:35). How, though, are others going to be blessed in giving unless we're willing to receive from them? We can't let our pride block the blessings of others. We should freely receive *and* freely give (Matt. 10:8). That's how God's economy of love works. If we give and receive with hearts filled with love, joy, and gratitude to God and to each other, then our whole world is filled with love. If we interrupt the flow by refusing to accept help from others, then we isolate ourselves from God's love and from those who are called to love us as Jesus has loved them.

SUMMARY

Jesus' humility toward us is the heart of his gentle, compassionate love for us. While pride creates walls between people, humility tears them down. To be humble, we need to be modest in our attitudes, our actions, and our speech. Our attitudes should be shaped by an accurate self-perception, and an awareness that we were made to live in loving interdependence with others. Our behavior shouldn't include showing off, and our speech should be free from boasting. Humility requires us to honor and submit to others, as well as to accept help when we need it.

APPLICATION

1. Meditate on Christ's modesty toward others and ask the Holy Spirit to test your heart to reveal any pride that you have toward others.

2. Ask the Holy Spirit to help you use your strengths to help others in need.

3. Ask the Holy Spirit to help you accept help from others in areas where you are weak. Just for practice, pull your car over somewhere and ask someone for directions—even if you know where you're going. See, that wasn't so bad, was it?

4. With God's help, try to get a handle on your tongue. Use duct tape if necessary (only kidding). Try to anticipate areas in which you would be tempted to brag, and plan to be silent in those areas. Or replace your bragging with modest statements that give glory to God.

5. Call someone who has done something for you, or who means a lot to you, and tell that person how important he or she is to you and to God. Or write that person a letter. Nobody seems to write actual letters anymore. The astonishment on his or her face will be all the thanks you'll need.

PART 5

OBEDIENCE

The Power of Christ's Love

Chapter 10

LOVE LETTERS FROM GOD

*If you obey my commands, you will remain in my love, just as I have
obeyed my Father's commands and remain in his love.*

—JOHN 15:10

*But if anyone obeys his word, God's love is truly made complete in
him. This is how we know we are in him: Whoever claims to live in
him must walk as Jesus did.*

—1 JOHN 2:5–6

How we handle a letter says a lot about what we think of the
sender.

The other day I came home after we'd been out of town a few
days and found a wad of mail in our mailbox. Most of us get mail
of one kind or another almost every day. I brought the mail into
the house and stood over the trash can, sorting. Life is too busy to
sit down and read every piece of mail, so we have to make quick
decisions about what to keep and what to pitch. So I sorted quickly:

Mail from people whom I don't know and who are trying to
sell something to me. *Throw away.*

Bills (ugh). Put in a pile to *deal with later.*

Magazines and newsletters. Put in a stack to read . . . *much later*
. . . maybe.

Letters from people I love. *Open immediately.* Stop everything,
sit down, and read right now.

In fact, if I get a letter from someone I love, I usually open it
and read it while standing in front of the mailbox. I don't even want
to wait to get inside the house.

As I was going through this sorting process, it occurred to me that in our lives, we all apply a similar sorting process to the Bible. If the Bible were in our mailbox, what would we do with it? Would we open it right then and there, like a love letter? Would we bring it inside and discard it, because it's trying to sell us something that we don't want to buy? Would we approach it dutifully, but with a slight sense of dread, like a bill? Or would we put it in a stack of stuff, telling ourselves that we'll get around to reading it sometime. Maybe. What is your reaction to the Bible?

And what about Jesus? When he walked the earth as a man, how did he react to the Bible? Did he throw out the words of Scripture, like junk mail, because they came from men, not God? Did he respond with dread or indifference, believing that they came from a harsh or distant God? Or did he embrace the teaching of the Scriptures because he believed that they came from his loving Father?

JESUS WAS PASSIONATE ABOUT THE BIBLE

To say that Jesus handled the words of the Old Testament with loving care is an understatement. The Bible was not something that Jesus treated as unimportant, or that he studied out of obligation with a slight sense of dread, when he got around to it. The words of the Bible were like food to Jesus. Or maybe like oxygen.

Even when Jesus was a young boy, he loved to study God's Word. When he was twelve years old, he and his parents traveled several days to come to Jerusalem for the Passover Feast. After the Feast, Jesus' parents started for home with a crowd of people, but Jesus stayed in Jerusalem without his parents knowing it. A day out of town, Jesus' parents realized that he wasn't with them. So they went back.

After three days, Mary and Joseph found Jesus. He was "in the temple courts, sitting among the teachers, listening to them and asking them questions" (Luke 2:46). When Jesus' parents told him that they'd been looking all over for him, Jesus said, "Didn't you know I had to be in my Father's house?" (Luke 2:49). Mary and Joseph didn't understand what Jesus was saying, but what he seemed to be saying was this: "You should know me well enough to know that I would probably be where I can study and teach the Scriptures—in my Father's house."

Jesus' life was the fulfillment of the words of the Bible. He fulfilled prophecy. He kept the commandments. He talked about the Bible when he sat at home, and when he walked along the road, and when he laid down, and when he got up (Deut. 6:7). When Jesus was hungry in the desert and Satan tried to tempt him with food, Jesus said, "Man does not live on bread alone, but on every word that comes from the mouth of God" (Matt. 4:4, quoting Deut. 8:3).

Jesus assured his followers that he didn't come to abolish the Old Testament law, saying, "I tell you the truth, until heaven and earth disappear, not the smallest letter, not the least stroke of a pen, will by any means disappear from the Law until everything is accomplished" (Matt. 5:18). Not the smallest letter. Not the least stroke of a pen.

And from the cross, when he was experiencing excruciating pain, Jesus spoke words from Psalm 22: "My God, my God, why have you forsaken me?" (v. 1). Jesus fulfilled the words of that psalm on the cross.

From start to finish, Jesus was passionate about the words of the Bible because he knew that they came from his loving Father. His passion reminds us of the words of Psalm 119: "I open my mouth and pant, longing for your commands" (v. 131). "Direct my footsteps according to your word; let no sin rule over me" (v. 133).

Although Jesus was passionate about God's Word, and the author of Psalm 119 was passionate about God's Word, "passionate" doesn't describe how many of us feel about the Bible. For me, for many years of my life, I confess that *passive* better describes how I've felt about God's Word. I certainly didn't "pant" when thinking about studying the Bible, as the psalmist did, or consider God's Word more important than eating, as Jesus did.

Apparently, I'm not alone. According to one study, 49 percent of Americans surveyed said that the statement "I believe the Bible has decisive authority over everything I say and do" applied completely to them, but only 28 percent said that the statement "I regularly study the Bible to find direction for my life" applied completely to them.[1] Another study found that only 18 percent of people thirty-six years of age or older base their moral choices on the Bible, while only 7 percent of adults ages eighteen to thirty-five base their moral choices on the Bible.[2] There's a huge disconnect here. Even among people who claim they believe that the Bible is the Word of God, not everyone studies the Bible regularly, and fewer still even look to the Bible to make moral decisions.

Is it important to be passionate—or at least diligent—about studying the Bible?

WHY WE SHOULD BE PASSIONATE ABOUT THE BIBLE

We should be passionate about the Bible because God intended the Bible to be received as a love letter that was written for us. The Bible describes the love story of God's relationship with his people—past, present, and future. It includes history, in the sense that it accurately documents God's love for his people in the past. But it also shows us how we can become living participants in his love story in the present, and provides us with a glimpse of our glorious future with him. In short, the Bible describes how God loves us, through his Son, Jesus Christ, and how we can love him back.

If we are passionate about the Bible, then we look forward to studying it and even to obeying its commands (Ps. 19:7–11). When our passion wanes, however, diligence and discipline need to take over, because God expects us to demonstrate our love for him and for Jesus by being obedient to his Word.

We may not associate love with obedience. But Jesus did. Jesus linked his love for God with his obedience to God (John 14:30–31). If we love God, we must follow Jesus' example of obedience (1 John 2:5–6).

Our love for Jesus is also expressed by our obedience to him. Jesus said, "If you love me, you will obey what I command" (John 14:15), and "You are my friends if you do what I command" (John 15:14). What did Jesus command? The Lost Commandment! He said, "My command is this: Love each other as I have loved you" (John 15:12).

We can't fully understand the Lost Commandment unless we read and study the Bible—the story of Jesus' love for us. We won't perceive how Jesus has loved us, or what he expects us to do today, unless we understand the words that he speaks to us through the Bible. As author Henry Blackaby said, "If the Christian does not know when God is speaking, he is in trouble at the heart of his Christian life!"[3]

Through obedience to God's Word, we live a life that is filled with the love, and the joy, and the power of Christ (John 15:10–12). In obedience, we rely on God's strength rather than our own, and live by God's power rather than our weakness (2 Cor. 12:9; 13:4). Obedience to God's Word, with the help of the Holy Spirit, puts us in the center of God's will, and we then experience God on a real and personal level, the way Jesus did.

If obedience to God's Word can yield all of this love, and joy, and power in our lives, then why aren't we more passionate and faithful about studying the Bible? How can we develop the kind of yearning for Scripture that Jesus and the author of Psalm 119 had?

HOW TO BECOME PASSIONATE ABOUT THE BIBLE

I don't have all the answers, but I've observed four factors that strongly influence whether we are passionate about studying the Bible. The first two have to do with our attitude, the third factor relates to how we study the Bible, and the fourth factor concerns our planning and scheduling. I'll introduce each factor with a question that we should ask ourselves.

Do You Believe That the Bible Is God's Word—For Real?

What is the Bible to you?

Everyone knows that talk is cheap. Saying what we believe about the Bible is not proof of our belief. Whether we try to do what the Bible says reveals our true convictions. It doesn't make any sense to follow the teaching of the Bible if we think it's a flawed collection of fairy tales. But if we really believe that the Bible is the

Word of God, then we would be foolish and sinful to ignore its teaching. So how do you feel about the Bible?

It's important to be honest with ourselves in response to this question. Some people think that those who believe that the Bible is the Word of God are either lying or gullible. I used to think that. I used to think that smart, educated people didn't believe in the Bible. Until I met several brilliant people who did. Then I read the Bible for myself and made up my own mind.

Believing that the Bible is the Word of God requires faith. We don't know everything, and we can't prove everything. But we rely on faith in lots of ways that have nothing to do with the Bible or God. In a way, faith means taking action even when we don't know everything we'd like to know, trusting that what we're doing is best. Without faith, we'd be paralyzed by inaction.

As a matter of intellectual and spiritual integrity, we need to make a decision whether or not the Bible is the Word of God. This decision involves both reason and faith. As we investigate the Bible, we find very compelling, reasonable evidence that the Bible is the Word of God, but the evidence and our reasoning can only take us so far. We don't have perfect knowledge, because we aren't God. Faith fills the gaps left by missing evidence or unresolved questions. But the gaps are not so large that an unreasonable leap of faith is required. In fact, unbelief is less reasonable than faith in the face of the evidence that the Bible is the Word of God. We can learn from others who have walked the road from skepticism to faith, and then wrote about their journey.

C. S. Lewis was a highly intellectual atheist while on the faculty of Oxford University. After Lewis grappled with the claims of Christianity, he went from being an atheist, to perhaps the most reluctant convert in England,[4] to one of the most eloquent defenders of the Christian faith to ever live. Lewis wrote several books that have become classics, including *Mere Christianity* (New York: Harper Collins, 2001).

Josh McDowell set out to refute the Bible and Christianity, and instead ended up becoming a Christian and accepting the Bible as the Word of God. McDowell is the author of *The New Evidence That Demands a Verdict* (Nashville: Thomas Nelson, 1999), which contains some of the findings that led McDowell to conclude that the Bible is God's Word. For more than forty years, McDowell has devoted his life to speaking and writing on Christianity.

Lee Strobel, an investigative journalist, followed a similar path. Lee received his law training at Yale Law School, and became the award-winning legal editor for the *Chicago Tribune*. He was an avowed atheist. When his wife became a Christian, Strobel set out to use his legal and investigative skills to *disprove* Christianity. He asked a dozen experts pointed questions about the reliability of the New Testament and the evidence for Jesus' resurrection. Following his investigation, Strobel felt compelled by the evidence to become a Christian. He is now a respected apologist for the Christian faith. Strobel's books include *The Case for Christ* (Grand Rapids: Zondervan, 1998), *The Case for Faith* (Grand Rapids: Zondervan, 2000), *The Case for the Creator* (Grand Rapids: Zondervan, 2004), and *The Case for the Real Jesus* (Grand Rapids: Zondervan, 2007).

Obviously, honest and smart people throughout history have rigorously investigated the claims and criticisms of the Bible and of the Christian faith, and then have concluded that the Bible is the Word of God. These conclusions have not been the result of blind faith, but rather informed faith. It would be spiritual malpractice to attempt to capture in just a few pages evidence of the Bible's accuracy that others have taken thousands of pages to lay out. But the arguments supporting the divine origin and authority of the Bible include evidence related to biblical manuscripts, archaeology, history, fulfilled prophecy, and statistical analysis. Some critics claim that science disproves the accuracy of the biblical account of creation, but Christians rebut these arguments with scientific evidence (see appendix B for an annotated list of suggested reading).

If we are not now persuaded that the Bible is the Word of God, then we owe it to God and to ourselves to place our skepticism at God's feet, and to ask him to show us his truth. He already knows about our skepticism, so we might as well admit it to him. Then we should pray for God's guidance, and dig into the Bible, and into some of the books that address our concerns. The books that I mentioned earlier might be a good starting point.

The ultimate test of the authority and wisdom of the Bible, however, probably comes from obeying what God tells us to do through the Bible, and then observing what happens over time. Our lives become living proof of the authority of the Scriptures. Sometimes, confidence in the Bible comes after obedience to its teaching, not before.

Even if we believe that the Bible is God's Word, we still have to make a decision about how to react to it.

Are You Willing to Do What the Bible Says?

Once we conclude that the Bible is the Word of God, are we willing to do what God tells us to do? Considering the statistical data at the beginning of this chapter, it seems that for many the answer is no. We know God speaks through the Bible, but, for a variety of reasons, we don't try to obey. We might be afraid. We might find our ways to be more attractive than God's ways.

The beauty of God's love is that he loves us even when we fail to obey him perfectly—as all of us do. His love through Jesus Christ covers our many instances of disobedience. We don't have to be afraid of failing. When we fail, God expects us to ask forgiveness, make amends, keep trying, and move forward.

God's ways are definitely better than our ways. There is no more joyful place to be than in humble obedience to Christ. If we embrace that fact in faith, our lives will never be the same. And if we claim that Jesus is our Lord, then obedience is our only alternative. It's the best alternative, by far.

If we believe that the Bible is God's Word, and are willing to obey it, then the next question has to do with understanding it. There's more involved than reading the plain meaning of the words.

Do You Know How to Understand What the Bible Is Saying to You?

Who wants to study something that they don't know how to understand or apply to their lives? Nobody I know. I think that's why many of us don't study the Bible. We want to know what God has to say, but we don't know how to figure out what he's saying *to us* in the pages of the Bible.

For years, I treated the Bible as though it were written *to* me, rather than *for* me. There's a big difference. If God wrote the Bible to me, in English, then I can simply read my Bible as though the words were intended to be read in twenty-first-century Maryland, in the context of my life.

But God didn't write the Bible *to* us. He caused it to be written *to* others, but *for* us as well. Here's what I mean. Each book of the Bible had a primary audience *to* whom it was written, often addressing specific situations or questions related to them. But God also caused the books of the Bible to be written *for* us, because through these same books, he intended to communicate universal truths and requirements to his followers throughout time and in all places.

If we want to understand what God is trying to say to us through the Bible, we first have to understand what he was saying to the original recipients of what we're reading. This first step is called *exegesis*. Next, we have to make a judgment, with the help of the Holy Spirit, whether God intended to speak universal principles through the verses in question, or whether God intended to confine the application of the Scriptures that we are studying to the place and time in which they were originally written. This second step is called *hermeneutics*. As a general principle, a Bible verse cannot mean *now* what God didn't intend it to mean *then*. The Holy Spirit then helps each of us to understand how to apply these universal truths and requirements in the context of our individual lives.

Why is this important? Because while good exegesis and good hermeneutics yield a rich understanding of what God is trying to say to each of us, bad exegesis and bad hermeneutics lead to serious misunderstanding of God's Word. We can't obey God, and tap into his love, joy, and power, if we don't understand what he is asking each of us to do.

Let me illustrate some of the challenges of exegesis through a story. I had the opportunity to live in Germany for the last two years of high school. Although I learned the language fairly quickly, I never spoke German like a German. One night, my German class went out to a comedy club. For about thirty minutes, I tried to understand what the comic was saying. I got a few jokes, but not nearly as many as my German friends, because I either couldn't quite understand what the comic was saying, or I didn't understand why it was funny. In other words, I didn't fully understand the *content* or the *context* of what the comedian was saying. Sometimes I didn't understand the literal meaning of his words. Other times, I knew the literal meaning of the words, but didn't understand the historical, political, or social context that made the words funny.

It's the same way with studying the Bible. To understand what we're reading, we begin by understanding the content of the Scriptures that we're studying. We look at how the book we're studying fits in the message of the Bible as a whole. Then we look at the structure and themes of the book that contain the verses we're studying. Next, we determine our text—the paragraphs or group of verses to which our primary verse belongs. And finally, we look at the verse that most concerns us, and the words of that verse. To better understand the meaning of important words within our text, it helps to have a dictionary that offers optional usages because it's likely that the language of the original biblical texts (Hebrew, Aramaic, or Greek) contains nuances of meaning that aren't captured completely in a single modern language word or phrase.

While content is important, so is context. We often know something about the human author who received God's inspiration to write the book of the Bible that we're studying, something about the original recipients of the writing, and where each lived. We can sometimes figure out what specific situation prompted the writing. Usually, we know approximately when the book was written. With all of this individual, relational, cultural, and historic context, we sometimes see new meaning in the content of the words of the Bible, and new applications of the text to our lives. We also avoid bad judgment that comes from taking verses out of context.

Here's a story about how our understanding of the Bible can run amok if we don't apply these principles. While I was writing the preceding few paragraphs, a young man from my church came over to say hello. Let's call him "George." During the course of the conversation, George remarked that several of the books that he'd seen on a shelf at our church didn't seem very helpful. "But that's okay," he said, "because the Bible says we don't need teachers. My brother shared some verses with me about this."

George is about eighteen years old. His brother—let's call him "Fred"—is about twenty-six years old. Both are extremely intelligent young men from a very strong Christian home.

I said, "I'd have to see those verses, George, because your interpretation doesn't seem right."

"I'll find them and e-mail them to you," George said, as he walked away.

About ten minutes later, I received a text on my cell phone: "1 John 2:26–27." I looked up the verses, which read as follows. I've italicized the part of the text that George was focusing on:

> I am writing these things to you about those who are trying to lead you astray. As for you, the anointing you received from him remains in you, and *you do not need anyone to teach you*. But as his anointing teaches you about all things and as that anointing is real, not counterfeit—just as it has taught you, remain in him.

A few minutes later, George came back to see me, wearing a wide grin. His brother, Fred, happened to walk over to see me at the same time, and joined in our conversation.

"George," I asked, "what do the verses that you texted me mean to you?"

"Just what they say."

"And what do they say to you?"

"That we don't need teachers, because of the anointing of the Holy Spirit on each of us."

"Well, George, are there any verses that you can think of elsewhere in the Bible that suggest that teachers are important?"

George stared back at me.

"Okay," I continued, "here are some that I can think of. First, Jesus commissioned us to help him make followers out of the entire world by teaching them [Matt. 28:19–20]. Second, God has given us teachers to prepare us for works of service, to build up the church, and to make Jesus' followers unified in mature faith [Eph. 4:11]. Third, one of the important criteria that we should look for in church leaders is their ability to teach [1 Tim. 3:2]. George, do these other verses suggest that you should take another look at your interpretation of 1 John 2:26 and 27?"

"Yeah, maybe so," George said.

"We'd have to take a look at these verses in the context of 1 John as a whole," I said, "but here's what these verses may be saying. John was apparently addressing a situation in which certain teachers were trying to lead Christians astray. John seems to be saying, 'Stay away from false teachers. If those are the only kind of teachers available to you, you don't need them. You can count on the fact that the Holy Spirit will instruct you.' But don't you think, George, that John would have wanted the recipients of his letter to listen to and value good teachers? Isn't John himself teaching the Christians to whom he is writing?"

"Yeah, I see what you're saying," George said.

And then George's older brother chimed in, "I guess I tend to take verses very literally."

When reading Scripture, it's easy to fall into the trap of missing the forest for the trees. Seeing the trees in proper perspective requires some training and some discipline. But a little training and a little discipline go a long way.

The understanding that we get from carefully studying the content and context of individual verses doesn't make us any less literal in our interpretation. Proper perspective helps us to better understand what God said to the original recipients of the books of the Bible, and what he is saying to us through those same books, today.

To learn how to understand the Bible and how it applies to us, it's helpful to read books like *How to Read the Bible for All Its Worth* by Gordon D. Fee and Douglas Stuart (Grand Rapids: Zondervan, 3rd edition, 2003), or *Living by the Book* by Howard G. Hendricks and William D. Hendricks (Chicago: Moody Publishers, 2007). The time invested in learning how to understand the Bible pays dividends for a lifetime.

If we believe that the Bible is God's Word, and if we're willing to try to obey it and understand it, then where do we start our study of the Bible? This leads us to my final question.

Do You Have a Reading Plan?

For many years, I considered it my church's responsibility to be my primary source of biblical instruction. Now I don't think so. Rather, the Bible seems to teach that I share the responsibility with my church, but that I have the primary responsibility to take the initiative and make the commitment to learn the Bible in a way that makes me a better follower of Jesus (Acts 17:11; 1 Cor. 9:24–27; Heb. 5:11–14).

In light of that responsibility, I think that we should each have a reading plan that is appropriate for us. By reading plan, I mean a reading list of books that help us understand the Bible's teaching, and a commitment to read and study the books on the list a certain amount of time each day. The list includes books of the Bible as well as other books. We should select the books and sequence our reading in such a way that we'll learn to better understand the teaching of the whole Bible as it relates to how God wants us to live our lives. Think of it as designing our own course on living in obedience to God's Word.

We may also choose to include seminars, audiotapes, podcast sermons, or other instruction on the list. The Internet makes a wealth of information available to us—even seminary classes—for free. But I've found that reading is the most important way to learn the Bible.

I don't mean to diminish in any way the importance of biblical instruction through the church or other more mature believers. Jesus loved us by teaching us, and our Bible teachers love us by teaching us. God wants us to learn from other people. But we also have to take responsibility for our own learning, rather than passively waiting for it to come to us.

Our obedience to the Word is also important to our learning. We need to actively pursue God's truth in the pages of the Bible, and then put what we learn into practice. That's what Jesus did. Otherwise, we won't even remember the most basic teaching of the Bible.

The writer of Hebrews addressed this matter. He was in the middle of trying to convey deep truth to his audience, when he realized that they weren't able to understand him because they hadn't bothered to learn and apply even elementary truths. Here's what he said:

> We have much to say about this, but it is hard to explain because you are slow to learn. In fact, though by this time you ought to be teachers, you need someone to teach you the elementary truths of God's word all over again. You need milk, not solid food! Anyone who lives on milk, being still an infant, is not acquainted with the teaching about righteousness. But solid food is for the mature, who by constant use have trained themselves to distinguish good from evil. (Heb. 5:11–14)

He could've been talking about me for much of my Christian life. Is there anything more strange or gross than an adult who stills expects to be fed milk out of a baby bottle? What about you? How much milk does your spiritual diet demand? We have to wean ourselves off spiritual milk through active learning and obedience.

A reading plan is a good start. Appendix B contains twelve principles for creating a reading plan that will help you grow to be a strong, mature follower of Jesus. It also contains a list of books that you may want to include in your plan.

SUMMARY

Jesus was passionate about the Bible. And even though he was the Word made flesh, he obeyed the teaching of the Bible. He ate, slept, and breathed Scripture until the day he died on the cross. Jesus treated the Bible as a love letter from God, written for him. As much as we would like to treat the Bible in this same way, we often don't. With the help of the Holy Spirit, we should explore why we are not as passionate about the Bible as Jesus was. We can begin by asking ourselves the four questions that are discussed in this chapter about how we approach the Bible. Our answers may reveal the path to restoring our passion for the Word.

APPLICATION

1. Characterize your reaction to the Bible in terms of passion level, on a scale of 1 to 10, with 1 being the "junk mail" end of the scale, and 10 being the "love letter" end of the scale.

2. Ask the Holy Spirit to show you what is preventing you from moving toward the 10 end of the scale.

3. Answer each of the four questions posed in this chapter that are directed toward the factors that influence your response to the Bible.

4. Ask God to help you overcome the obstacles that make it difficult for you to respond to the Bible as a love letter from him.

5. Create a reading plan that addresses your obstacles, and that broadens and deepens your grasp of the Word of God. See appendix B for help in creating your plan.

ASK AND IT'S YOURS

You may ask me for anything in my name, and I will do it.
—JOHN 14:14

When my wife and I were engaged, I was in school in Chicago and she worked in Washington, D.C. We saw each other only every few months, so we spent hours and hours on the phone. I mean hours. What did we talk about? Everything and anything. Our dreams. Our fears. Silly stuff that happened to us during the day. Our plans. And how much we loved one another.

That's what prayer should be like. We should talk to God all the time, about everything and anything. Our dreams. Our fears. Silly stuff that happened to us during the day. His plans for us. And how much we love one another. God wants his church to be a house of prayer (Matt. 21:13).

We talk to God because we love him and want him in our lives. We want him to help us be obedient to what he has called us to be. And in order to love others as Jesus loves us, we need God's guidance and help.

When we pray for others, we love them by joining in their struggle (Rom. 15:30). How and when we pray affects whether our prayers are answered. Jesus taught us the key to effective prayer.

THE KEY TO EFFECTIVE PRAYER

The purpose of talking to God is not just to get him to do something for us. We want to shower him with our praises, confess our sins and receive forgiveness for them, and thank him for his blessings on our lives. But we often ask God to do something when we talk to him.

How do we know whether God will do what we're asking him to do? What requests can we make of him that we know he will grant?

The Bible teaches that, "The prayer of a righteous man is powerful and effective" (James 5:16). Our righteousness comes from Jesus, by our faith in him (Rom. 3:22) and not from our natural selves apart from Christ. Apart from Christ, we are not righteous by what we do. No one is; not even one person (Rom. 3:10). So the first key to effective prayer is to commit our lives to Jesus as our Lord and Savior, and to live by faith in him, through the Holy Spirit.

But is that all? Does God grant every request of every Christian? Of course not. It matters what we ask him to do. Not only must we be considered righteous by virtue of our relationship with Jesus Christ, but our request has to be righteous. Prayer is righteous if it is part of a right choice. How do we know if what we're asking is part of a right choice?

What's in the Name of Jesus?

Jesus said, "You may ask me for anything in my name, and I will do it" (John 14:14). That's an exciting promise. If we ask God for the right something in the right way, Jesus himself will do it for us—if it's in Jesus' name.

What does Jesus mean by "in my name"? That's the key. In this context, "name" implies the authority and character of Jesus.[1] In other words, we can't just end our prayers by saying "in Jesus' name," and expect our requests to be granted. There's nothing wrong, of course, with ending our prayers this way. It's probably a good reminder that our requests must be consistent with Jesus' authority and character. But to pray effectively, we need to know Jesus' character well. The Lost Commandment helps us.

The Lost Commandment in Prayer

We find an important key to effective prayer in the gospel of John. Focus on the words *if* and *then* in these passages: "*If* you obey my commands, you will remain in my love, just as I have obeyed my Father's commands and remain in his love. . . . My command is this: Love each other as I have loved you. . . . *Then* the Father will give you whatever you ask in my name" (John 15:10, 12, 16, emphasis added). If we want to obey the Lost Commandment, and ask God for help, he will give us what we need. Our request is in Jesus' name because his helping us obey the commandment that he gave us—the Lost Commandment—is consistent with Jesus' character and authority.

We can't obey the Lost Commandment in our own strength. We need the power of Christ living within us to do it. Jesus wants us to acknowledge this fact in prayer by asking him for help. That's one of the ways we remain in him and he remains in us, as he intended.

Let me give a practical example—prayers concerning forgiveness of others. One of the ways that Jesus loves us is by forgiving us. So in keeping with the Lost Commandment, Jesus taught us to love our enemies and to pray for those who persecute us (Matt. 5:44), just as he loved his enemies (us), and prayed for those who persecuted him. Even while Jesus was being crucified, he prayed, "Father, forgive them, for they do not know what they are doing" (Luke 23:34).

When the disciples asked Jesus to teach them to pray, Jesus included these words in what we now call the Lord's Prayer: "Forgive us our debts, as we also have forgiven our debtors" (Matt. 6:12). "Forgive as the Lord forgave you" (Col. 3:13) is part of the Lost Commandment.

So it's absolutely clear that, according to the Lost Commandment, Jesus wants us to forgive others. It's just as clear that we usually don't want to! Our feelings are hurt. We're embarrassed. We've been injured. We've been wronged. Forgiveness is contrary to our natural desire for revenge. Why do you think revenge is such a popular theme in movies and books? Because revenge appeals to a universal human instinct.

So if we're going to forgive others as Jesus forgives us, we need the supernatural power of the Holy Spirit to help us. We need to ask for help from Jesus. We can't do it on our own.

What should we say to God when we ask him for this help? Many of us learned to pray using the acronym "ACTS." ACTS stands for adoration (worship, praise), confession, thanksgiving, and supplication (requests). If we combine the ACTS format with the Lost Commandment, here's what we might pray:

Adoration   "Father, you are holy and righteous and loving and forgiving. No one compares to you. You're the only God. You love me so much that you sent your Son, Jesus, to die for me on the cross. I've made a lot of wrong choices and deserve to die for them. But because of Jesus, you have forgiven me. Thank you, Father.

Confession   Father, you've told me that I need to forgive others as you have forgiven me. I know that I'm supposed to forgive. But I confess that I haven't forgiven my brother [let's call him "Joe"], and I don't want to, because he did something bad to me and hurt me. When I see him now, Father, all I want to do is rip his face off [keeping it real]. But I know that this is a sin, Father. I've done so many things wrong, and you forgave me. My sin crucified Jesus, and you forgave me anyway. If I don't forgive Joe, Father, I know it's an insult to you. It's like my saying that I don't appreciate that Jesus died so that I could be forgiven. Forgive me, Father, for my sin of unforgiveness.

Thanksgiving Father, thank you for forgiving me because I believe in your Son as my Lord and Savior. Thank you for sending your Holy Spirit to live inside of me. Thank you for helping me to forgive others as Jesus has forgiven me.

Supplication Father, I can't forgive Joe without your help. Please change my heart, and strengthen my will. Help me to be humble in your sight, and in Joe's sight. Help me to forgive Joe as you have forgiven me. I'm going to go see Joe now, Father. Be with me as I try to reconcile with him. In Jesus' name I pray. Amen."

I can say with certainty, and based on experience, that God will answer that prayer, because it's in Jesus' name. We may have to pray it more than once. We will almost certainly have to wrestle with hard feelings toward Joe. Joe may not react as he should when we go to him. He may continue to act like a jerk until the day he dies. But we will be able to forgive Joe for his sins, through the power of the Holy Spirit, as Jesus has forgiven our sins.

Using this ACTS format, we can ask God to help us love others in the many ways that Jesus has loved us. The elements of Christ's love that are covered in this book are good places to start: joy, relationship with God, mission, humility, obedience, forgiveness, and service, all are central to Christ's command to love others as he has loved us. Other characteristics of Christ's love are important as well. But these seven elements are the core of his love.

Listening to God

Prayer is supposed to be a conversation with God, but I tend not to let him get a word in edgewise. I tend to look at prayer as my speaking to God, but I forget that he is also trying to speak to me. How do we listen to God's side of the conversation? Through attentive silence and expectant observation.

Attentive silence means pausing after asking God something, to allow God to speak to our hearts. His voice is not usually audible with our ears; it's discerned within our thoughts—the thoughts that occur to us after we have spoken to him. We have to pay attention in order to hear God's voice over the chatter of our own thoughts. The Holy Spirit helps us to tell the difference between his voice and our thoughts.

We can ask God to clarify what he is saying, the same way that we would in a human conversation. We might say something like, "Father, I think that what I heard you say is ——. Please confirm that I heard you correctly." Or, "Please explain what you mean by ——." Or, "What's the next thing that you want me to do in keeping with what you just told me?" Each time we ask God something, we need to pause for a few moments to listen for God's answer. If we just keep talking, how do we expect to hear him?

God often confirms what he has said to us in prayer in other ways as well. In answer to what we asked him in prayer, he speaks to us through the Bible, our circumstances, and other Christians. But we need to pay attention through expectant observation to hear his answer. By expectant observation, I mean that we should expect God to speak in these ways, and pay close attention to what we feel drawn to read in the Bible after we pray, to what happens to us in our daily lives after we pray, and to what other people say after we pray. We should also actively seek the advice of mature Christians when we're trying to discern God's will. God often speaks to us through others.

Prayer of the kind I'm describing is not just something we do with our eyes closed, by ourselves. When do we pray?

WHEN AND WHERE TO PRAY

As members of Christ's church, we are called to pray continually (1 Thess. 5:17). If there's one thing you can say about Jesus, it's that he prayed a lot. When he needed to make an important decision, Jesus prayed. He prayed all night before choosing the twelve apostles (Luke 6:12). When he felt anxious or sad, Jesus prayed. He prayed for hours in the garden of Gethsemane to prepare to die on the cross (Matt. 26:36). When he was thankful to God, Jesus prayed. He prayed to thank God just before he fed several thousand people with only a couple of fish and a few pieces of bread (Matt. 14:19). The written words of God in the Scriptures, and the spoken words of God in prayer, were the bread of life to Jesus when he walked the earth as a man. And Jesus is the bread of life to us (John 6:35).

Where did Jesus pray? Often he prayed by himself; often with his disciples. Sometimes he prayed in public, not to be showy, but to teach others to pray and to bear witness to God.

To love like Jesus, we need to pray like Jesus. Prayer should be a natural part of our lives. I've been blessed by Christian friends who taught me what it means to make prayer as important and as natural as breathing. I once served on the board of directors of a Christian organization. We faced many difficult decisions together. Very often, we'd be right in the middle of an intense discussion when, David, a doctor friend of mine, would say, "Hold on a second. We need to pray about this right now." And we would. That happened all the time, and God blessed us with wisdom and resources as a result of our desire to do what he wanted us to do.

I have another friend who's a Christian editor. If you talk to her on the phone, or listen to her speak to an audience, she'll pray frequently and spontaneously. I mean, she'll weave prayers in between the sentences that she's speaking to you, as though there are three people in the conversation at all times. And there are. Jesus is the third person (Matt. 18:20). My friend takes that seriously, so she brings Jesus into the conversation through her prayers.

If we pray to obey and to walk in the path of God's Word, Jesus will answer our prayers. After putting God's Word into practice, and praying that the Holy Spirit will help us to obey, we're ready to take the next step. We're ready to teach others how to obey—by example.

SUMMARY

To pray effectively, our prayers need to be in the "name of Jesus," meaning that they should be consistent with his character and purposes. The Lost Commandment can help us to pray effectively. We need to pray in order to have the power and wisdom necessary to obey the Lost Commandment. Because Jesus gave us the Lost Commandment, if we ask God to help us obey the Lost Commandment, then we can be certain that we're praying in the name of Jesus. Prayer involves not just speaking to God, but listening and watching for his answer.

APPLICATION

1. Ask the Holy Spirit to give you an area of your life to pray about.

2. Meditate on the Scriptures that pertain to that area of your life.

3. Pray the Lost Commandment as it applies to that area of your life, using the ACTS format.

4. After your prayer, ask the Holy Spirit to tell you what to do next. Listen in silence, carefully.

5. If what you're told is consistent with the teaching of Scriptures go do it. If not, you didn't hear right, so ask again and keep listening.

Chapter 12

SHOW THEM HOW IT'S DONE!

Follow my example, as I follow the example of Christ.
—1 Corinthians 11:1

For several years of my life, I studied and taught a very tough style of karate called "Kyokushin," which means "ultimate truth" in Japanese. Kyokushin doesn't teach about Jesus—who is the Way, the Truth, and the Life—so it doesn't literally teach the ultimate truth of life. But it does teach some valuable and enduring truths that are consistent with the teachings of Christ. Kyokushin teaches the value of humility and honor, that strength comes through struggle, that everyone should be both a student and a teacher, and that the purpose of strength is peace.

When it comes to teaching, Kyokushin stresses that teachers must teach from experience. We can't learn to fight from someone who hasn't fought a lot. We don't learn to fight well out of a book—even a really good book—unless someone with experience also tells us and shows us how. Our learning starts with explanation and demonstration. But learning something well requires application. We have to actually do what we're taught. Ultimately, the only way to learn how to fight well is to fight.

In the Bible, Jesus told us how to love one another. Through his life and the lives of his apostles, Jesus also *showed* us how to love one another. Now it's our turn. We need to love one another, and learn from our experiences. Our chief *sensei* is the Holy Spirit, who guides and teaches us. His experienced assistant instructors are our seniors in the faith. Our pastors and elders. Our parents. Our godly friends with more experience in the faith than we have. The ones who are walking the talk in the love of Christ. We should find them, listen to them, and follow their example.

Whatever we learn in this way, from sound teaching and our personal experience, Christ sends us out to teach. Jesus said, "As the Father has sent me, I am sending you" (John 20:21). We become apostles of Christ; *apostles* literally meaning "sent ones."[1] Every Christian, whether we are white belts in the faith or experienced black belts, has something to teach others. Here are three principles of teaching to take on the road with us.

TEACH BY EXAMPLE

Jesus sent us out to make disciples of all nations (Matt. 28:19). Disciples of Christ are people who learn, understand, and obey Jesus' teaching.[2] These people commit their lives to Christ as Lord and Savior, which makes them converts, then they follow through on their commitment by following Jesus and his teaching. It's the follow-through that makes a convert a disciple.

If converts are left to fend for themselves, without their being taught and shown how to follow Jesus, it's like leaving a newborn infant on the street. It's a hateful, irresponsible thing to do. It certainly isn't following the Lost Commandment.

When Jesus called his disciples, he didn't spend a mere few minutes with them by the Sea of Galilee, have them commit their lives to him, and then say, "See you later." What did he do? When he called Peter, Andrew, James, and John, Jesus said, "Come, follow me" (Matt. 4:19). They needed to follow him to hear his teaching, but more importantly, they needed to see him live his teaching and they needed to receive his correction. Then they were ready to be sent out as teachers to repeat this process:

1. Proclaim the love of Christ, the gospel.
2. Invite others to respond to Jesus' love as converts.
3. Teach (disciple) them to love others as Christ loves them.
4. Send the disciples out as teachers of Christ's love, to repeat the process.

That's how the love of Christ is supposed to spread throughout the world: through obedience to the Lost Commandment.

The apostle Paul taught and demonstrated by example this principle of teaching others how to be disciples of Christ. Discipling is one huge game of follow the leader, whose name is Jesus. Paul wrote, "Follow my example, as I follow the example of Christ" (1 Cor. 11:1). Paul reminded the Corinthians that what he received from the Lord, Paul passed on to them (1 Cor. 11:23; 15:3). To his student and friend Timothy, Paul wrote, "Set an example for the believers in speech, in life, in love, in faith and in purity" (1 Tim. 4:12).

The writer of Hebrews also encouraged believers to follow their Christian leaders. He wrote, "Remember your leaders, who spoke the word of God to you. Consider the outcome of their way of life and imitate their faith" (Heb. 13:7).

Are we ready to rise to the challenge of setting an example for others? Christ has sent us out into the world to do this. The world is supposed to learn obedience to the Lost Commandment by watching our example. The world should know Jesus' love for them by experiencing our love for them, in obedience to the Lost Commandment. Jesus said, "By this all men will know that you are my disciples, if you love one another" (John 13:35). We need to stand up on our feet as Jesus' disciples, step up to his challenge by following the Lost Commandment, and step out into the world that so desperately needs his love.

TEACH THE WHOLE TRUTH

When Jesus sent us into the world to make disciples, he told us to teach others to obey *everything* that he commanded us (Matt. 28:19–20). Everything. The whole truth.

The New Testament Scriptures repeat this instruction several times. After Jesus' crucifixion and resurrection, the apostles went out to preach the gospel. It didn't always go over well. On one occasion, the high priest and all his associates, who were members of the party of the Sadducees, got jealous of the apostles, so they threw them into jail (Acts 5:17–18). "But during the night an angel of the Lord opened the doors of the jail and brought them out. 'Go, stand in the temple courts,' he said, 'and tell the people the *full* message of this new life'" (Acts 5:19–20, emphasis added).

The angel must have known that the apostles would be tempted to omit the controversial parts of the message. So the angel made a point of emphasizing that the apostles were to teach the "full message" of Christ. And they did. Even though they got arrested again, and were flogged, they continued to teach the message of Christ. As Peter and the apostles told the high priest, "We must obey God rather than men!" (Acts 5:29). So "day after day, in the temple courts and from house to house, they never stopped teaching and proclaiming the good news that Jesus is the Christ" (Acts 5:42).

Jesus spoke just what his Father God taught him (John 8:28). He explained what was said in all the Scriptures concerning himself (Luke 24:27). We, too, need to be equally faithful in teaching the full message of Christ from the Bible. We need to be more concerned about a loving and true message than we are about how people will react.

Why would we be tempted to teach something less than the full message of our new life in Christ? Because it doesn't always go over well with our listeners. The apostle Paul warned that there'd come a time when people would turn away from sound biblical teaching, and look for teaching that matches what they want to do, rather than what God wants them to do (2 Tim. 4:3). These people gravitate toward teachers who intentionally distort the truth to win followers (Acts 20:30). Let's not be one of those false teachers.

Jesus lost disciples because some of them thought his teaching was hard (John 6:60–66). If we are faithful to Jesus' teaching, should we expect a different result? Jesus said, "He who listens to you listens to me; he who rejects you rejects me; but he who rejects me rejects him who sent me" (Luke 10:16).

TEACH EVERYONE

Jesus didn't sit still very much. His mission of love and salvation required him to keep moving so that he could spread his teaching as widely as possible. On one occasion, Jesus taught a crowd and cast out demons in a synagogue. "News about him spread quickly over the whole region of Galilee" (Mark 1:28). Immediately after he left the synagogue, he visited Peter and Andrew's house, where he healed Peter's mother-in-law (Mark 1:29–31). That evening, after sunset, the whole town gathered at Peter and Andrew's door, wanting Jesus to heal them (Mark 1:32–33)! Can you imagine what that must have been like for Jesus? I get claustrophobic just thinking about it.

Well, the next morning, while it was still dark, Jesus got up, went off by himself, and prayed. But Peter and his buddies went looking for him. I mean, the guy couldn't get a minute to himself! They told Jesus, "Everyone is looking for you!" (Mark 1:37). And the sun wasn't even up yet!

How would we have responded to Peter? I might have said to Peter, "Wow, great! We're going to have to find a bigger house, and get organized, so that we can serve all these people." But that's not what Jesus said. He said, "Let us go somewhere else—to the nearby villages—so I can preach there also. That is why I have come" (Mark 1:38). He went through *all* the towns and villages, teaching in *all* their synagogues, and preaching the good news of the kingdom of God to *all* people (Mark 9:35). He refused to stay put when there were so many people in other places who needed to hear the gospel.

Jesus said that we're supposed to teach everyone, in all nations (Matt. 28:19). We're supposed to teach ourselves, too, of course, and not just to avoid sin and hypocrisy. We won't know how to teach others unless we apply the teaching to ourselves (Matt. 7:3–5).

We may not have to go across the world. We can start by walking across the house to our family members, across the street to our neighbors, and across the hall to our coworkers. Wherever we are, we should always be prepared to give a gentle, respectful, reasoned answer to anyone who asks us why we believe in Jesus (1 Peter 3:15). But we shouldn't get too comfortable where we are when there are people in towns and villages around the world who have never heard the name of Jesus and have never heard the gospel. We've got to go to them, or help others go to them, to fulfill our commission to teach the world to obey all that Jesus has commanded us. Jesus said, "As the Father has sent me, I am sending you" (John 20:21). We've got to get going.

SUMMARY

Jesus has called us to teach the entire world how to be his disciples. We need to obey and to teach the way he did. We should teach by example, *showing* others how to follow Jesus rather than just telling them how. We should teach all that Jesus commanded us (including the Lost Commandment), rather than just what people want to hear. Finally, we should spread our teaching throughout the earth, rather than confining it to the same people. Jesus told us to get going with his message.

APPLICATION

1. Make it part of your mission in life to teach the Lost Commandment by example. Teach the world about love by loving others as Jesus loves you.

2. Always consider yourself Jesus' student. Ask him and others to point out areas of your life in which you can better love others as Jesus loves you. Respond well to correction, even if you feel a little embarrassed or offended.

3. Plan to take a short-term mission trip to some place unlike where you live. Ask the Holy Spirit where you should go.

4. Consider supporting—or being—a missionary of the gospel.

PART 6

FORGIVENESS

The Strength of Christ's Love

Chapter 13

LET IT GO

Forgive as the Lord forgave you.
— Colossians 3:13

I know a man who was an adult before he learned that he had a great-grandfather who was still alive. We'll call him Doug. Apparently, Doug's great-grandfather had deeply offended Doug's grandfather (we'll call him William) decades earlier. So not only did they not speak to each other, but Doug's entire family treated his great-grandfather as though he were dead.

When Doug found out about his great-grandfather, he tried to get William to forgive him. Christ had forgiven William, Doug reminded him, and so William should forgive his father. William's response was, "I will never forgive him! Never!" And he was angry that Doug had asked him to forgive his father. The grandfather acted as though it were disloyal for Doug to even suggest forgiveness. As far as Doug knows, his grandfather and great-grandfather never reconciled. But Doug was able to meet his great-grandfather, and praised God for that opportunity.

Here's a less dramatic story about unforgiveness. I was sitting at a picnic table full of Christians. As I enjoyed the summer breeze and my macaroni salad, a friend of mine told me a story. His adult son, also a Christian, had run into some problems with his neighbors in his apartment building. The neighbors had done something to annoy his son. I think it had to do with playing music too loudly. They had words, and now the son was planning his revenge, the father explained, smiling.

What I find troubling about these stories—and I think I could tell two dozen more—is that they're stories about Christians who refused to forgive others even though, as Christians, they had received the forgiveness of Christ. Some of us feel absolutely entitled to punish those who have offended us. The punishment might be passive, such as avoiding any relationship with them. That way, we can punish them, while still looking pious. Or it might be active punishment, such as our saying or doing something in retribution. Some of us live as though "don't get mad, get even" is in the Bible.

THE LOST COMMANDMENT OF FORGIVENESS

Only 55 percent of Christians surveyed say that the statement, "God's grace enables me to forgive people who have hurt me," applies completely to them.[1] For many Christians, then, "Forgive as the Lord forgave you" (Col. 3:13) could be called the Lost Commandment of forgiveness. Yet it echoes throughout the New Testament. The apostle Paul told the Romans, "Accept one another, then, just as Christ accepted you, in order to bring praise to God" (Rom. 15:7). He told the Ephesians, "Be kind and compassionate to one another, forgiving each other, just as in Christ God forgave you" (Eph. 4:32).

The commandment to forgive is part of the Lost Commandment, because forgiveness flows out of love. To love others as Jesus loves us requires us to forgive others as Jesus has forgiven us. We can't love others without wanting to forgive them.

Most of us have experienced the pain of unforgiveness by either refusing to forgive, or by not receiving forgiveness when we've hurt someone by mistake or by choice. Either way, unforgiveness causes pain by destroying relationships, which isolates us from each other and from God. It robs us of God's complete joy.

Many of us would probably lose our reluctance to forgive, and have confidence that God empowers us to forgive, if we clearly understood *God's* view of forgiveness. We need to hear this warning: God won't tolerate our unforgiveness. The Bible couldn't be clearer.

According to Jesus, if we don't forgive others, God won't forgive us. It's just that simple. Jesus said, "For if you forgive men when they sin against you, your heavenly Father will also forgive you. But if you do not forgive men their sins, your Father will not forgive your sins" (Matt. 6:14–15). We can't ask God for forgiveness if we hold anything against anyone (Mark 11:25). Anything. Against anyone. As it is said in James, "Judgment without mercy will be shown to anyone who has not been merciful" (James 2:13). Can you think of anything that you hold against anyone?

In fact, if we haven't forgiven someone, we can't pray the Lord's Prayer without lying to God. Unless, of course, we skip our request for forgiveness. When we pray, "Forgive us our debts, as we forgive our debtors," we are also praying these words of the Lord's Prayer, according to the gospel of Luke: "Forgive us our sins, for we also forgive everyone who sins against us" (Luke 11:4). We need to think about that before we pray the Lord's Prayer again.

If we realize, even while we are praying the Lord's Prayer, that we hold something against someone, Jesus said that we should forgive the person then and there, so that God may forgive us our sins (Mark 11:25). We forgive others by walking with faith through the five-step process of reconciliation, the way Jesus did (see pages 167–68 and 176–87).

Jesus tells a chilling parable that illustrates the consequences of unforgiveness. He said that the kingdom of heaven is like a king who wanted to settle accounts with his servants (Matt. 18:23). A servant who owed a large debt asked for more time to pay, but the king in his mercy forgave the entire debt and let him go (Matt. 18:24–27). The forgiven servant then encountered someone who owed him money and who also asked for more time to pay. But the forgiven, yet unmerciful, servant had the man thrown into prison until he could pay (Matt. 18:28–30).

Word got back to the king of what had happened. The king was furious. "'You wicked servant,' he said, 'I canceled all that debt of yours because you begged me to. Shouldn't you have had mercy on your fellow servant just as I had on you?' In anger his master turned him over to the jailers to be tortured, until he should pay back all he owed" (Matt. 18:32–34). And then Jesus added this terrifying statement: "This is how my heavenly Father will treat each of you unless you forgive your brother from your heart" (Matt. 18:35). The Greek word translated *heart* here signifies a person's entire being, including that person's thinking, emotions, and will.[2] We have to forgive others with everything we've got. That's what God demands.

We should be willing to forgive others just because our unforgiveness makes God unhappy. We shouldn't have to talk about the severity of our punishment if we disobey. It reminds me of a discussion I had with my college-age daughter, Lauren, concerning her curfew when visiting home. Lauren wanted to come home later than I would have liked her to come home. I was struggling with whether I should make an issue of it. On the one hand, she was a young adult. On the other hand, she was still young enough to be under our roof. Lauren got upset because she said I wouldn't let her come home when she wanted.

"But Lauren," I said, "I haven't said that you can't do what you want."

"I know, Dad," she responded, with tears welling up in her eyes, "but you pout! A lot!" Lauren loves me enough to care about whether I'm happy. I don't have to threaten to kick her out of our house to get her attention.

I don't want to get tangled up in a theological argument about whether or not God is going to "kick us out of his house" if we don't forgive others. Forgiveness of others, however, is so fundamental to giving our lives to Jesus as our Lord and Savior that unforgiveness calls our faith into question—which means that we may never have been in God's house in the first place.

Do we really want to find out exactly what God means when he says he won't forgive us if we don't forgive others? Is unforgiveness of any offense worth taking that kind of a risk?

By God's grace, Jesus was able to forgive *us* for nailing him to the cross. By this same grace, in the power of the Holy Spirit, *we can* give and receive forgiveness as Jesus commanded. But where do we start? We can start by trying to understand why forgiveness is so important to God, and what it means to forgive.

WHY FORGIVENESS IS SO IMPORTANT TO GOD

Love is only as strong as its capacity to forgive. Without forgiveness, we can't have lasting relationships with either God or others. Family relationships and lifelong friendships can end in an instant because of disputes over minor matters. Slights can escalate into major battles. Major offenses can turn into full-scale family feuds. It's impossible to estimate how much pain has been caused throughout the world, throughout time, as a result of unforgiveness. Without forgiveness, sin would destroy the unity of the family of God one relationship at a time.

The point of forgiveness is to preserve and restore loving, lasting relationships with God and others. God wants to have a real, personal, loving, and everlasting relationship with each one of us, and he wants us to have that same kind of relationship with others (John 17:20–23; Eph. 3:14–15). He wants everybody to work together, to help each other, and to enjoy each other, celebrating together the joy of his love for us and of our love for each other. That's what God wants. That's an important part of what it means to experience complete joy.

But our sin gets in the way. Sin drives a wedge between us and God, and between us and each other. Because we're prone to sin, our relationships with God and others are prone to separation. And we don't have the strength to overcome our own sin. We need God's power.

The only antidote to sin is forgiveness that flows from God's sacrificial love for us. We love because he first loved us (1 John 4:19), and we forgive because he first forgave us. God sent his only Son to die on the cross in order to make forgiveness possible—not only God's forgiveness of us, but our forgiveness of each other. Jesus conquered our sin and the resulting death of our relationships with God and others when he died on the cross for us. He is willing to extend his forgiveness to us. All we need to do is acknowledge that he saved us, and promise to follow him as our Lord. We acknowledge that he saved us by confessing our sins to him, and acknowledging that he died on the cross to pay the price for our sins. We promise to follow him as our Lord by committing to doing our best, with his help, not to sin again. And when we sin again, despite our intentions not to, we confess our sins to him, and experience the forgiveness that he has already extended to us.

God also has a plan to restore our relationships with each other when sin separates us—a plan that mirrors his plan to restore our relationship with him. The plan is that we forgive others *as the Lord forgave us*. But what does that mean, and how is it possible?

WHAT FORGIVENESS MEANS

So what is forgiveness? First, forgiveness is based on a decision, not a feeling. Forgiveness is deciding not to let our own reaction to other people's sins and failings interfere with God's plan for unity. It requires that we react to other people's offenses based on what Jesus did *for* us, not based on how we feel about what others did *to* us. The decision is then followed by a process of reconciliation, which we'll discuss a little later.

Two Greek words that have slightly different connotations are translated in the New Testament as forgive or forgiveness: *aphiēmi* and *charizomai*. If we take the meaning of these two words together, we get a better sense of what forgiveness means.

Aphiēmi is the word most often used by Jesus when talking about forgiveness. It's the word he uses in the Lord's Prayer. The word emphasizes what we do when we forgive. *Aphiēmi* literally means "to send away."[3] Figuratively, both the *punishment* for sins, and the *offense* itself are, as far as God is concerned, cast away.[4]

Charizomai is the word most often used by the apostle Paul when talking about forgiveness, including in the verse that introduced this chapter (Col. 3:13). It means "to give an unconditional favor."[5] It's a gift of grace, thus emphasizing what we receive in return for our forgiveness: nothing. Forgiveness is a gift.

When God forgives us, he casts our sin and the punishment that we deserve far away from him and us—as far as the east is from the west (Ps. 103:12). God's forgiveness is a gift of grace, purchased with the blood of Christ that was shed for us on the cross. We can't earn our forgiveness from God. The price is too large. And Jesus has already paid the price for us. But what we *can* do is thank God every day for forgiving us, not only by praising God in our prayers, but also by paying his forgiveness forward into the lives of others.

"Well, sure," you might say. "Easier said than done." My father deserted our family. My wife cheated on me. My kids never visit me.

I . . . am . . . in . . . pain. Anger rages inside me like a forest fire in a drought. How can I possibly forgive others as Jesus forgave me?

You can't. You can't by yourself. But you must. You must with God's help. The Holy Spirit, working by and with the Word in our hearts, can pour living water into our hearts, transform our attitudes, and empower our steps so that we can forgive others as Christ forgave us. Let's ask the Holy Spirit to show us what God's Word teaches us about Jesus' six attitudes of forgiveness.

SIX ATTITUDES OF JESUS' FORGIVENESS

If we find it difficult to forgive as Jesus forgave us, it may be because we don't have the same attitudes toward the sins of others that Jesus has toward our sins. Our wrong attitudes can encumber our obedience to God's commandments. Let's compare our attitudes to Jesus' attitudes, so that with the help of the Holy Spirit, we can conform our attitudes to his.

Six attitudes helped Jesus to forgive us as he walked the hard road of the reconciliation process, even as it led him to the cross. Each of these attitudes concerns Jesus' view *of God* (at the time Jesus was a man), rather than his attitudes toward us. In these attitudes of forgiveness, we find an important, overarching theme—that to overcome the sin of others through forgiveness, we need to focus first on the love of God *for us*, and then focus on the love of God *for others*. The Lost Commandment helps us to maintain this focus.

Acknowledge God's Sovereignty

Jesus knew that God is sovereign. God is all-knowing, all-powerful, and ever-present. He has the ability and the authority to direct how the events of our lives unfold. He is in charge. God has the right to be the most important being in our lives.

Jesus responded to God's sovereignty by committing his life to glorifying God in all situations—including when Jesus suffered at the hands of men. Jesus' suffering didn't cause him to question God's sovereignty. Instead, Jesus *affirmed* God's sovereignty in the midst of his suffering. In the garden of Gethsemane, as Jesus prepared himself for the cross, he said, "My Father, if it is possible, may this cup be taken from me. Yet not as I will, but as you will" (Matt 26:39).

If we question God's sovereignty, we tend to focus on ourselves and blame others when we've been offended, rather than try to understand God's sovereign purpose. How do we react when others offend us? Do we commit the dispute to God in prayer, or do we lash out at those who have offended us?

Trust God's Goodness

Jesus knew that God is good *all the time*, and not just when Jesus' life was free from difficulty. God was good when Satan tempted Jesus in the desert. God was good when crowds tried to seize Jesus, when the Pharisees plotted against Jesus, and when the apostles abandoned Jesus. God was good when Herod killed Jesus' relative and friend, John the Baptist. God was good all the way to the cross. In fact, Jesus said, "No one is good—except God alone" (Mark 10:18).

Jesus' confidence in the sovereignty of God, and in the goodness of God, enabled Jesus to place his complete trust in God. In the words of Job, Jesus' attitude toward God was, "Though he slay me, yet will I hope in him" (Job 13:15).

When he lived as a man, Jesus saw sin in the context of God's good plan to save sinners from sin and death. He didn't regard sins against him as an unexpected, strictly personal affront, or as a distraction from the mission that God gave to him. His appropriate response to our sin was central to his God-given mission.

How do we react when offended? Do we thank God for his goodness in giving us an opportunity to demonstrate the gospel? Do we see our response to the offense as part of our God-given mission? Or do we allow our personal desires to turn into demands that cause us to judge and punish others?

Appreciate God's Love

Jesus said, "As the Father has loved me, so I have loved you" (John 15:9). His love for us was a response to God's love for him. Jesus appreciated—he understood and valued—God's love for him, and that appreciation was demonstrated to God through Jesus' love for us, in obedience to God's commands.

Because he loves us, God has offered us forgiveness for our sins. If we have accepted God's forgiveness by accepting Jesus as our Savior and Lord, then God commands us to demonstrate our appreciation to him by forgiving others as he has forgiven us. Our forgiveness of others directly reflects the degree to which we understand and value the forgiveness that we have received from God through Jesus' death on the cross. We should *tell* God that we are grateful for his forgiveness, but it's even better to *show* him that we are grateful by forgiving others as he has forgiven us. If we tell God that we appreciate his forgiveness, but don't forgive others, we end up communicating ingratitude and hypocrisy.

Have we adequately thanked God for his forgiveness through our forgiveness of others? Christians should be the most forgiving people on earth, because we should be very aware of how much we have been forgiven by the grace of God.

Hunger for God's Righteousness

Jesus hungered for God's righteousness on earth. He deeply desired to have God's righteousness reflected in his life, through obedience to God's Word. When John the Baptist did not want to baptize Jesus, "Jesus replied, 'Let it be so now; it is proper for us to do this to fulfill all righteousness'" (Matt. 3:15).

Jesus demonstrated both his desire for righteousness *and* his love as he reacted to the sin of others. God's righteous holiness demands punishment when we disobey God. But in his love, God offers us mercy and forgiveness through Jesus Christ. The gospel combines righteousness with forgiveness in love. So when Jesus encountered sinners, he had the courage to proclaim righteousness by pointing out sin, and calling for repentance. He spoke the truth in love, so that we could grow spiritually (Eph. 4:15). But he also had the compassion and the love to forgive our offenses, so that we would not be preoccupied by fear of punishment as we grow (Rom. 8:15).

Jesus calls on us to have this same desire for righteousness in our lives, and in the lives of those around us. He commands us to pursue God's kingdom and his righteousness as our first priority

(Matt. 6:33). We should, in fact, hunger and thirst for righteousness (Matt. 5:6).

Do we have the courage to pursue righteousness in our lives, and in the lives of others? Can we admit when we are wrong, and then take steps with God's help to be changed? Do we have the courage to speak the truth in love to someone who has hurt us, so that both we and they can grow in righteousness?

Desire God's Community

Jesus values relationships and community more than the accomplishment of particular tasks. If he were task oriented, Jesus wouldn't have bothered to associate with the apostles (or us), because he doesn't need any of us to accomplish anything. Yet God invites each of us to join him in his work on earth, because he wants to be with us. He wants us to experience joy as we grow in our maturity and in our knowledge of him.

God also wants us to be in community with each other, as a family. He is our heavenly Father, and Christians are brothers and sisters to one another (Matt. 12:49–50). Christians should be even closer to each other, in fact, than are members of a family; we should be as close as members of one body. Our relationships with each other are supposed to help us "grow up into him who is the Head, that is, Christ. From him the whole body, joined and held together by every supporting ligament, grows and builds itself up in love, as each part does its work" (Eph. 4:15–16). Working together, and "speaking the truth in love" to one another (Eph. 4:15), we are meant to grow both as individuals and as a faith community.

Jesus' five steps of forgiveness—which I call the "process of reconciliation" and discuss below—are a vital part of this personal and community growth process, because they enable us to improve ourselves and each other. "As iron sharpens iron, so one man sharpens another" (Prov. 27:17). We sharpen ourselves and each other through the reconciliation process.

Because Jesus is relationship and community oriented, he chooses to look at us with compassion rather than condemnation. He focuses on our faith, rather than on our fallibility. He proclaims our promised future, rather than dwelling on our past. Jesus

LET IT GO

chooses to think about what is excellent or praiseworthy about us, as we should choose to think about what is excellent or praiseworthy about each other (Phil. 4:8).

And what about us? Are we relationship oriented or task oriented? Do we react to the failings of others with compassion or condemnation? Do we focus our attention on the wrongs that others have done in the past, or do we choose to concentrate on what is praiseworthy about them, and what we can do to serve them in the future?

Be Willing to Imitate God's Sacrifice

If the cross demonstrated anything, it was that Jesus was willing to make the ultimate sacrifice to purchase our forgiveness. He had done absolutely nothing wrong, yet he was willing to die an excruciating death to save us from our sins. We did nothing to deserve that sacrifice.

Jesus doesn't ask that we repay him for his forgiveness. We couldn't if we tried. But he does want us to pay his forgiveness forward to others who need our forgiveness. We should be willing to bear *our* cross by forgiving others because Jesus bore *his* cross to forgive us.

Are we willing to make personal sacrifices in order to forgive others? Are we willing to let go of our grudges, our paybacks, and our demands, for the sake of the cross?

As our attitudes conform to Jesus' attitudes of forgiveness, it becomes easier to step out in faith, and follow Jesus' five steps of forgiveness.

FIVE STEPS OF JESUS' FORGIVENESS

Jesus didn't adopt attitudes of forgiveness and then remain aloof from us and our sin. He didn't disassociate from sinners, ignore ungodly remarks, condone sinful situations, or avoid uncomfortable confrontations. On the contrary, Jesus loves us much too much to walk away from our sins that way. He came to earth not only to die for our sins, but also to lovingly, truthfully, and compassionately *confront us with our sins*. He wants us to come face-to-face with

167

our sins so that we will turn away from *them*, and toward *him*. In him and in him *alone*, we find true love, healing, power, purpose, and complete joy. Jesus' forgiveness requires loving confrontation because without this confrontation, there would be no redirection toward him—no repentance. And there's another benefit. The teaching, rebuking, correcting, and training in righteousness that comes from this loving confrontation also helps each of us to be equipped for the good work that God wants us to do.

As we look at the pattern of Jesus' life, we see that his forgiveness involved five steps that comprise a process of reconciliation with God. Each step can be characterized by one word:

1. *Go.* Jesus took the initiative by coming from heaven to earth to bring us the message of the gospel. He accepted this mission of love and salvation from God in humble obedience to God's calling. Forgiveness was at the core of the mission, the purpose of which was to restore God's relationship with us.

2. *Show.* Speaking the truth in love, Jesus shows us both our sin and the path to our salvation in him. He didn't come to condemn us; he came to save us (John 3:17) and to reconcile us to God through him (2 Cor. 5:18). He wants us to have a full, abundant life (John 10:10).

3. *Confess.* Jesus expects us to respond appropriately to what he has shown us. First, he expects us to confess our offenses to him, and to ask his forgiveness. He promises in advance to grant us this forgiveness.

4. *Repent.* Jesus also expects us to repent of our sins, meaning that he wants us to agree that we'll try not to sin again, and that we'll do what we can to repair the damage that we've done to others.

5. *Forgive.* If we confess and repent, then we are assured that Jesus will forgive us (Rom. 10:9–10; 1 John 1:9). Out of love for us and for God, Jesus forgives us by not punishing us, not reminding us of our sin (1 Cor. 13:5), and not separating from us. He conquers our sins by forgiving them, and giving glory to God.

Jesus now commands us to love others as he has loved us by following this same process of reconciliation (Matt. 18:15–17). Through the process of reconciliation, each of us—offenders and offended, sinners and sinned against—become more like Jesus.

HOW WE BEGIN TO FORGIVE

How do we begin to forgive? How do we find strength to initiate the reconciliation process? The same way we begin everything we do in the name of Jesus. We begin at the foot of the cross, in prayer, and with a decision to take action with the help and power of the Holy Spirit.

Pray

We shouldn't try to forgive someone without praying first. Forgiveness is very difficult. There's no reason to even try without the help of the Holy Spirit. As we pray, it may be helpful to use the ACTS format to focus our attention. Here are some specific suggestions concerning each part of our prayer:

Adoration. Praise God for his incredible, generous mercy toward you. God's love for us is boundless and unbelievable. What can we say in praise of someone who gave his only Son to save our eternal lives? Words are not enough, but give it a try.

Confession. Confess any sins that you have not yet confessed, including the sin of unforgiveness. Spend some time considering your own many sins, mistakes, wrongdoings, and shortcomings—particularly the ones that may have contributed to the offense that you are forgiving. We need to confess and repent of our sin in order to see clearly how we should respond to the sin of others (Matt. 7:3–5).

Francis A. Schaeffer, the late theologian, once spoke to a man about how divisions that arose in the Brethren church during World War II were healed.[6] Hitler, in order to better control the church, passed a law that required all churches to unify. The Brethren churches split over how to respond. Some complied. But some disobeyed, and many of their members were killed in concentration camps.

After the war, wide divisions remained between the members of these two groups. Feelings ran deep and emotions high. Elders from both groups came together in a quiet place to try to resolve their disagreements. They decided that for several days, each man would do nothing except "search his own heart concerning his own failures and the commands of Christ."[7] Then they met together.

What happened then? The man told Schaeffer, "We just were one."[8] Understanding our own sinfulness is critical to forgiving the sin of others.

Thanksgiving. Thank God for his forgiveness of your many sins. Thank Jesus for dying for your sins. Thank him for enabling you to forgive, through the power of the Holy Spirit. Thank him for giving you the opportunity to love someone else as he has loved you by forgiving them.

Supplication. Ask for an opportunity to share the gospel of Christ with the offender, and to demonstrate the gospel of Christ through forgiveness. Ask the Holy Spirit to empower you to forgive the offender with your whole heart. He will give you strength, protection, and boldness to speak to the offender. He will help you and the other person to confess and repent of the sin that caused the problem. He will comfort you and ease your pain.

Reconcile Immediately

If the offender is still alive, forgiveness without attempting to engage in the process of reconciliation is unforgiveness. If possible, we should begin the reconciliation process immediately. In the next chapter, we discuss how to reconcile.

SUMMARY

God commands us to forgive as we have been forgiven in Christ. Forgiveness requires that we decide to react to other people's wrongdoings based on what Jesus did *for* us, not based on what others did *to* us. It is the process of reconciliation with others that demonstrates and reenacts the gospel for those who have offended us. This process involves five steps characterized by the words *go, show, confess, repent,* and *forgive.* We find these steps easier to take if we share Jesus' six attitudes of forgiveness, and keep in mind God's warning that he will not forgive us if we refuse to forgive each other. In most cases, forgiveness requires us to attempt to reconcile with others immediately. We need God's help to accomplish this, and should ask for his help in prayer.

APPLICATION

1. Pray that the Holy Spirit will show you whom you have not forgiven.

2. Make the decision to forgive that person in the name of Jesus.

3. Compare Jesus' attitudes of forgiveness to your attitudes, and ask the Holy Spirit to conform your attitudes to those of Christ.

4. Prepare to take the steps of the reconciliation process by praying. Using the ACTS format, ask the Holy Spirit to help you forgive.

5. Begin the reconciliation process immediately, if possible. (See the next chapter for more guidance about the reconciliation process.)

Chapter 14

GET IT TOGETHER

First go and be reconciled to your brother; then come and offer your gift.

—Matthew 5:24

Our sins separate us from others through the anger and pain that they cause. Forgiveness and reconciliation are the only ways to restore these relationships.

The word that's translated as *reconcile* in the New Testament means "change" and "exchange."[1] Through our cooperation with the Holy Spirit in the reconciliation process, our attitudes change to the attitudes that enabled Christ to forgive. We exchange our angry feelings for Christ's love. We go from hurting each other to helping each other.

Why should we bother with reconciliation? Why can't we forgive from a distance, and avoid a messy, inconvenient, face-to-face meeting? Because Jesus said so, and because forgiveness from a distance doesn't restore our relationships the way God intended.

THE LOST COMMANDMENT
OF RECONCILIATION

As we said in the previous chapter, God links his forgiveness of us to our forgiveness of others. Jesus lived, died, and rose from the dead to restore our relationship to God *and* each other. God reconciled us to himself in Christ, not counting our sins against us because of Jesus' sacrifice on the cross (2 Cor. 5:18–19). God then committed the message of reconciliation to us: "We are therefore Christ's ambassadors, as though God were making his appeal through us" (2 Cor. 5:20).

We are all supposed to have a reconciliation ministry (2 Cor. 5:16–20). The process of reconciliation expresses both God's justice and God's mercy, so that each of us will become more righteous and more loving as we learn to live in godly harmony with others. It is a demonstration—a reenactment—of the gospel. The process of reconciliation expresses to someone who has offended us the way that God offers forgiveness to *all* of us through Jesus. Our message should be, "Be reconciled to God and others!"

If we as Christians haven't reconciled to others, then God says that his relationship with us is on hold until we do. On hold?! Yes. In the Sermon on the Mount, Jesus said that anyone who is angry with his brother would be subject to judgment (Matt. 5:22). "Therefore," Jesus said, "if you are offering your gift at the altar and there remember that your brother has something against you, leave your gift there in front of the altar. First go and be reconciled to your brother; then come and offer your gift" (Matt. 5:23–24). God wants us to stop whatever we're doing to go reconcile with anyone with whom we have a disagreement. It's that important to him.

In this passage (Matt. 5:21–24), Jesus drove home the need for our reconciliation to others in four ways. First, he compared anger to murder, implying that in God's eyes, to be angry with our brother is as serious as murdering him (Matt. 5:21–22).

Second, in the original language, Jesus changes from the plural form of *you*—someone in the southern United States might translate this as "y'all"—to the singular form of *you*—as in, "I'm talking specifically and personally to you." The shift is at the word *therefore* in Matthew 5:23, when Jesus talks about leaving our gift at the altar to go and reconcile. It's as though in the sermon, Jesus inserted your name after the word *therefore*, like this: "Therefore, Dave, if you're offering your gift at the altar . . . ." He's getting really personal here.

Third, we have to understand Jesus' words in the context of the Jewish religion of his day. In the Old Testament, God commanded Jews to atone for their sins through animal sacrifices. In

Jesus' time, these sacrifices were offered at the temple in Jerusalem. Without the animal sacrifice as atonement for sin, the worshipper would still be subject to God's judgment.

These sacrifices, however, weren't sufficient if the worshipper's sin was intentional. Before a sacrifice could be offered for an intentional sin, the worshipper had to confess the sin to the person offended, and be truly penitent.[2] True penitence included doing whatever was possible to compensate the injured person for the harm done to him or her. So, for example, a worshipper could not come to offer a sin offering for stealing something without first confessing the theft, promising God not to do it again, and returning the stolen item to its owner. Jews knew that not even the sacrifices offered on the Day of Atonement would be sufficient for someone who was not first reconciled to his neighbor.[3]

Fourth, consider the embarrassment and inconvenience involved in obeying Jesus' command. In order to offer an animal sacrifice, a Jew would have to spend time traveling—often considerable distances—to the temple in Jerusalem. For Jews from Jesus' home town of Nazareth, this would have been a trip of about ninety miles.

After arriving at the temple, the worshipper would walk through a series of courtyards carrying the animal—first through the Court of the Gentiles, then the Court of Women, then the Court of Men, until he reached the Court of the Priests. At that point the worshipper would hand the animal to the priest to hold. The worshipper would then press his hands on the animal as a ceremonial way of transferring his sins to the animal, and he would pray, "I entreat, O Lord; I have sinned, I have done perversely, I have rebelled; I have committed [here the sacrificer specified his sins]; but I return in penitence, and let this be for my covering."[4]

If at this point in offering his gift to God, the worshipper remembered that he'd failed to reconcile with someone, this is what Jesus said should be done: stop right there, leave the gift at the altar, go and be reconciled, and then come back and offer the gift. Now imagine the embarrassment of having to say to the priest, "Hold on. I have something to go take care of. I have to leave my gift here." Then the worshipper would have to walk back out through all the courts of the temple, and all the way home, to reconcile with his brother. And then walk all the way back to the temple, possibly with another animal, to offer his gift at the altar.

Today, Jesus is still telling us through this passage to stop whatever we're doing in order to go and be reconciled to our neighbors. If we're standing in the middle of a baptismal font about to be baptized, and remember our brothers have something against us, we should tell the pastor to stop, because Jesus says, "Go." Go out of the water, get into our cars, and go reconcile with our brothers. If we're praying before we take communion, and there remember that our neighbors have some things against us, we should stop taking communion, because Jesus says, "Go." Put down the piece of bread, go find our neighbors, and be reconciled. If we're sitting at a meal saying grace, and remember that our neighbors have something against us, we should stop eating and excuse ourselves from the table. We should go to our telephones, go see our neighbors, and go be reconciled. Jesus says, "Go, go, go!"

It doesn't matter whether our "brothers" have something against us, as in this verse, or whether we have something against our "brothers." The command is still, "Go!" (Matt. 5:23–24; 18:15–17).

But isn't it sometimes a good idea to ignore an offense, letting it roll off of us like water off a duck's back? Although it's praiseworthy for someone to be willing to overlook an offense (Prov. 19:11), I believe that God usually wants us to go be reconciled—if it is, in fact, an offense. Isolated incidents that are just annoying, rather than truly offensive, might be overlooked. But anything that may indicate a deeper problem between people, anything that lingers in our memories, and anything that has any potentially negative effect on our relationships with other people or on the reputation of Christ should be addressed in the reconciliation process. We also need to be on guard against the human tendency to avoid the reconciliation process by characterizing an offense as an insignificant annoyance. So when in doubt, go!

Okay, so we go to our neighbors to be reconciled. How does the Bible say that should work exactly? Again, we should walk in Jesus' footsteps by following the five-step reconciliation process.

HOW TO RECONCILE

As we said in the previous chapter, biblical reconciliation involves five steps (Matt. 18:15–17):

1. *Go.* The parties meet face-to-face, if possible. Usually, the meeting should be just between the parties, in order to protect confidentiality.

2. *Show.* The person who was offended shows the other person his or her fault. But that's not all there is to be done. The person who was offended should begin by (a) affirming his or her relationship with the offender (to the extent a relationship exists), (b) confessing his or her own sins to the offended person—the sins that contributed to the disagreement, (c) repenting of the sins that contributed to the disagreement by pledging to take specific steps to remedy any harm that was caused, and to do things differently in the future, and (d) assuring the offender of forgiveness, if the offender will admit to and repent of his or her part in the dispute.

3. *Confess.* The offender admits and agrees that he or she was wrong. If the offender will not confess, then the offended person tries again by meeting with the offender as well as other people who agree that an offense has occurred. And if that doesn't work, then the offended person involves the offender's church by asking for a meeting with the offender and the offender's pastor. And if that doesn't work, the offended person relates to the offender as a non-Christian—meaning that the offended person still loves the offender, but doesn't relate to him or her as though both share a common commitment to Christ. Forgiveness is conditioned on confession and repentance.

4. *Repent.* The offender says, "I won't do it again"—and means it. The offender also agrees to restitution to the extent possible, meaning that the offender does what he or she can to right the wrong by giving time, money, or whatever it takes to undo the harm that the offender caused. The purpose of this restitution is partly to help the person who

was offended, but mostly to demonstrate true repentance on the part of the offender. If the offender cannot afford to make restitution, then the offended person still must forgive the offender, because Christ has forgiven the one who was offended. Restitution can also help an offender to focus on the need to change his or her behavior in the future, which helps the offender to pursue the righteousness to which Christ calls him or her.

5. *Forgive.* The injured person forgives the offender by (a) letting go of the offense in his or her heart, (b) not punishing the offender, (c) resuming his or her relationship with the offender (although changes in the relationship may need to be made for the benefit of both parties to minimize the chances of further injury), and (d) committing not to bring up the offense in the future, unless truly necessary.

Sadly, this process doesn't always restore a relationship with an offender. An offender may be dead, dangerous, or determined not to participate in the reconciliation process appropriately. We can't control all of the factors that lead to reconciliation, because it takes two to reconcile. But we need to make sure that we do everything that is appropriate to reconcile from our side of the dispute (Rom. 12:18).

I'll illustrate the five steps of the reconciliation process by way of a personal story.

The Kick

I studied Kyokushin karate until I went to graduate school, and then I had to stop. I was a brown belt, but I just didn't have time, and then moved to a place where there weren't any Kyokushin schools.

At the age of forty-three—after twenty years—I returned to training. Two years later, I was asked to test for black belt.

Kyokushin karate is a style of karate that is very physically demanding and emphasizes hard fighting. My black belt test was given over a period of three days—Thursday night through Saturday late afternoon. I had overcome several injuries and an unrelated surgery in the six months before the test, so I thought it was somewhat of a miracle to be ready. When I arrived at the test location, I prayed that God would allow me to glorify his name through my test. I also prayed that he protect me.

Thursday night went well. I fought several times and felt strong. Friday was filled with all kinds of training and testing, but not much fighting, until late afternoon. Then the fighting began for real. I was paired against a series of black belts whose job it was to push me very hard physically.

In my third fight, I was paired against a twenty-year-old black belt named Jason, who had great kicks. He wasn't part of our school, so we didn't know each other. The fight went for a few minutes, with me pretty much chasing Jason around the ring. It wasn't that I was beating him up badly. I was just trying to stay close to him so that it would be harder for him to hit me with his kicks.

And then came the kick I couldn't stop. From very close range, Jason did a vicious, jumping back-spin kick that hooked around my blocking arm. His heel caught me with full force on the right side of my face, about an inch below my temple, breaking my jaw in two places. My lower right jaw was fractured, and my lower left jaw was broken in two pieces. No, the rules didn't permit hard contact to the face. But it happened.

I was taken to a local hospital, where an X-ray confirmed that my jaw was broken. Two of my black belt friends then drove me to my hometown hospital three hours away. The next day, an oral surgeon put my jaw back together with a titanium plate, and wired my mouth shut. That's the condition I was in when I took Lauren to the concert that I mentioned in chapter 2.

How did I feel just after I was injured? Obviously, I felt physical pain—though not nearly as much pain as you'd think. But what I really felt was anger and disappointment. I didn't know whether, at my age, my body could stand getting ready for another test. I felt angry that Jason had not controlled his kick. I confess that I even felt angry at God for not protecting me in the way I expected him to. At the time, I certainly couldn't see how having my jaw broken did anything to glorify God. What I had in mind was a dramatic, triumphant, successful completion of my black belt test! That's obviously not what God had in mind. At least not that day.

So now you have the background for my illustration of how to be reconciled. Here's how the five steps of reconciliation played out in this case.

Go

I knew that God wanted me to see Jason as soon as I could, and I was told that he wanted to see me as well, when I was ready. I wanted to take the initiative. Jesus came to me, so that I could be forgiven. Jason needed me to love him as Jesus had loved me. He had sinned against me, as I have also often sinned against God and others. He needed to know how to be reconciled to me, just as Jesus had told me how to be reconciled to God.

More importantly, I had no idea whether Jason knew Jesus. I wanted to love Jason as Jesus loves me, so that Jason would know that Jesus loves him. Jason needed to know, if he didn't already, that Jesus invites him to a personal relationship with God. And God wanted me to hand that invitation to Jason personally, if I had the opportunity.

Sure, I could've said to myself, "Jason kicked me! He should come to me!" And I would've been right. But Scripture says, "Go!" Not later. Right now. If we wait more than a brief time for our hard feelings to go away, we're not being obedient to God's Word. Our hard feelings also don't really go away. They just fester and imbed in our hearts, and eat us alive. In my experience, the longer we wait, the more likely we are to come up with rationalizations as to why we shouldn't go.

I needed to have surgery first, and had to be discharged from the hospital. But within a few days, I arranged to meet Jason. The Bible requires a face-to-face meeting, if possible, and our electronic age hasn't changed that. Tone of voice and body language communicate more than 90 percent of our message. There's no good substitute for a face-to-face meeting.

Show

Before I went to see Jason, I prayed that God would soften my heart, and give me the right words to say. I needed the Holy Spirit

179

to remind me of his presence throughout the process. I knew that I couldn't do anything without God.

My first meeting with Jason was at his karate school. We sat alone in his teacher's office. Reconciliation is supposed to be private and confidential (Matt. 18:15), although, at times, a peacemaker might be needed to facilitate the discussion (more about that in the next chapter). If the offender is dangerous, another person might be needed for safety reasons.

If Jason were a Christian, which he apparently wasn't, we would have begun our meeting in prayer, and invited the Holy Spirit to help us. I prayed silently by myself instead.

I didn't have to say much to show Jason his mistake. He knew he'd made a mistake. And I couldn't say much, because my teeth were wired shut! I did explain some of my feelings about the injury, and the impact of the injury on me and my family. Finally, I pointed out to him what he already knew—that if his kick had landed an inch or two higher, he might have killed me.

As I spoke to Jason, I tried, with God's help, to be aware of my tone, my body language, and my words. I wanted to communicate in every way possible that, although he had hurt me, I still loved him as Jesus loves me. I tried not to make any assumptions or inflammatory accusations that went beyond the facts as I knew them. Assumptions are often wrong. Inflammatory accusations that attack a person's character are wrong on several levels. They're not loving. They're counterproductive. And they're often false.

The purpose of showing someone his or her mistake in the reconciliation process is to help that person understand why what he or she did was wrong, and how that person's sin hurt others. We have to speak hard truths, but we have to do it in love (Eph. 4:15). The offender should feel guilt when he or she hears what we say. Not guilt that grinds the offender down—guilt that motivates the offender to complete the reconciliation process correctly, which leaves no regret (2 Cor. 7:10).

I didn't do anything to Jason to justify what he did to me. That was clear from the outset. But it's often the case that when we speak to others about how they've offended us, we learn that we've offended them as well. To glorify God through the meeting, everyone has to remain humble and receptive to hearing what the other person has to say.

We should never forget to pray, or underestimate the power that God makes available to us through prayer, in the process of reconciliation. I prayed silently throughout my meeting with Jason. Had Jason been a Christian, we would've also prayed periodically throughout the meeting.

Confess

We know whether someone has listened to us in the reconciliation process if what we say results in an honest, open discussion, and a confession. "I'm sorry if you think I did you wrong" is not a confession. "I did what I did because you did something wrong" is not a confession. "I'm sorry if I hurt your feelings" is not a confession, although we might appreciate hearing that.

Jason listened to me, and immediately admitted his wrong. He also admitted to something that I didn't, in fact, know he had done. He confessed that he had kicked me in the head on purpose, not by accident. That was a shock. He did it out of fear and frustration. But it was intentional.

If the offender doesn't say what he or she did wrong, and what he or she should've done right, then the person hasn't really confessed to anything. Confession sounds like, "I was wrong when I [fill in the specific details of what was done wrong]. I should have [fill in the details of what should have been done]. Will you please forgive me?"

What if the offender doesn't confess? Then the Bible tells us to come back to the offender with two or more persons who were witnesses to the offense, and to repeat the process (Matt. 18:16). If that doesn't work, then we're supposed to "tell it to the church" (Matt. 18:17). Most churches don't have a formal reconciliation ministry, so the best approach is usually to ask the senior pastor of the offender's church about how to proceed with this step, and get as close as possible to what Jesus intended.

If the person doesn't attend church, then we have the choice of either dropping the matter or going to court to resolve the dispute.

But secular court probably won't do our relationship with the offender any good, or bring the offender to a place of repentance.

Repent

Both Jason and I agreed that his kick was an isolated incident. It was clear from our meeting that he didn't intend to do it again. But what if he had? Would I have been obligated to forgive him again? Most of us have heard the saying, "Fool me once, shame on you. Fool me twice, shame on me."

I certainly sympathize with the sentiment of that old saying. But it's not biblical. If our offenders do wrong to us again, and repeat this reconciliation process genuinely, we would have to forgive them in the name of Jesus (Matt. 18:21–22). We might need to take steps to protect ourselves in the future—like deciding not to trust them again in the same situation—but we'd have to forgive them.

As it happens, Jason later continued to have anger management problems in his karate school, and his teacher eventually had to tell him that he would not be permitted to fight. I genuinely regret that. But it was necessary.

Forgive

I told Jason that I forgave him. And I meant it. I explained to him why I was forgiving him. I told him about Jesus, and how Jesus had forgiven me. I explained that I had made many mistakes and poor decisions in my life, and unless Jesus had died for my sins, I would have been eternally separated from God.

Without Jesus, I wouldn't have had the strength to forgive him. But because of the love of Jesus, I genuinely cared about Jason and his well-being. I wanted him to know, and he needed to know, that I forgave him from my heart. Jason was genuinely relieved to hear this. We shook hands.

Jason and I then agreed to have lunch. When we got together the second time, I gave him a Bible and a book about Christianity, and we talked more about Jesus. I would love to say that Jason accepted Christ then and there. He didn't—but at least I had the opportunity to plant a seed.

By the way, four months after the accident, I was awarded my black belt. Eight months after that, I had to continue the fighting test that was interrupted by my injury. This time, I didn't break anything.

RECONCILING WHEN WE ARE THE OFFENDERS

How does the reconciliation process work when we are on the other side of an offense—when we sin, rather than are sinned against? Or what if we don't think that we have done anything wrong, but we know that someone else thinks that we have wronged them? Are we obligated to go through the reconciliation process, and if so how does that process compare to what the Bible teaches us to do when others sin against us?

Yes, as we said earlier, the Bible tells us to go through the reconciliation process (Matt. 5:23–24). The reconciliation process involves essentially the same five steps, with understandable differences. Here are some observations on each of these steps as they relate to this type of reconciliation:

1. *Go.* In going, have a spirit of humility, and resist the temptation to be defensive. This requires the help of the Holy Spirit, so we should pray before going, and as we go.
2. *Show your sin.* We might call this step "show what we know, and ask them to show the rest." By that I mean that if we are going to someone whom we have offended, we may not know entirely what we've done wrong, or even whether the person is offended. Therefore, we show the person what we know about what we have done, and ask them to show us how we have offended them. We need to be willing to listen for the purpose of understanding what happened from the other person's point of view, without being defensive.
3. *Confess.* Where we understand and agree with the other person concerning what we have done wrong, we admit our fault. Where we disagree with their perception of the events, we express our perception, our intention to be loving and true, and our desire to be reconciled.

4. *Repent*. We come to an agreement about what should change in the future.
5. *Ask for forgiveness*. We ask the person for forgiveness. If they are reluctant to forgive from their heart, we ask them why. Some aspect of the confession or repentance steps may have to be repeated. But if they still will not forgive, it is appropriate to speak the truth in love concerning the Bible's teaching on the necessity of forgiveness.

The objective of following this process is to honor and give glory to God by doing everything that we can, in his name and with his help, to be reconciled to others. Here is a story that illustrates this process. Unfortunately, it does not have a happy ending as far as the relationship was concerned.

Hank and Dan (not their real names) were old friends. Both are Christians. They met in school, were in each other's weddings, and shared many happy and sad experiences together, like brothers. After they finished school, they became business partners.

Their business relationship lasted for several years. Hank wanted to make changes in the business, and when Dan wouldn't agree, Hank terminated the business relationship. In the process of dissolving their business relationship, Hank and Dan said and did things that hurt their personal relationship. The hurt was not acknowledged at the time, but became apparent after the dissolution of the business, when the two friends stopped seeing and talking to each other.

After several months of not hearing from Dan, Hank sensed that the dissolution of the business had damaged his personal relationship with Dan significantly. He began to reflect on what he had done wrong, or may have done wrong, in the course of severing his business relationship with Dan. Hank wanted to try to follow the steps of biblical reconciliation to restore his relationship with Dan. This is what Hank did:

Go

Hank called Dan and asked to have lunch with him. Dan agreed. At lunch, Hank began in prayer.

Show Your Sin

After praying, Hank said something like this: "Dan, we've been friends for years. We've been through a lot together. We went to church together while we were in school. We were in each other's weddings. We were business partners. We've been together during good times and difficult times, as good friends and brothers in Christ.

"But since we dissolved our business partnership, our personal relationship has been strained. We haven't been in touch with one another, and we haven't tried to spend time together. I don't want it to be this way any more, Dan.

Confess / Repent

"I think that I have done some things that were wrong in the process of our break up of the business. Here is what I think God is showing me I did wrong: [Hank described the ways he thought he had sinned against Dan]. Dan, I ask your forgiveness for doing these things. I didn't mean to make these mistakes, but they were mistakes. I want to do what it takes to make things right between us.

Ask to Show

"I'm also sure that there must be other things that I've done wrong that I don't even realize. Will you please show me how I have offended you, so that I can ask your forgiveness for these sins as well?"

Dan's Response

At this point, Hank hoped that Dan would open up, affirm their relationship, and point out where Hank had fallen short as a friend and business partner. He had hoped to discuss what went wrong, to confess what he had done wrong, and then to receive Dan's forgiveness. After this, if it seemed appropriate, Hank might have also shown Dan how Hank thought Dan could have behaved better, in the hope that Dan would respond with his own confession and repentance, and Hank would then express his own forgiveness.

But unfortunately, that's not what happened. Instead, Dan essentially denied that Hank had offended him. Dan then explained the lack of contact between the old friends this way. "Hank, we both have a lot of friends, and busy schedules. We can't keep up with everyone." To this, Hank responded, "Dan, we both have other friends and busy schedules. But I only have one of you in my life. We have a shared history that can't be duplicated. I can't replace you with someone else. I love you, and want to be your friend. I'll make an effort to continue our relationship. But I can't do it myself, and I won't chase you if you don't reciprocate." After making several attempts to continue his relationship with Dan, Hank had to accept the reality that the relationship was over from Dan's point of view. The two men have not spoken for several years.

By refusing to communicate what's wrong, the offended person makes it impossible for the offender to repent or to ask forgiveness in a meaningful way. Refusing to participate in the reconciliation process in this way is a form of revenge. The injured person withdraws from the relationship as retribution for the offense, but denies what he or she is doing in order to conceal his or her unforgiveness.

In some ways, this form of revenge is more insidious than overt revenge, because while overt revenge is obvious to all, this revenge is veiled by lies. The greatest of these lies may be the one that we tell to ourselves: that our actions are justified because we have chosen to "turn the other cheek" (Matt. 5:39). Turning the other cheek means abandoning our desire for revenge, not abdicating our responsibility to reconcile.

ADAPTATIONS TO THE RECONCILIATION PROCESS

The biblical process of reconciliation obviously can't always be performed exactly the way Jesus described. It may be impossible, practically speaking, to go to the other person physically. The cost of travel to where that person lives, for example, may be prohibitive. In that case, the next best way of "going" may have to do, like calling the other person on the telephone.

It may be unwise to meet with the other person alone, if meeting alone will likely expose the injured person to physical or emotional abuse. In that case, the injured person may need to take someone with him or her to offer protection, but that "protector" should not get in the way of the reconciliation process. If these adaptations are necessary, what's important is to remain as true to the principles of the reconciliation process as possible under the circumstances. But we shouldn't skip steps of the reconciliation process entirely, or use the obstacles that are present in our circumstances as excuses for failing to attempt reconciliation.

WHEN THE RECONCILIATION PROCESS DOESN'T BRING RECONCILIATION

What if this reconciliation process doesn't reconcile us to the offender? If it's clear that the other person is in the wrong, then Jesus said that we should treat the offender "as you would a pagan or a tax collector" (Matt. 18:17). Remember that the author of this gospel, Matthew, was a tax collector! Tax collectors were notorious for collecting unauthorized money for their own personal benefit. They were considered crooks.

Treating someone as a pagan or a tax collector doesn't mean taking revenge on that person. It simply means relating to the offender as an unbeliever. The offender should not take communion and should not be permitted to continue as a member of a church. But he or she should be permitted to attend church and should be treated lovingly, as all people should be treated. This is not so much a punishment as it is recognition of the reality that the offender really doesn't know Jesus. The offender's refusal to acknowledge his or her wrong and ask forgiveness is proof of that person's unbelief.

We can't always control our circumstances and we definitely can't control how others react to the reconciliation process. All we can do is the best we can with God's help, so that "as far as it depends on [us, we] live at peace with everyone" (Rom. 12:18). The outcome of the process is not our responsibility—that's in God's hands.

SUMMARY

Reconciliation with others involves a five-step process—the same five steps that Jesus took to reconcile us to God. We go to the person with whom we have a dispute, show that person what he or she has done wrong, receive his or her confession, accept that person's repentance, and forgive him or her. The process may need to be adapted to fit our circumstances and the nature of the dispute. We need God's help to accomplish this process, and to restore the relationship that was damaged by our wrongs or the wrongs of others. Our responsibility is to be as faithful to the principles of this process as possible under our circumstances. If the other parties do not respond in kind, we are not responsible for their reaction.

APPLICATION

1. With a piece of paper and pen in hand, ask the Holy Spirit to give you the names of every person whom you may have offended, or who has offended you.

2. Pray for each person on your list, that by following the reconciliation process, you will love that person as Jesus has loved you. Pray that each one will be blessed as you attempt to reconcile with that person.

3. Ask the Holy Spirit to help you to reconcile properly with those whom you have offended.

    a. With the help of the Holy Spirit, and in preparation for your face-to-face meetings, write out genuine confessions of your offenses against each person. Consider how you can assure each person of your repentance. What steps can you take to ease that person's pain or to right your wrong?

    b. Ask that the Holy Spirit make it possible for you to see everyone on your list face-to-face, and soon.

4. Ask the Holy Spirit to help you to reconcile properly with those who have offended you.

a. With the help of the Holy Spirit, and in preparation for your face-to-face meetings, write out how you will lovingly but truthfully explain how each person has offended you. Remember not to make assumptions or false accusations. Demonstrate love and humility from start to finish.

b. Ask that the Holy Spirit make it possible for you to see everyone who has offended you face-to-face, and soon.

5. Start making calls and meeting with people, beginning with those whom you have offended. Pray a lot for God's help.

6. Be relentless in your loving pursuit of reconciliation. This is your ministry. Take it seriously.

Chapter 15

SHUTTLE DIPLOMACY

Blessed are the peacemakers, for they will be called sons of God.
—MATTHEW 5:9

After the October 1973 Arab-Israeli war, tension between Israel and Egypt remained high. A cease fire was in effect, but several unresolved issues jeopardized continued peace. Israel encircled and threatened to destroy the Egyptian Third Army. In an effort to help the parties disengage from their hostilities, United States Secretary of State Henry Kissinger spent two years flying back and forth between the Israeli and the Arab capitals. He urged the nations to make peace, and helped them find the specific terms under which peace might be achieved. As a result, peace agreements were signed in 1974 and 1975. Kissinger's approach to mediating this conflict became known as "shuttle diplomacy."

God's son, Jesus, in coming to earth, engaged in a peacemaking mission to end the conflict between God and people. The sin of mankind—of each one of us—caused the conflict. Jesus helped us understand the terms of peace, and made peace possible through his death on the cross. He didn't negotiate peace between the parties, like Kissinger did, because God doesn't negotiate. But in love, he conveyed the terms that make peace with God possible.

Jesus not only explained how to be at peace with God, but also demonstrated how to experience peace with other people. Peace with God begins when we accept the love that he has given us through Jesus Christ. Peace with other people is possible when we demonstrate the love of Christ to them, through the same humility, forgiveness, and service that Christ demonstrated to us.

While peace with God through Christ is a sure thing, peace with others is not. We need to remember that even Jesus did not experience peace with all other people. He was, after all, crucified. Sometimes, no matter what we do, others may choose to be at war with us, but our mission is to be at peace with them, to the extent possible (Rom. 12:18).

A peacemaker helps those who are at war with each other to walk the path of peace, which is straightened, paved, and lit by the love of Christ.[1] The path of peace is the biblical process of dispute resolution that leads away from hostility and toward forgiveness and reconciliation. A peacemaker mediates this process. Sometimes, one of the parties to a dispute invites the peacemaker to help. But sometimes, if prompted by the Holy Spirit, the peacemaker intervenes uninvited.

What if one or more of the parties to the dispute are not Christians? Is there anything that a Christian peacemaker can do to help? Yes, but obviously the approach to the dispute changes. I serve as a court-appointed mediator in suits that have been brought in state court. I can't explicitly discuss Jesus or biblical teaching on forgiveness and reconciliation in cases assigned to me. But before and during the mediation process, I do pray that the Holy Spirit will help me to mediate peace between the parties. And I can use some of the principles of dispute resolution that Jesus teaches us in the Bible.

If we, as potential peacemakers, haven't walked the road of forgiveness and reconciliation in our own lives, then we aren't much help as guides to others. We need to be experienced guides to help others walk the path of peace. Otherwise, we're the blind leading the blind.

Not all of us are ready or able to begin a peacemaking ministry, any more than we're ready or able to open a medical practice or other profession that requires special gifts, abilities, and training. But we can all learn the basic principles of peacemaking, just like we can learn first aid. If we find someone who is bleeding badly, the best person to help them is probably an emergency room doctor. But if more qualified help isn't available immediately, then we may have to give first aid.

So it is with peacemaking. Sometimes, we encounter a relationship that's bleeding to death, and there's no one else to help. God may call us at least to stop the bleeding long enough to get the parties to a more qualified peacemaker. And if we're all they have, then we ask the Great Physician to help us, and we do the best peacemaking job we can.

PEACEMAKER QUALIFICATIONS

If you're looking for a peacemaker to help you with a conflict, or think God may be leading you into a peacemaking situation, here are some attributes of a capable Christian peacemaker:

- *Christian maturity.* Peacemakers who have walked with Christ for many years should know the path of peace best. Ideal peacemakers have strong spiritual discipline in the areas of prayer and Bible study. Their lives should bear the fruit of the Holy Spirit: love, joy, peace, patience, kindness, goodness, faithfulness, gentleness, and self-control (Gal. 5:22).
- *Commitment to Christian unity.* Peacemakers can't be peace breakers. They shouldn't be involved in "quarreling, jealousy, outbursts of anger, factions, slander, gossip, arrogance, [or] disorder" (2 Cor. 12:20). They shouldn't cause division in the church (Rom. 16:17; Titus 3:10). They should be able to keep confidences.
- *Excellent communication skills.* Peacemakers should be "quick to listen, slow to speak and slow to become angry" (James 1:19). They should be capable of speaking the truth in love (Eph. 4:15). And they should be capable of restating what someone has said in a way that promotes understanding and reduces hard feelings.
- *Peacemaking knowledge and experience.* Peacemaking is learned through experience. Peacemakers should have experience in forgiving and in being forgiven by others, as well as in the process of face-to-face reconciliation. Peacemaking can't be fully learned without actually doing it.

We can see the value of these peacemaking attributes as we study the peacemaking process.

THE PEACEMAKING PROCESS

Depending on our situations and our qualifications, we may either be called to give peacemaking first aid, or to try to facilitate the full peacemaking process.

Peacemaking First Aid

The primary purpose of peacemaking first aid is to encourage the parties to a dispute not to make any rash decisions, and to engage in the reconciliation process. Rash decisions in reaction to an offense can greatly widen the gap between disputing parties. Rashness can compound an offense, multiply pain, and harden hearts.

Motivating others to reconcile can be difficult. Our best chance is to listen to enough of their stories to see the need for reconciliation, then talk to them about Jesus' teaching on forgiveness and reconciliation. As Jesus taught us, we should emphasize that reconciliation should be as confidential as possible (Matt. 18:15).

We should resist taking sides in the dispute, because a peacemaker must maintain a degree of neutrality. But we need to show compassion for the feelings of each of the disputing parties. The balance between neutrality and compassion is obviously difficult to strike. The Holy Spirit helps us to set the tone of our peacemaking efforts and keep our balance.

What if our encouragement to forgive and reconcile doesn't work? Then we keep encouraging. If we have access to both parties, then we may try to talk to both of them separately, and shuttle back and forth in an effort to help the parties understand one another and come together. But if we only have access to one of the parties, then we only talk to that person.

Throughout the process, from start to finish, we ask the Holy Spirit to guide us. Without God, we can do nothing in the peacemaking process. We need the discernment and the power that only God can give us, through the Holy Spirit.

Unless we feel called and qualified to act as a face-to-face facilitator, we would leave that part of the peacemaking process to others.

The Full Peacemaking Process

The full peacemaking process mirrors the reconciliation process. The peacemaker has four important roles: intervention, facilitation, instruction, and exhortation.

Intervention. Our natural human instinct is to stay out of other peoples' fights, and if we don't have a relationship with either party to the dispute—or a strong stake in the outcome of the dispute—that's probably a God-given instinct (Prov. 26:17). Usually, we won't get involved in shuttling between the parties or facilitating their face-to-face discussion unless invited by at least one of the parties. But if we know both parties in the dispute—particularly if they are both Christians—then we may be called to intervene in the dispute without an invitation.

No matter how gently the peacemaker approaches the situation, the fact that he or she is intervening puts the peacemaker's relationship with the disputing parties at risk. When Doug intervened in the dispute between his grandfather and great-grandfather, Doug's grandfather, William, deeply resented it. Doug believes that his peacemaking efforts permanently hurt his relationship with William. We all wish it weren't so, but that's the price of peacemaking. It's a price we should be willing to pay to save the disputing parties from the potential consequences of unforgiveness.

Facilitation. A peacemaker facilitates the reconciliation process by making it easier for the parties to meet and to talk. Initially, a peacemaker usually shuttles back and forth between the disputing parties to encourage them to meet for the purpose of reconciliation. Even before the parties get together, the peacemaker can begin to build bridges of understanding and compassion between them. A peacemaker might say something like, "I know that the two of you have been friends for years. It would be a shame to lose your relationship over this." Or, "I know that there are hurt feelings on both sides here."

Once the parties agree to meet, the peacemaker can facilitate the scheduling process. Calendar conflicts can become an excuse not to meet. The peacemaker can help avoid this problem. As we discussed in previous chapters, the parties should meet as soon as is reasonably possible.

If the peacemaker attends the face-to-face meeting, his or her primary purpose is to help provide a framework within which the disputing parties can conduct the reconciliation. The peacemaker should suggest that the meeting be opened in prayer. Ideally, each person should pray. Each should ask the Holy Spirit to help the parties glorify God and understand each other in the meeting. Each should pray for assistance in being humble and teachable. If the parties cannot bring themselves to pray, then the peacemaker should touch on these points.

Once the discussion begins, the peacemaker should encourage the parties to take turns discussing their issues in the dispute. As the discussion proceeds, the peacemaker makes mental notes of areas in which the parties share common ground of any kind. The parties should be encouraged to speak directly to one another, rather than to the peacemaker. During this portion of the process, the peacemaker may actually say very little.

In order to verify a correct understanding of what is being said, the peacemaker should reflect back to each party what he or she understands each party to be saying. This is a form of active listening. It helps the peacemaker to understand both parties. It also helps each party to better understand the other's point of view.

The way the peacemaker uses language can inflame or quell the emotions of the parties to the dispute. Although the restatement should include both the content and the emotion of what is being said, it may help if the peacemaker softens the rhetoric in two ways. First, the restatement should include words that make clear that what is being said is the speaker's point of view. If the dispute is over something that was supposedly stolen, the peacemaker would not say, "So, Joe stole your horse." He or she would say, "So, you think that Joe stole your horse." The second statement is equally true, but allows for the possibility that the speaker is mistaken in his or her perception.

Second, the peacemaker can use language that avoids drawing conclusions. In the horse theft dispute, for example, the peacemaker might say, "So, Harry, what you're saying is that your horse is gone and that you think Joe took it." "Took it" is less emotionally charged than "stole it." The phrase also allows for the possibility that Joe may have borrowed the horse, intending to bring it back.

Often, the "go" and "show" phases of the reconciliation process discussed in chapter 14 reveal that misperceptions contributed to the dispute. All of us are prone to jump to conclusions about what others have done, based on our understanding of the facts. Jumping to conclusions can be a sin in and of itself, because it can involve assuming the worst about others, rather than giving them the benefit of the doubt.

After the parties to the dispute have each described the facts and circumstances as each sees them, the peacemaker then attempts to turn the conversation gently toward identifying potential ways of resolving the dispute. Here's where confession and repentance should take place.

The peacemaker will likely have to take a more active role in the discussion at this point. He or she might say something like, "Joe, what I hear you saying is that you now believe you made a mistake in the way you handled the situation, and you regret your mistake. Would you be willing to speak directly to Harry now, to tell him that, and to ask his forgiveness." Or the peacemaker might ask, "What can be done to make things right here?"

The peacemaker is not the ultimate judge of who is right and who is wrong. God is. The peacemaker can direct the parties' attention to issues and to approaches, but it's not the peacemaker's place to determine whether Joe or Harry is wrong.

Instruction. The peacemaker should instruct the parties on the peacemaking process, and the urgent need for biblical forgiveness and reconciliation.

When it comes to the dispute itself, however, the peacemaker should be more neutral, or risk losing credibility with both parties in the dispute. Still, the peacemaker can offer some gentle assistance. The peacemaker might say, for example, "A Scripture comes to my mind as we talk about this situation—John 13:34–35. How do each of you think that this text applies to your situation?" The peacemaker may think that the Scripture directly resolves the dispute, but probably shouldn't say so. If the parties don't see it that way, the peacemaker might ask follow-up, open-ended questions, or might even suggest an interpretation for discussion, but should not pronounce a judgment based on the Scripture. That's not the role of the peacemaker.

The discussion between the parties shouldn't focus just on their individual thinking and feelings about what's right and wrong. Most of all, the parties should be seeking God's will for the resolution of the dispute. Therefore, it's best if all parties have their Bibles with them for reference. Periodically, throughout the discussion, the parties should be encouraged to pray together to seek God's wisdom and will.

Exhortation. Although the peacemaker should remain neutral for the most part, there is a place for exhortation by the peacemaker. This has to be done carefully and prayerfully. An exhortation can be implicit or explicit.

An implicit exhortation might sound something like, "Harry, I'm having a hard time understanding why you think you have the right to ask Joe to give you ten times the value of the horse that he took from you." The statement asks for a clarification. But implicitly it says, "Harry, I recommend that you back off of your request for ten times the value of your missing horse, unless you can show Joe a biblical right to that kind of compensation."

A direct exhortation might sound something like, "I recommend that you strongly consider the consequences of withholding forgiveness here." This kind of exhortation should be used sparingly, to maintain neutrality.

A CALL FOR PEACEMAKERS

Whether you're giving peacemaking first aid, or conducting the full peacemaking process, you can count on God's help. Jesus, our Prince of Peace, calls us to walk in his way, on the path of peace, toward unity with each other and with God. Our world is filled with division and disagreement. We need more peacemakers to sow the love and peace of Jesus into a world that is constantly at war with itself. "Peacemakers who sow in peace raise a harvest of righteousness" (James 3:18). I pray that all of us will learn peacemaking first aid, and that many of us will be called to be highly capable and available peacemakers.

For more information on the peacemaking process, I recommend Ken Sande's book entitled *The Peacemaker: A Biblical Guide to Resolving Personal Conflict* (Grand Rapids: Baker Books, 2004). You may also want to visit the Web site of Peacemaker Ministries (http://www.peacemaker.net) for information on how you or your church can receive training in peacemaking, or how you can find a certified Christian conciliator near you.

SUMMARY

Peacemakers are those who help others to forgive and reconcile by facilitating the process of biblical dispute resolution. The process sometimes begins with the peacemaker shuttling back and forth between the disputing parties, urging them to forgive and reconcile with each other. If the peacemaker is called to do so and has the necessary training, the peacemaker may also act as a mediator when the parties meet to discuss their dispute. The full peacemaking process roughly parallels the steps of biblical reconciliation. We need more trained peacemakers to help us find the path of peace that Jesus made possible through his love for us.

APPLICATION

1. Pray for an opportunity to be a peacemaker.

2. Learn the principles of peacemaking and apply them in your family and in your church.

3. Ask God whether you should make peacemaking one of your ministries, and if he says you should, pursue your ministry seriously. Find a more experienced peacemaker to learn from. Read books and take a course on Christian mediation.

PART 7

SERVICE

The Soul of Christ's Love

Chapter 16

FEET AND HANDS

Now that I, your Lord and Teacher, have washed your feet, you
also should wash one another's feet. I have set you an example that
you should do as I have done for you.

—JOHN 13:14–15

Jesus was about to eat his last supper with his disciples. The evening meal was being served. Satan had already prompted Judas to betray Jesus, but Jesus knew that God had placed all things under his power.

In that moment, we would expect Jesus to be thinking about himself. Memories of his life. Thoughts of returning to his heavenly Father. The pain that he would endure the next day on the cross. Things like that.

But not Jesus. In that moment, Jesus chose to show the apostles the full extent of his love by performing an amazing act of humble service for them. He got up from the table, took off his outer clothing, wrapped a towel around his waist, and washed the disciples' feet (John 13:1–5).

In the society of Jesus' time, the first thing that guests did when they entered a house or a tent was to wash their feet. Everyone wore sandals, and the host didn't want his guests to track their smelly, dirty feet into his home. Foot washing was also a matter of hospitality—it refreshed tired travelers.

In an ordinary home, the host furnished the water, and the guests washed their own feet. But in the home of a rich man, the washing was done by a slave. It was considered the lowliest of all services.[1] When Jesus took off his outer clothing and wrapped a towel around his waist, he was then dressed like a servant or a slave.

That's how much Jesus loves us! He's willing to serve us by personally meeting our most basic human needs. He doesn't say that a job is beneath him. He's not afraid to get his hands dirty. He wants to change our hearts by touching our lives with his loving service to us.

Why didn't the apostles wash their own feet when they arrived for the Last Supper? Why were they willing to eat their meal with Jesus while having dirty feet? Why, when Jesus stood up and dressed like a slave, didn't every one of them jump up and say, "Oh, Lord Jesus! Please forgive us! We'll all dress like servants and wash *your* feet. And then we'll wash our own!"

To their shame, that's not what the apostles did. All but Peter let the Lord of heaven and earth work like a slave to wash their feet without a word of protest. When Peter protested, Jesus said, "You do not realize now what I am doing, but later you will understand" (John 13:7).

Jesus didn't make Peter wait long for an explanation. He said, "Now that I, your Lord and Teacher, have washed your feet, you also should wash one another's feet. I have set you an example that you should do as I have done for you. I tell you the truth, no servant is greater than his master" (John 13:14–16). In effect, Jesus said, "A new command I give you: serve one another. As I have served you, so you must serve one another. In this way all men will know that you are my disciples, if you serve one another." It's the Lost Commandment of service.

How serious is Jesus about this command that we serve others? Very serious. Jesus treats our service—or lack of service—as given directly to him (Matt. 25:40, 45). So if we wash one another's feet by serving one another in love and humility, we wash Jesus' feet. And if we sit around at the spiritual table of our lives refusing to wash our own feet, let alone the feet of others; if we are waiting to be served, rather than serving; if we consider certain tasks beneath our dignity or our calling, and ignore the basic human needs of others—then we are guilty of great sin. We are guilty of idolatry and pride by putting ourselves above Jesus. We are guilty of ingratitude toward Jesus for his service to us. And we are guilty of failing to love others as Jesus has loved us. Christ calls us to roll up our sleeves and get our hands dirty in service to others and to him.

Each of us needs to ask the Holy Spirit to help us answer these questions: When it comes to service to others, do I act like Jesus did at the Last Supper? How do my attitudes and my actions need to change to be the loving, humble servant that Jesus called me to be? To whom do I need to go to ask forgiveness for my lack of loving service?

Today we can begin a new life of service to Jesus and others. We can begin by better understanding the Bible's teachings on service.

WHY WE SERVE

Jesus has asked us to serve others as he has served us. We shouldn't need any more motivation than that. But it's part of our human nature to ask, "What happens if I disobey? What are the consequences of disobedience both while I'm alive and after my body dies?" These questions go the heart of our relationship with God and what it means to be a Christian.

Our lives as Christians shouldn't focus on how little we have to do to get to heaven, or how severely we'll be punished for disobedience of God on earth. How would God feel about such an attitude? As a father, I can only imagine the pain and disappointment I'd feel if my children only helped around the house when they thought I would kick them out or punish them if they didn't help.

"Lauren, would you please wash the dishes?"

"If I don't, are you going to kick me out of the house?"

"Well . . . no I won't. But I need some help."

"Wow, great. No, I won't help you."

"Elizabeth, would you please wash the dishes?"

"Dad, you just told Lauren you won't kick us out of the house if we refuse to help you. So no, I won't help you."

I'd feel hurt, unloved, and disappointed. That's not how we want God to feel.

We don't perform works of service to *become* members of God's family. We perform works of service *because* we are members of

God's family, and we love him. Would I throw my daughters out of the house for their refusal to help? Of course not. But I would be unhappy, and at some point I'd have to ask myself, "Are these girls really part of our family? Maybe they only look like our daughters. Maybe there was a mistake at the hospital, and someone else's daughters were sent home with us because daughters aren't supposed to treat their fathers this way."

The teaching of the Bible is clear. We don't earn the right to be God's children through our works of service. My next door neighbor's daughter could come and work in my house morning, noon, and night. That wouldn't give her the right to be adopted as my daughter. No matter how much we work, God doesn't owe us anything. Compared to God's pure holiness, "all our righteous acts are like filthy rags" (Isa. 64:6).

We are God's children by his grace alone, through our faith in Jesus Christ as our Savior and Lord (Rom. 10:9–10). "For it is by grace you have been saved, through faith—and this not from yourselves, it is the gift of God—not by works, so that no one can boast" (Eph. 2:8–9). God doesn't want us bragging about our works. He doesn't want us to claim that we've earned the right to be in his family. God adopts us into his family through Christ as a demonstration of his grace and mercy.

Jesus told the thief who hung next to him on the cross, "I tell you the truth, today you will be with me in paradise" (Luke 23:43). The thief couldn't jump down off the cross and do anything. He was about to die. He was permitted into paradise because he acknowledged Jesus as his Lord and Savior (Luke 23:40–43).

But there's no such thing as faith without works of service, except when service is impossible because the believer is about to die or is completely incapacitated—like the thief on the cross. Faith without works is dead faith (James 2:17). We need live faith to be alive in Christ. Otherwise, we'll remain dead in our sin. And sin will continue to separate us from God from now into eternity, unless we accept Jesus' invitation to be our personal Lord and Savior, in true faith.

Our faith and actions should work together; our faith should be made complete by what we do (James 2:22). As our Lord, Jesus sees to it that we have works of service to do. In faith, we should do these works of service to his glory.

In fact, God created us in Christ to perform works of service, and he prepared the work for us in advance (Eph. 2:10). He equips us for service by giving us his Word (2 Tim. 3:16–17). Our pastors and teachers are responsible for preparing us for works of service (Eph. 4:11–12). Christ instructs our service through prayer, and he empowers us to serve through his Holy Spirit.

Our service to one another should be out of our love for Jesus and one another, not out of pure obligation (Gal. 5:13). The greatest love of all is to lay down our lives in service to our friends, the way Jesus did (John 15:13). Laying down our lives for each other doesn't just mean dying for one another. It also means living for one another. We should lay down our lives every day for those whom we are called to love.

Whoever tries to withhold his own life from others will lose it. But whoever gives his life away to others, out of love for Jesus and the gospel, will find it (Mark 8:35). We experience complete joy when we serve others. By doing good works and sharing ourselves, we take hold of "the life that is truly life" (1 Tim. 6:19).

WHOM WE SERVE

The whole world needs help—literally. We find it hard not to get discouraged when we think about how much hunger, sickness, loneliness, and pain fill the earth. In the face of all of this need, how does each of us decide whom to serve? Chapter 18 discusses how we can discern Christ's calling to serve.

As Christ leads us and we are able, we should do good to all people (Gal. 6:10), but we should especially serve three groups of people.

Family

God has placed each of us within certain family and church relationships. The Bible is clear that special love and duty are owed to parents, spouses, children, and those who belong to the family of believers in Jesus Christ. Husbands must love their wives as

Christ loved the church (Eph. 5:25) and as their own bodies (Eph. 5:28). Wives must submit to their husbands as to the Lord (Eph. 5:22). Marriage, in fact, involves mutual submission, each spouse to the other (Eph. 5:21). Fathers are commanded to teach their children about the Lord and his ways and not to frustrate them (Eph. 6:4). We are commanded to honor our fathers and mothers (Exod. 20:12; Matt. 15:4). Finally, we are called to do good to all people, especially to those in Jesus' family, who have entrusted their lives to him as Savior and Lord (Gal. 6:10).

Those in Urgent Need

Although just encountering someone with a need doesn't necessarily mean that we're the ones to meet the need, God puts some people in our paths who urgently need our service. I'll talk more about that in chapter 18. The more urgent the need and the fewer alternatives these people have, the more likely we are the ones whom God has appointed to help them.

The parable of the good Samaritan is an example. The Samaritan was traveling from Jerusalem to Jericho when he came across a naked man who had been beaten half to death by robbers. A priest and a Levite—religious people who should have known better—ignored the man. But the Samaritan took pity on the man, bandaged his wounds, and made sure he would be cared for at a local inn at the Samaritan's expense (Luke 10:30–35).

My wife and I got help from a Good Samaritan on a trip to see our daughter Elizabeth play in a marching band competition. We were a hundred miles from home and about a hundred miles away from the competition when we discovered, at a rest stop, that we had a flat. It was on a Sunday evening, so our options were limited. As we sat in a fast-food restaurant trying to figure out what to do, a man named Steve walked up to us and offered to help.

"I'm a salesman. I have to be at a meeting in Bethlehem [Pennsylvania] tomorrow, but I'll give you whatever help I can until then."

As it turned out, even though Steve drove a different kind of van than we did, his full-sized spare fit our vehicle perfectly. So he loaned it to us. He also helped us change the tire in the rain. We took off for the band competition and made it with only ten minutes to spare. We later learned that, after he left us, Steve stopped to help another motorist with car trouble.

When I returned the spare tire to Steve, I asked him whether he often helped people like this. I also asked him why he did it.

"Several years ago, I had to take this sales job, and it put me on the road for most of the week," Steve said. "That meant I couldn't become as involved in my church as I wanted. So I prayed that the Lord would use me to serve others when I travel. The very next day, I started running into people who needed help. And it's been like that ever since. That was five years ago."

God wants us to be available to those in urgent need, like Steve is. All we need to do is ask him, and we'll begin to see others who need our service.

The Poor

The poor are often the most in need of our service, but they're also the most overlooked. For the sake of discussion, the poor includes the sick, the oppressed, and the lonely. The sick are the poor in health. The oppressed are the poor in justice. The lonely are the poor in relationships.

Throughout the Bible, God commands us to serve the poor. Through the prophet Isaiah, he said, "Is not this the kind of fasting I have chosen: to loose the chains of injustice and untie the cords of the yoke, to set the oppressed free and break every yoke? Is it not to share your food with the hungry and to provide the poor wanderer with shelter—when you see the naked, to clothe him" (Isa. 58:6–7).

Caring for the poor is one of the most important ways that we demonstrate the love of Christ. Jesus made himself poor for our sakes so that through his poverty we could become rich (2 Cor. 8:9). When James, Peter, and John sent the apostle Paul and Barnabas to the Gentiles, all they asked them to do was to remember the poor (Gal. 2:10). In love, Jesus asks us to follow in his footsteps by serving the poor.

If we completely overlook the poor, our faith in Jesus is in question and we risk God's judgment. Jesus said that when he returns, God will condemn those who neglect the poor. God will say, "Depart from me, you who are cursed, into the eternal fire prepared for the devil and his angels. For I was hungry and you gave me nothing to eat, I was thirsty and you gave me nothing to drink, I was a stranger and you did not invite me in, I needed clothes and you did not clothe me, I was sick and in prison and you did not look after me" (Matt. 25:41–45). Whatever we do for the poor is credited to us as though we did it for God himself. Whatever we refuse to do for the poor, we refuse to do for God himself.

We have to find the poor, look at them with compassion, and serve them as though we are serving the Lord himself. The poor in money and health are easy to find. The poor in relationships or justice may be less obvious if we don't look for them with the help of the Holy Spirit, but we should ask God to show us whom he has chosen for us to serve.

HOW WE SERVE

If we understand the way God has shaped us as individuals, then we also have insight into how we can best serve God and whom we are to serve. Our personalities, spiritual gifts, abilities, passions, and experiences make each of us uniquely valuable for specific kinds of service. Depending on the circumstances, we should choose ways of serving that take best advantage of our unique value and our circumstances, like Steve the traveling salesman did.

But it's important to keep two things in mind. First, God may ask us to serve in unexpected and uncomfortable ways. Is anybody really comfortable washing feet? God may call us to very uncomfortable service, either to fill a need or to help us grow in maturity. Mother Teresa demonstrated the humble attitude that we should have toward service. She considered herself to be "God's pencil. A tiny bit of pencil with which he writes what he likes."[2]

Second, we can trust that when God calls us to serve, he gives us what we need to serve. We need, of course, to listen carefully for God's voice. We do this by meditating on his Word, seeking his will in prayer through the Holy Spirit, evaluating our circumstances with spiritual discernment, and listening to godly counsel. Then it's time to step out in faith to serve, trusting that God will give us what we need.

SUMMARY

When Jesus washed the feet of the disciples, he provided us with an example of loving others by serving them. We should serve others as an expression of our love for Jesus and our faith in him. Our families, others in urgent need, and the poor should receive our greatest service. When we serve the poor, the sick, the oppressed, and the lonely, God accepts our service as though it were performed directly for him. Likewise, if we refuse to serve those in need, God treats our refusal as though we refuse to serve him.

APPLICATION

1. Ask Jesus to give you his heart for service. Tell him you'll do anything he asks you to do. That's what it means to follow Jesus as our Lord.

2. Ask the Holy Spirit to show you who in your life needs your service, and what needs to be done. Then do it as soon as you can.

3. Go looking for opportunities to serve the poor. Ask the Lord to allow you to feed them, clothe them, and visit them in their hour of need. Then take action.

Chapter 17

DOLLARS AND SENSE

Freely you have received, freely give.
—Matthew 10:8

Jesus gives us a simple choice: serve God or serve money. We can't serve both; we'll love one and hate the other (Matt. 6:24). So we must choose. And we make our choice by the way we make our money, and by the way we give our money away. We choose to serve God by making our money honestly and fairly. We also choose to serve God by giving our money freely to those who are in need. God gives freely to us so that we can give freely to others (Matt. 10:8).

The love of money is the root of all kinds of evil. It can cause us incredible grief. It may even cause us to wander away from our faith (Matt. 13:22; 1 Tim. 6:10).

One day, a rich young man walked up to Jesus and asked him, "Teacher, what good thing must I do to get eternal life?" After claiming that he had kept various commandments, the young man asked Jesus, "'What do I still lack?' Jesus answered, 'If you want to be perfect, go, sell your possessions and give to the poor, and you will have treasure in heaven. Then come, follow me.'" At that, the young man went away sad, because he had great wealth (Matt. 19:16–21). He made his choice.

After the young man left, Jesus told his disciples that it's very hard for a rich man to enter the kingdom of heaven. In fact, it's practically impossible. Jesus said, "Again I tell you, it is easier for a camel to go through the eye of a needle than for a rich man to enter the kingdom of God" (Matt. 19:24). This expression about a camel passing through the eye of a needle was common among the Jews, and signified something impossible, not something improbable.[1] (In the United States, we might say something like, "It's easier for a pig to fly than it is for a rich man to enter the kingdom of God." We all know that pigs don't fly.) But then Jesus added, "With man this is impossible, but with God all things are possible" (Matt. 19:26).

Jesus told not only the rich young man to sell all his possessions and give to the poor; he said the same thing to the disciples (Luke 12:33). The difference is that the disciples made a different choice than the rich young man: they did what Jesus said, and decided to serve God rather than money. So we can't rationalize Jesus' statement: we can't conclude that Jesus told the rich man to sell his possessions only because the rich man had a bad attitude toward money. Hording money is bad in and of itself.

So what does the Bible teach us about giving? Here are nine biblical principles to guide us.

CHRIST IS THE SECRET TO CONTENTMENT

We can't help but notice that the rich are often the most miserable people we know. Those who are rich by worldly standards can still be unhappy if they compare themselves to others who have greater wealth than they have. Covetousness and greed are never satisfied, because they always focus on what we don't have, rather than on what we do have.

If we always look at those who have more than we have, we're not only miserable, but we usually can't see those who are truly poor, even though they're all around us. Much of the world lives in abject poverty—hungry, naked, sick, lonely, and afraid.

The apostle Paul said, "I have learned the secret of being content in any and every situation, whether well fed or hungry, whether living in plenty or in want. I can do everything through him who gives me strength" (Phil. 4:12–13). The secret to contentment is not money. It's God and his Son, Jesus Christ. When we find our contentment in Christ, we're free from the bondage that material possessions can place on us. Then we're free to give to the poor cheerfully, as God wants, and experience the true joy of giving (2 Cor. 9:7).

WE CAN'T OUTGIVE GOD

When we give to the poor according to godly principles, God will not allow us to outgive him. Jesus said, "Give, and it will be given to you. A good measure, pressed down, shaken together and running over, will be poured into your lap. For with the measure you use, it will be measured to you" (Luke 6:38).

If we give generously, God will give generously to us because through our giving we fulfill God's desire to demonstrate his love to the poor. The Bible assures us that God will make us rich in every way so that we can always be generous to those in need (2 Cor. 9:10–11). What an incredible joy it is to express God's love to others in this way.

Jesus assured the disciples that if they gave to the poor, they would lay up treasure for themselves in heaven—treasure that would endure (Matt. 6:19). We should all deposit a generous amount of our wealth in heaven through our gifts to the poor.

GOOD STEWARDSHIP IS PART
OF GODLY GIVING

Good financial management is part of godly giving. We should manage our affairs so that we are able to pay our debts as they become due (Rom. 13:8). We should minimize our reliance on debt, because debt can enslave us (Prov. 22:7). Sound budgeting, savings, and investment help us to provide for the needs of our families and the poor.

In order to give as God intended, we may need to make adjustments to our circumstances and our lifestyles. Obviously, this can take time. It's important to seek God's will for our finances, and to make the adjustments that he directs, even if it requires a significant change in our circumstances.

TEN PERCENT OF OUR GROSS INCOME GOES TO THE CHURCH

At least 10 percent of our gross income (the tithe) should be given to our churches. If we don't tithe, God says that we're robbing him (Mal. 3:8–9). But if we tithe, God says that he will bless us. Through the prophet Malachi, God said, "'Bring the whole tithe into the storehouse, that there may be food in my house. Test me in this,' says the LORD Almighty, 'and see if I will not throw open the floodgates of heaven and pour out so much blessing that you will not have room enough for it'" (Mal. 3:9–10).

Will we get rich if we tithe? Not necessarily. And if we do, we're probably supposed to give away more money!

I can say from firsthand experience that God makes good on his promise concerning tithing. My wife and I have been married for twenty-five years. For most of those years, we've tithed, and always had what we needed. In the years when we have not tithed, we not only didn't have any more money than in years when we tithed—we seemed to have more difficulty making ends meet. I can't give any explanation for this, other than that God is true to his Word.

We might ask whether this Old Testament tithing requirement was eliminated in the New Testament. No New Testament text suggests that we are expected to give less, now that our Savior, Jesus Christ, has come. If anything, we're probably expected to give more.

On a practical note, we may find it easiest to tithe if we have the tithe taken out of our paychecks or bank accounts automatically. Modern technology can help reduce the temptation of holding back money that we owe to God.

Most church members—no matter what Christian denomination—don't come close to tithing. Can you imagine how financially strong the church would be if everyone tithed?

ELIMINATE EXTRAVAGANCE

Jesus told a parable about a rich man who built bigger and bigger barns to store his goods, so that he could have years of leisure

(Luke 2:14–21). Doesn't that sound a little like the retirement planning of our world today?

But that's not God's retirement plan. God said to the man, "You fool! This very night your life will be demanded from you. Then who will get what you have prepared for yourself?" (Luke 12:20).

God gives us wealth not so that we can take the rest of our lives off in a retirement of leisure. God gives us wealth not so that we can buy extravagant cars and houses and toys. James wrote, "Now listen, you rich people, weep and wail because of the misery that is coming upon you. Your wealth has rotted, and moths have eaten your clothes. Your gold and silver are corroded. Their corrosion will testify against you and eat your flesh like fire. You have hoarded wealth in the last days" (James 5:1–3).

God's retirement plan is heaven itself. He wants us to take joy in living life on earth to the fullest. He wants us to serve him by serving others until the day we die and go to be with him. And when we see him face-to-face, we'll take joy in hearing him say, "Well done, my good and faithful servant."

Am I saying that it's not godly to save money? Of course not. But we should ask God to help us discern the difference between ungodly hoarding and godly saving. Our motivation and our objectives can make our financial plans righteous or unrighteous.

LOOK AT THE POOR WITH COMPASSION

Many of us have seen television appeals for charitable giving to help the sick, the hungry, and the homeless. Some of these commercials are almost unbearable to watch. Sometimes we feel so overwhelmed by the suffering that we look away.

We have to stop looking away. Jesus never looks away from suffering. When he walked the earth, he looked at people in need with compassion (Matt. 9:36; 14:14; 15:32; 20:34). He didn't blame the poor for being poor. Jesus helped them, and so should we.

The Greek word that is translated as *compassion* in the verses in Matthew could be defined as "a gut reaction that leads to urgent action."[2] As the apostle John asked, if we have material possessions, see someone in need, and don't take pity on him, how can the love of God be in us (1 John 3:17)?

SACRIFICE TO GIVE

Jesus became poor for our sakes (2 Cor. 8:9). We should be willing to sacrifice in order to give to the poor. We may not have to take a poverty vow, but we should certainly take a vow to increase our giving to those in poverty. We should be willing to give up at least some of what we have in order to help those who have nothing at all.

BEYOND THE TITHE, GIVE PRIMARILY TO THE POOR

Our giving should be directed primarily toward the poor, in the broadest sense of the word. We should take the time to pick charities that make good use of our gifts. There are independent organizations whose mission it is to confirm the financial stewardship of Christian charities, so it's becoming easier to pick appropriate ways to get our help to the poor.[3] As always, we should ask the Holy Spirit to give us discernment in making wise choices.

GIVE TO GLORIFY GOD

The purpose of our giving is not only to help the poor, but also to give glory to God. Our hope is that through our giving, those who receive our help will know that we are Christians because we love them as Christ loved us (John 13:35). We hope that they will give praise and thanks to God for what we do for them (2 Cor. 9:11). To accomplish this objective, there are times when we should explicitly acknowledge God as we make our gift. God is the one who gave us the money to give to the poor. We want to properly give him credit. The Holy Spirit helps us discern when it's best to give anonymously, when we should acknowledge God explicitly, and how we can best give God the glory.

We shouldn't care about receiving credit for our giving. At times, allowing ourselves to be recognized can encourage other donors to give. But if we sense that this recognition makes it difficult for us to remain humble, then it would be better to give anonymously (Matt. 6:3).

Wouldn't it be wonderful to see universities and hospital wings named after the Lord Jesus Christ? They would stand as monuments to the love of Jesus.

SUMMARY

The Bible tells us that we have received freely from God and so we should give freely to others. Giving is, in fact, one way we serve God and others. Nine biblical principles, however, should guide our giving: (1) when we make the decision to serve God and find our contentment in Christ, we experience the joy of giving; (2) we can't outgive God; (3) good budgeting is part of godly giving; (4) ten percent of our gross income should go to the church; (5) eliminate extravagance; (6) look at the poor with compassion; (7) sacrifice to give; (8) beyond giving to church, give primarily to the poor; and (9) give to glorify God.

APPLICATION

1. Ask the Holy Spirit to teach you how to find contentment in Christ, and to protect you from the temptations of covetousness and greed.

2. Create a budget that shows where you spend your money.

3. Make sure that your budget includes your tithe.

4. Eliminate extravagance from your lifestyle and retirement plans, so that you can give more money to the poor. Sell items that you really don't need, and give the money to the poor, in the name of Jesus.

5. Evaluate your spending and savings habits according to biblical principles of giving.

6. Resolve to give more than your tithe, and direct the giving toward a church or reputable charities that serve the poor.

WHO'S NEXT IN LINE?

Then, because so many people were coming and going that they did
not even have a chance to eat, he said to them, "Come with me by
yourselves to a quiet place and get some rest."

—MARK 6:31

Sometimes, love means saying "no" or "not now." With the help of the Holy Spirit, we should discern God's boundaries and priorities for our lives and for the way we serve. His boundaries require us to say "no" to some service and giving opportunities; his priorities sometimes require us to say to others, "Not now" or "If I have time."

How could it possibly be loving to say "no" or "not now"? Because every time we say "yes" to one activity, we also say "no" to another activity. We're faced with trade-offs.

Humility helps us to see our boundaries and set our priorities in obedience to the Lost Commandment. In humility toward God, we recognize that we can't do anything without Jesus (John 15:5). If we try to do something without Jesus—or something that only Jesus is supposed to do—our efforts won't promote a loving relationship with him. Jesus wants us to recognize him as Lord by working with him, and through him, and for him, not apart from him.

In humility toward others, we should acknowledge that others can often do many things better than we can. God limits our personal capabilities and our callings intentionally so that we have to work within loving relationships with others to accomplish the missions that he gives us. We were meant to function within a body of believers (1 Cor. 12:12–31), as a Christian family, all working together. That's what makes God smile. In God's army of faith, we're not supposed to be an army of one.

So in this chapter, we'll discuss how to discern and observe our God-given boundaries and priorities as we obey the Lost Commandment.

THE BOUNDARIES OF OUR CALLING

A woman came into my office asking for help on behalf of a non-profit, secular organization. She wanted me to take a leadership role in the organization because it had organizational and financial problems. I didn't want to. I suggested that someone who worked for me instead take the position. But somehow I ended up taking the position anyway. And I spent tens, if not hundreds, of hours helping the organization. In retrospect, though my intentions were good, taking the position was a mistake.

Many of us are too helpful for God's own good. We think that we have to meet any need that we encounter. The word *no* doesn't seem to be in our vocabularies. We may think that we're obeying the Lost Commandment by running ourselves ragged—but we're not. Rather, we're doing our own work and not doing the good works that God planned for us to do (Eph. 2:10).

We need, then, a survey of our God-given boundaries. We need to see whether the way we use our time and money is within God's calling on our lives. So, like a surveyor looks through a transit to set an accurate property line, we have to sharpen our focus on where God's will sets our boundaries.

Surveying the Boundaries of Our Calling

God puts boundaries on our calling to keep us focused on what he wants us to do. He doesn't want us to do some things, even if they seem helpful or loving to others. How do we discern God's boundaries?

The answer is, prayerfully and carefully. Here are some questions that may help us to discern whether God wants us to invest time or money in an activity:

1. Do we believe that God wants us to engage in the activity based on the words of the Bible, prayer, our individual circumstances, and the advice of trusted Christian advisers, including our spouses or our parents? God usually confirms his calling through more than one means.
2. Is this an activity that meets one of our basic human needs such as nutrition, rest, or exercise?
3. Does the activity fall within the thrust of our ministries, based on our personalities, gifts, abilities, passions, and experience?
4. Are we meeting an emergency need that cannot easily be met by others?
5. If the activity is something related to recreation, can it be done primarily on Sunday (the day God designated for rest)? Can we participate in the activity and still meet our giving and budgetary guidelines?
6. Can we participate in the activity without jeopardizing our abilities to meet higher priority needs?

The more time or money involved in the activity, the more the activity should, of course, be scrutinized. But the answer to at least some of these questions should be "yes" before we commit a lot of time or money to an activity.

Are there any bright lines that God draws to define the boundaries of our calling to obey the Lost Commandment? For example, do our obligations under the Lost Commandment extend beyond our Christian family of faith?

Our Boundaries Extend Beyond Our Churches

In trying to find God's boundaries, some of us are tempted to exclude non-Christians from the scope of the Lost Commandment. Many of the Scriptures that we've discussed throughout this book use words that seem, at first blush, to support this view.

The words of the Lost Commandment itself, for example, were spoken to a room full of Christians. When Jesus told them to love "one another" as he had loved them, was he drawing a boundary that excluded non-Christians from the scope of the commandment?

Here's another example. When Jesus said that we were to reconcile with our "brother," was he only talking about other Christians? Are non-Christians excluded? Can we let our disputes with non-Christians go unresolved?

Even the Golden Rule says that we're supposed to love our "neighbors" as ourselves. But the question is, "Who's our neighbor?" The Golden Rule was first given to the Jews (Lev. 19:18). At the time, Jews mostly lived next to other Jews. So was God saying that Jews have to love "as themselves" only other Jews?

The answer is that we're supposed to love everyone as Jesus has loved us, whether they share our faith in Jesus or not. Here are eight ways that we know that the boundaries of our love extend beyond our church walls:

1. *Jesus' teaching on love was all-inclusive.* When Jesus said that we should love one another as he has loved us, he didn't say "only" one another. He didn't say, "Don't love non-Christians." Many Jews of Jesus' time thought that they were free to hate their enemies. Jesus' response was that the Jews (and we) are supposed to love and pray for our enemies (Matt. 5:43–48). A man once asked Jesus, under the Golden Rule, "Who is my 'neighbor'?" The man was really asking Jesus, "Who am I not obligated to love?" Jesus told the parable of the good Samaritan to give his answer: we can't exclude anyone from our love simply because of who they are (Luke 10:29–37). Jesus put his teaching into practice by demonstrating his love for the Samaritans, who were considered enemies of the Jews. He loved them by spending time with them and teaching them (John 4:9–26, 39–43). We have to be willing to love anyone whom God calls us to love.

2. *Jesus' love for us came before we were Christians.* Jesus loved us before we became Christians (Rom. 5:8). "We love because he first loved us" (1 John 4:19). So under the Lost Commandment, we need to love others as Jesus loved us—even though they aren't Christians.

3. *One purpose of the Lost Commandment is evangelism.* Jesus said that everyone would know that we are his disciples

if we obey the Lost Commandment (John 13:35). There's nothing distinctive about loving others who love us (Luke 6:32–33). Our Christian love for non-Christians attracts them to Christ in the same way that Jesus' love for us attracted us to him.

4. *God's passion is for the lost.* To emphasize how much God loves those who don't know him yet, Jesus told three parables in a row: the parables of the lost sheep, the lost coin, and the lost son (Luke 15:3–32). We need to have that same compassion for the lost.

5. *God loves the whole world.* God so loved all the people of the world that he sent his Son to save us (John 3:16–17; 12:47), even though many of us hate Jesus (John 7:7). *We* shouldn't withhold God's love from anyone, because *God* hasn't withheld his love from anyone—even us!

6. *Jesus demonstrated love toward everyone.* When Jesus walked the earth as a man, he didn't exclude anyone from his love. He was criticized for spending time with people considered to be immoral. But he said that he came to invite sinners to follow him (Matt. 9:12). Even while Jesus was being crucified, he asked God to forgive his crucifiers (Luke 23:34).

7. *God's direction to the apostles was, "Do good to all people."* After Jesus ascended into heaven, God continued to lead Christians to love unbelievers as Christ had loved them. God sent Peter to Cornelius the Gentile, and showed Peter that he should not call *any* man impure or unclean (Acts 10:28). God also inspired Paul to write, "As we have opportunity, let us do good to all people" (Gal. 6:10).

8. *Jesus' Great Commission to us is all encompassing.* Jesus told us to go out into "all the world" (Mark 16:15), to "all nations" (Matt. 28:19; Luke 24:47). He commanded us to preach the gospel to "all creation" (Mark 16:15), teaching them to obey everything that he has commanded us (Matt. 28:20), including the Lost Commandment. As God sent Jesus into the world in love (John 3:16), so also Jesus sends us into the world in love (John 20:21).

We need to survey and re-survey our God-given boundaries to make sure that we are within the boundaries that he has established for our service and our giving. But we can't exclude non-Christians. We have to love them as Jesus has loved us.

But are boundaries enough? No, they're not. Once we've surveyed and established God's boundaries, we then need to establish priorities to help us live within those boundaries.

PRIORITIES

Priorities help us to allocate our time and money within the boundaries God has given to us. While boundaries help us determine what we'll do or not do, priorities help us determine what to do in the next hour, in the next day, or in the next year. Boundaries help us determine what goes on our to-do list. Priorities help us to decide the order in which we work on the tasks on our to-do list.

Priorities also help us to deal with the unexpected. Just when we think we have a handle on the use of our time or money, something usually happens that requires us to reassess our decisions. An unexpected need arises. Something costs more than we thought it would. Priorities are useful because they help us to make necessary adjustments to our planning without losing sight of our God-given boundaries.

Our Planning Versus God's Plans for Us

I confess that I've always found it difficult to set priorities with confidence. Recently I was frustrated by the low level of billable work that I'd accomplished in my law practice. Time that I could've spent making money was instead spent helping others who couldn't afford to pay me. True, some of the activities that had taken me away from my law work probably should've been declared out-of-bounds through a proper survey. But that wouldn't have solved all my time problems.

So one day, in order to get on top of my problem, I decided to list the priorities for my day. Starting with the first priority, I blocked off time on my calendar to accomplish each task. My obvious intention was to refuse to do anything other than what I'd planned for my day.

And then two phone calls came in to my office. The first call involved a family that was going to be evicted from their home unless someone helped them. But they didn't have money to pay me. They didn't have much time to look for someone else to help them either. They were desperate.

Their need was within the thrust of my calling as an attorney. So, after praying briefly, I felt led to help them. And God found a way, through my help, to keep a roof over their heads.

Within an hour, a second call came in with a similar plea for help. Honestly, I thought my head was going to explode. My priority list was going out the window. But after some prayer, I felt led to help the second caller as well. God's grace was sufficient for me, and my head didn't explode.

Did I make the right decisions? I think so. But if I made the wrong decisions, I made them for the right reasons. In each case I made the decisions based on prayer and in faith that God was leading me to help. In both cases, I thought that I was following the Lost Commandment as Jesus intended.

If the phone had rung a third time with a similar need, would I have accepted that third client as well? I don't know. But I do know that God promises not to overload us beyond our abilities (Matt. 11:28–30).

We need lists, calendars, and budgets to be good stewards of the time and money that God has entrusted to us. But in humility, we need to realize that Jesus is Lord of our calendars and our wallets. He'll change our plans and our spending according to his will. We can plan all we want, but God determines what we should do (Prov. 16:9) and what purposes should be accomplished through our work (Prov. 19:21). Our plans succeed when they are a response to God's will (Prov. 16:3).

Our Desires Versus God's Desires for Us

Through the Holy Spirit, God wants to give us pure hearts (Ps. 51:10; Acts 15:9). And then he wants to give us the desires of our hearts (Ps. 37:4; Matt. 5:8). If we make it our first priority to seek God and his will for our lives, he'll take care of everything else (Matt. 6:33).

To find God's will for our lives, we have to make a conscious effort to understand—and usually reject—the priorities that the world tries to impose on us (Rom. 12:1–2). The world's expectations tend to diverge from God's expectations in the areas of work and leisure.

Work. We need to work in order to provide for our families (1 Tim. 5:8). But the world tends to look at work differently than God looks at work.

First, the world tends to measure success by the size of our bank accounts, while God measures our success by the size of our love for him and one another. If we try to live up to the world's standards of success, accumulating possessions that we really don't need, we can easily find ourselves sacrificing time that we should be spending with the Lord, with our families, and in service to others.

Second, the world tempts us to look for our identities in our careers and in our credentials, rather than in Christ. Our greatest claim to fame should be found in God's name: that we are known as Christians by our love for others, through our obedience to the Lost Commandment.

Third, the world expects us to pick whatever career pays the most, no matter what the work demands of us. The world sees our careers as separate from our Christian service. But Jesus is Lord of all—including the marketplace. In Christ, our career should be a vocation as well—a calling to serve him through our service to others, in obedience to the Lost Commandment.

Finally, the world accepts work as a hobby or a means of escaping our personal lives. A Washington lawyer once told me that his firm looked at divorce as a sign of commitment to the firm. He passed it off as a joke, but almost every lawyer in the firm was divorced or single.

But work isn't supposed to be a hobby or an escape. If we no longer need to work to make money, then we should ask Jesus whether we can be of better service to him in a way that doesn't necessarily involve making money. Or maybe we should be giving away all of the money that we earn, because others need the money more than we do.

If we find ourselves using work to run away from relationships with the Lord, our spouse, or our children, then we should ask the Lord whether we should quit our jobs and do something else. Or maybe we should just go home and love our families the way Jesus has loved us—sacrificially, selflessly, and compassionately.

Leisure. Even Jesus had to rest from his work in order to strengthen himself for service (Mark 6:31). But the world tends to make leisure the goal of work. Some of us thank God it's Friday because we live for the leisure that we have on weekends. We look forward to going home from work so that we can watch television. We work hard to increase our opportunities to pursue our hobbies. Some of us spend incredible amounts of time and money on hobbies or other amusements that have no positive impact on others.

There's nothing wrong with leisure, hobbies, or weekends. But if we make leisure a higher priority than service in obedience to the Lost Commandment, then we make leisure our god. We won't bear the fruit that Jesus intended us to bear, and we won't experience the joy of life in Christ. But when we use rest and fun to restore our strength so that we can love others in obedience to the Lost Commandment, then we have life that is truly life.

SUMMARY

Following the Lost Commandment not only involves saying "yes" to service and giving opportunities, it also involves saying "no" or "not now." God doesn't call us to serve or give in response to every opportunity. Our God-given boundaries distinguish the work that God has called us to do from the work that God has called others to do. When faced with an opportunity to give or to serve, we need to prayerfully re-survey God's boundaries in our lives. As we do so, we should remember that we are called to love all people according to the Lost Commandment, and not just those inside the church. Our God-given priorities define what we do now rather than later.

We should be flexible when making plans so that we will be receptive and responsive to God's changes to our schedule.

APPLICATION

1. Pray that the Holy Spirit helps you to see the boundaries that God intends to establish in your life. Ask him to show you how you need to adjust the way you spend your time and money in order to obey the Lost Commandment.

2. Ask those with whom you live what they think of the way you've been spending your time and money. Listen carefully, without being defensive. God often speaks to us through those whom we love.

3. Survey your calendar and your checkbook. Based on God's principles of service and giving, compare what you're doing to what you hear the Holy Spirit telling you to do.

4. Take out a piece of paper and draw a vertical line down the middle of it. Label the left column "+" and the right column "–". In the "+" column, list activities that you think God wants you to add or emphasize. In the "–" column, list activities that you think God wants you to eliminate or de-emphasize.

5. Make an action plan. What are you going to do and who are you going to call in order to draw more godly boundaries in your life?

6. Implement your plan to establish God's boundaries in your life.

7. For the activities that are still inbounds, make a plan for how much time and money you're going to spend on each activity per week or per month. Show your plan to your loved ones for their comments, and make adjustments.

8. Make to-do lists based on godly priorities every day, and do the most important things first.

9. Be flexible. You never know when God will call you, asking you to fill a need that's not on your list, but is on his list for you.

CONCLUSION

Life is pointless and joyless without God's love.

Though it may come as a surprise to us, practicing obedience to the Lost Commandment *is* the point of our lives. The Lost Commandment requires us to love others as Jesus does by:

- Putting our relationship with God first
- Being determined to accomplish our God-given mission
- Having a heart of humility
- Using the power that only comes from obedience to God
- Strengthening our relationships with forgiveness
- Making service the soul of our existence

Our obedience to *this* commandment—not the Golden Rule—brings complete joy to Jesus and to us (John 15:10–12). Jesus, in fact, intended to replace the Golden Rule with the Lost Commandment, so if we continue to follow the Golden Rule because we think that *it* is the greatest commandment, we miss Jesus' point. We also miss what Jesus really wants *from* us and *for* us. Joy. Complete joy! He loves us that much.

Our love for others in obedience to the Lost Commandment flows out of our relationship with God, made possible by Christ's death for us on the cross. God invites us to experience his love for all eternity. We accept his invitation by personally acknowledging to him and others that Jesus died for our sins, rose from the dead, and reigns in our lives as Savior and Lord. Once we do this, and understand who we are in Christ, God's love begins to heal the wounds that we have experienced in the world.

God requires that each of us continue Jesus' determined mission to change our lives and our world with his love. Our lives change when, with the help of the Holy Spirit, we focus our minds and our hearts and our strength on understanding how Jesus has loved us, so that we can love others the same way. Our world begins

227

to change when we pay Jesus' love forward by loving others as he loves us, *and by teaching them to do the same.*

We can't accomplish our missions without humble hearts. Jesus loved God by humbly acknowledging God's sovereignty. He made his Father's purposes and glory more important than his own objectives and acclaim. So must we. Jesus loved others by humbly serving them, as though he were the least important person among them. So must we. As Jesus' servants, we cannot be above our Master.

Humility enables us to live our lives in God's power, through our obedience to him. In faith, we pursue God's will for our lives. We study his Word with the assistance of the Holy Spirit. We speak to him with affection and reverence as our Father. We listen intently to his words in response to our prayers. We allow him to teach us what it means to love others as he has loved us, and then in the power that he gives us through the Holy Spirit, we love him *and* others by following in Jesus' footsteps. As we follow Jesus, we learn from him, and teach others by example. Our words and our actions should follow *Jesus'* example of love, rather than reflect *our* ideal of love.

We also obey the Lost Commandment by forgiving and serving others, as Christ has forgiven and served us. Forgiveness strengthens our love for others by protecting it from the ravages of sin. Relationships that are characterized by criticism are destined to die, but relationships that are grounded in grace and forgiveness can last forever. If we carry the message of Christ's forgiveness into every dispute we encounter, the peace of Christ will begin to fill our world with love and joy.

Jesus also expresses his love for us by serving us, as he provides for our practical, physical, and emotional needs. Service is the soul—the essential expression—of Jesus' love for us. As Jesus has served us, so we must serve others. Just as Jesus has given us our daily bread, so also we should love others by sharing our bread with them. Freely Jesus has given to us; freely we should give to others. We need to serve and give to others as though we were serving and giving to Jesus himself. God has given us boundaries and priorities for our calling to serve him, so that we will know how to allocate our time and our money in accordance with the Lost Commandment.

By following the Lost Commandment, we experience the joy of living in communion with Christ. We better understand his love and suffering for us as we love and sacrifice for others in the same way. Our love for Jesus deepens as we see him active in our lives, and in the lives of those whom we love in his name.

If we practice obedience to the Lost Commandment, our daily lives become acts of worship that fill us with Christ's love. In Christ, we can have complete joy through a life that is truly life. His love, expressed through us, bears fruit that will never die.

We have missions to accomplish in Christ. May we all transform the world together through Christ's love, until all of us join in one chorus of voices to sing praises to our God, whose very being is love. "For from him and through him and to him are all things. To him be the glory forever! Amen" (Rom. 11:36).

SCRIPTURES THAT ECHO THE LOST COMMANDMENT

Notice how many of these Scriptures deal with the seven principal elements of Christ's love: joy, relationship with God, mission, humility, obedience, forgiveness, and service. Note the connections between the love that God and Jesus have shown for us, and our obligations to demonstrate this same love to others.

Scripture	Text
Matt. 5:9	Blessed are the peacemakers, for they will be called sons of God.
Matt. 5:11–12	Blessed are you when people insult you, persecute you and falsely say all kinds of evil against you because of me. Rejoice and be glad, because great is your reward in heaven, for in the same way they persecuted the prophets who were before you.
Matt. 5:23–24	Therefore, if you are offering your gift at the altar and there remember that your brother has something against you, leave your gift there in front of the altar. First go and be reconciled to your brother; then come and offer your gift.
Matt. 6:12	Forgive us our debts, as we also have forgiven our debtors.
Matt. 6:14–15	For if you forgive men when they sin against you, your heavenly Father will also forgive you. But if you do not forgive men their sins, your Father will not forgive your sins.
Matt. 7:1–2	Do not judge, or you too will be judged. For in the same way you judge others, you will be

Scripture	Text
	judged, and with the measure you use, it will be measured to you.
Matt. 10:8	Freely you have received, freely give.
Matt. 18:32–33	Then the master called the servant in. "You wicked servant," he said, "I canceled all that debt of yours because you begged me to. Shouldn't you have had mercy on your fellow servant just as I had on you?"
Matt. 22:37–40	Jesus replied: "Love the Lord your God with all your heart and with all your soul and with all your mind." This is the first and greatest commandment. And the second is like it: "Love your neighbor as yourself." All the Law and the Prophets hang on these two commandments.
Matt. 25:40	The King will reply, "I tell you the truth, whatever you did for one of the least of these brothers of mine, you did for me."
Matt. 25:45	He will reply, "I tell you the truth, whatever you did not do for one of the least of these, you did not do for me."
Mark 8:34–35	Then he called the crowd to him along with his disciples and said: "If anyone would come after me, he must deny himself and take up his cross and follow me. For whoever wants to save his life will lose it, but whoever loses his life for me and for the gospel will save it."
Mark 8:38	If anyone is ashamed of me and my words in this adulterous and sinful generation, the Son of Man will be ashamed of him when he comes in his Father's glory with the holy angels.
Luke 6:27–38	But I tell you who hear me: Love your enemies, do good to those who hate you, bless those who curse you, pray for those who mistreat you. If someone strikes you on one cheek, turn to him the other also. If someone takes your cloak, do not stop him from taking your tunic. Give to everyone who asks you, and if anyone takes what

Scripture	Text
	belongs to you, do not demand it back. Do to others as you would have them do to you.

If you love those who love you, what credit is that to you? Even "sinners" love those who love them. And if you do good to those who are good to you, what credit is that to you? Even "sinners" do that. And if you lend to those from whom you expect repayment, what credit is that to you? Even "sinners" lend to "sinners," expecting to be repaid in full. But love your enemies, do good to them, and lend to them without expecting to get anything back. Then your reward will be great, and you will be sons of the Most High, because he is kind to the ungrateful and wicked. Be merciful, just as your Father is merciful.

Do not judge, and you will not be judged. Do not condemn, and you will not be condemned. Forgive, and you will be forgiven. Give, and it will be given to you. A good measure, pressed down, shaken together and running over, will be poured into your lap. For with the measure you use, it will be measured to you.

Luke 12:16–21

And [Jesus] told them this parable: "The ground of a certain rich man produced a good crop. He thought to himself, 'What shall I do? I have no place to store my crops.'

"Then he said, 'This is what I'll do. I will tear down my barns and build bigger ones, and there I will store all my grain and my goods. And I'll say to myself, "You have plenty of good things laid up for many years. Take life easy; eat, drink and be merry."'

"But God said to him, 'You fool! This very night your life will be demanded from you. Then who will get what you have prepared for yourself?'

"This is how it will be with anyone who stores up things for himself but is not rich toward God."

Scripture	Text
John 6:57	Just as the living Father sent me and I live because of the Father, so the one who feeds on me will live because of me.
John 10:14–15; 17	I am the good shepherd; I know my sheep and my sheep know me—just as the Father knows me and I know the Father—and I lay down my life for the sheep. . . . The reason my Father loves me is that I lay down my life—only to take it up again.
John 13:14–15	Now that I, your Lord and Teacher, have washed your feet, you also should wash one another's feet. I have set you an example that you should do as I have done for you.
John 13:20	I tell you the truth, whoever accepts anyone I send accepts me; and whoever accepts me accepts the one who sent me.
John 13:34–35	A new command I give you: Love one another. As I have loved you, so you must love one another. By this all men will know that you are my disciples, if you love one another.
John 14:12	I tell you the truth, anyone who has faith in me will do what I have been doing. He will do even greater things than these, because I am going to the Father.
John 14:15–17	If you love me, you will obey what I command. And I will ask the Father, and he will give you another Counselor to be with you forever—the Spirit of truth. The world cannot accept him, because it neither sees him nor knows him. But you know him, for he lives with you and will be in you.
John 14:21	Whoever has my commands and obeys them, he is the one who loves me. He who loves me will be loved by my Father, and I too will love him and show myself to him.
John 14:23–24	Jesus replied, "If anyone loves me, he will obey my teaching. My Father will love him, and we will come to him and make our home with him.

Scripture	Text
	He who does not love me will not obey my teaching. These words you hear are not my own; they belong to the Father who sent me."
John 15:10–14	If you obey my commands, you will remain in my love, just as I have obeyed my Father's commands and remain in his love. I have told you this so that my joy may be in you and that your joy may be complete. My command is this: Love each other as I have loved you. Greater love has no one than this, that he lay down his life for his friends. You are my friends if you do what I command.
John 15:20–21	Remember the words I spoke to you: "No servant is greater than his master." If they persecuted me, they will persecute you also. If they obeyed my teaching, they will obey yours also. They will treat you this way because of my name, for they do not know the One who sent me.
John 17:15–23	My prayer is not that you take them out of the world but that you protect them from the evil one. They are not of the world, even as I am not of it. Sanctify them by the truth; your word is truth. As you sent me into the world, I have sent them into the world. For them I sanctify myself, that they too may be truly sanctified.
	My prayer is not for them alone. I pray also for those who will believe in me through their message, that all of them may be one, Father, just as you are in me and I am in you. May they also be in us so that the world may believe that you have sent me. I have given them the glory that you gave me, that they may be one as we are one: I in them and you in me. May they be brought to complete unity to let the world know that you sent me and have loved them even as you have loved me.
John 20:21	As the Father has sent me, I am sending you.
John 21:16	Again Jesus said, "Simon son of John, do you truly love me?" He answered, "Yes, Lord, you

Scripture	Text
	know that I love you." Jesus said, "Take care of my sheep."
Acts 1:8	But you will receive power when the Holy Spirit comes on you; and you will be my witnesses in Jerusalem, and in all Judea and Samaria, and to the ends of the earth.
Rom. 15:7	Accept one another, then, just as Christ accepted you, in order to bring praise to God.
1 Cor. 11:1	Follow my example, as I follow the example of Christ.
2 Cor. 1:5–6	For just as the sufferings of Christ flow over into our lives, so also through Christ our comfort overflows. If we are distressed, it is for your comfort and salvation; if we are comforted, it is for your comfort, which produces in you patient endurance of the same sufferings we suffer.
2 Cor. 5:20	We are therefore Christ's ambassadors, as though God were making his appeal through us.
Gal. 6:2	Carry each other's burdens, and in this way you will fulfill the law of Christ.
Eph. 4:32	Be kind and compassionate to one another, forgiving each other, just as in Christ God forgave you.
Eph. 5:1–2	Be imitators of God, therefore, as dearly loved children and live a life of love, just as Christ loved us and gave himself up for us as a fragrant offering and sacrifice to God.
Eph. 5:21–32	Submit to one another out of reverence for Christ.
	Wives, submit to your husbands as to the Lord. For the husband is the head of the wife as Christ is the head of the church, his body, of which he is the Savior. Now as the church submits to Christ, so also wives should submit to their husbands in everything.
	Husbands, love your wives, just as Christ loved the church and gave himself up for her to make her holy, cleansing her by the washing with water

Scripture	Text
	through the word, and to present her to himself as a radiant church, without stain or wrinkle or any other blemish, but holy and blameless. In this same way, husbands ought to love their wives as their own bodies. He who loves his wife loves himself. After all, no one ever hated his own body, but he feeds and cares for it, just as Christ does the church—for we are members of his body. "For this reason a man will leave his father and mother and be united to his wife, and the two will become one flesh." This is a profound mystery—but I am talking about Christ and the church.
Eph. 6:7–8	Serve wholeheartedly, as if you were serving the Lord, not men, because you know that the Lord will reward everyone for whatever good he does, whether he is slave or free.
Phil. 2:5–7	Your attitude should be the same as that of Christ Jesus: Who, being in very nature God, did not consider equality with God something to be grasped, but made himself nothing, taking the very nature of a servant, being made in human likeness.
Col. 3:13	Forgive as the Lord forgave you.
1 Tim. 6:18–19	Command them to do good, to be rich in good deeds, and to be generous and willing to share. In this way they will lay a treasure for themselves as a firm foundation for the coming age, so that they may take hold of the life that is truly life.
Heb. 6:10	God is not unjust; he will not forget your work and the love you have shown him as you have helped his people and continue to help them.
Heb. 12:1–3	Therefore, since we are surrounded by such a great cloud of witnesses, let us throw off everything that hinders and the sin that so easily entangles, and let us run with perseverance the race marked out for us. Let us fix our eyes on Jesus, the author and perfecter of our faith, who

Scripture	Text
	for the joy set before him endured the cross, scorning its shame, and sat down at the right hand of the throne of God. Consider him who endured such opposition from sinful men, so that you will not grow weary and lose heart.
James 2:13	Judgment without mercy will be shown to anyone who has not been merciful. Mercy triumphs over judgment!
1 Peter 1:22–23	Now that you have purified yourselves by obeying the truth so that you have sincere love for your brothers, love one another deeply, from the heart. For you have been born again, not of perishable seed, but of imperishable, through the living and enduring word of God.
1 Peter 2:20–21	But if you suffer for doing good and you endure it, this is commendable before God. To this you were called, because Christ suffered for you, leaving you an example, that you should follow in his steps.
1 Peter 4:10–11	Each one should use whatever gift he has received to serve others, faithfully administering God's grace in its various forms. If anyone speaks, he should do it as one speaking the very words of God. If anyone serves, he should do it with the strength God provides, so that in all things God may be praised through Jesus Christ. To him be the glory and the power for ever and ever. Amen.
1 John 1:7	But if we walk in the light, as he is in the light, we have fellowship with one another, and the blood of Jesus, his Son, purifies us from all sin.
1 John 2:5–6	But if anyone obeys his word, God's love is truly made complete in him. This is how we know we are in him: Whoever claims to live in him must walk as Jesus did.
1 John 3:16–17	This is how we know what love is: Jesus Christ laid down his life for us. And we ought to lay down our lives for our brothers. If anyone has material possessions and sees his brother in need

Scripture	Text
	but has no pity on him, how can the love of God be in him?
1 John 4:7	Dear friends, let us love one another, for love comes from God. Everyone who loves has been born of God and knows God.
1 John 4:11–12	Dear friends, since God so loved us, we also ought to love one another. No one has ever seen God; but if we love one another, God lives in us and his love is made complete in us.
1 John 4:19–21	We love because he first loved us. If anyone says, "I love God," yet hates his brother, he is a liar. For anyone who does not love his brother, whom he has seen, cannot love God, whom he has not seen. And he has given us this command: Whoever loves God must also love his brother.
Rev. 3:21	To him who overcomes, I will give the right to sit with me on my throne, just as I overcame and sat down with my Father on his throne.

HOW TO CREATE A READING PLAN

H ere are twelve principles for creating a reading plan:

1. *Buy a good study Bible.* Buy a respected translation of the Bible that includes study notes, a concordance, maps, and introductions to each book of the Bible. My favorite is the *NIV Study Bible,* but there are other good ones. I don't recommend that you use paraphrase Bibles, like the *Living Bible* or the *Message,* as your primary Bible.

2. *Make a commitment.* Commit to spending a certain minimum amount of time per day reading. I would suggest 20 or 30 minutes per day. Many people find that it's helpful to pick a time and a place, almost as though they are making an appointment with God. I have found that a more flexible approach seems to work better for me. I try to pray and read in the morning, before I get going with my day, but I also take whatever I'm reading wherever I go, and look for moments here and there when I can read for a few minutes.

3. *Pray before reading.* Each time you sit down to read, whether it's the Bible or some other book, remember to pray. Ask the Holy Spirit to help you to understand what God wants you to glean from your reading.

4. *Learn how to learn.* Even if you have been blessed with years of education and spend your work-life learning new things, invest time up front in improving your ability to learn. Not

just learning how to learn the Bible, but also learning how to learn in general. I've been blessed by some great books on learning that I put at the top of the list of recommended books included in this appendix.

5. *The Bible is the key.* Whether we read the Bible, or read books about the Bible, our primary objective should be to learn the Bible. We should spend significant amounts of time reading the Bible itself, and not fall into the trap of only reading what others have written about the Bible. Once we understand how to read the Bible in context, we should evaluate all other teaching carefully in light of biblical teaching. I have included a chart at the end of this appendix that lists steps to take and questions to answer for the purpose of understanding and applying the Bible to our lives.

6. *Get the big picture.* Try to get at least an overview-level of knowledge about the structure, themes, and historical context of the Bible. You may find it helpful to attend seminars that are offered on the Old and New Testament by Walk Thru the Bible Ministries, Inc. (http://www.walk thru.org), which provide a broad overview of the Bible in a fun way. You should plan to read and/or listen to the entire Bible more than once, with the intention of understanding the principal themes that are developed throughout the entire Bible: God's sovereignty and holiness, his love for us despite our imperfection, his relationship with Israel and the church, and his plan to redeem us through the work of Jesus Christ on the cross.

7. *Initially, focus on key New Testament books.* After learning more about learning how to learn, I recommend careful study of these books in the following order: John, Acts, Romans, Galatians, Ephesians, Philippians, Colossians, Hebrews, and Revelation. That's nine of the twenty-seven

books of the New Testament. Then I recommend you start at the beginning and read all the way through the New Testament, creating a short outline of each book.

8. *Read the Old Testament.* It's important to study the Old Testament. Read it through and study it from the beginning, just as you did the New Testament.

9. *Memorize and meditate on key verses.* As you study the Bible, ask the Holy Spirit to show you particular verses that you need to know and apply. Memorize these verses and mull them over in your mind, considering how they apply to your life. Write the memory verses on note cards that you carry around with you. Tape the verses to the mirror of your bathroom and look at them as you get ready for your day. Consider memorizing larger chunks of Scripture that seem particularly important to you. Scripture memorization and meditation yield huge benefits (Ps. 1:1–3).

10. *Address specific questions.* At times, we all have issues that concern us. Such issues relate to relationships, family, jobs, finances, health, you name it. The Bible offers wisdom on all of these. Ask the Holy Spirit to help you find answers to the questions that are on your mind. In addition to the Bible, read other great books that are based on the Bible and are written about these subjects.

11. *Invest in study materials.* As your finances permit, consider investing in additional materials, such as an audio version of the Bible, books on biblical history, a Bible dictionary, and a complete concordance. Getting an audio Bible and downloading sermons onto an MP3 player can turn even a short commute into one of the best parts of your day.

12. *Participate in Bible study with others.* Find Bible studies where the Bible is taught well, and participate in them. We are encouraged by and learn from the insight of others.

BOOK RECOMMENDATIONS

Any number of books may be helpful to you. To get you started, though, here are some titles that I recommend as supplements to your Bible reading.

Books on Learning How to Learn

I would recommend both of these books for the top of your reading list, because they help us become more effective learners:

Mortimer J. Adler and Charles Van Doren, *How to Read a Book* (New York City: Simon & Schuster, Inc., 1972). A classic book that has sold about seven million copies since it was originally printed in 1940, this book will help you become a more effective reader of the Bible as well as anything else you read.

Mortimer J. Adler, *How to Speak/How to Listen* (New York City: Simon & Schuster, Inc., 1983). Teaches us how to speak and listen more effectively, improving our ability to learn from and relate to others.

Books on How to Understand the Bible

Either of the first two books below (both of them if you have time) give a great introduction to how to read the Bible. The third and fourth books go deeper into these subjects.

Howard G. Hendricks and William D. Hendricks, *Living by the Book* (Chicago: Moody Press, 1991).

Gordon D. Fee and Douglas Stuart, *How to Read the Bible for All Its Worth*, 3rd edition (Grand Rapids: Zondervan, 2003).

Gordon D. Fee, *New Testament Exegesis: A Handbook for Students and Pastors* (Louisville: Westminster John Knox Press, 2002).

Douglas Stuart, *Old Testament Exegesis: A Handbook for Students and Pastors* (Louisville: Westminster John Knox Press, 2001).

Books Relating to the Inerrancy of the Bible

Lee Strobel, *The Case for Christ* (Grand Rapids: Zondervan, 1998). Experts answer pointed questions about the biblical account of Jesus' life and death on the cross.

Lee Strobel, *The Case for the Creator* (Grand Rapids: Zondervan, 2004). Experts answer pointed questions about the biblical account of creation.

Josh McDowell, *The New Evidence That Demands a Verdict* (Cambridge University Press, 1999). This book is organized in outline format, and has a great deal of evidence pertaining to the accuracy of Scripture.

Books About the History and Culture of the New Testament Era

F. F. Bruce, *New Testament History* (New York City: Doubleday, 1969). A biblical scholar describes the history of the Middle East from approximately 400 B.C. to approximately A.D. 200.

Eduard Lohse, *The New Testament Environment* (Nashville: Abingdon Press, 1976). Excellent discussion of the political, religious, and cultural movements within Judaism and the Hellenistic-Roman environment that framed biblical writings from approximately 400 B.C. to approximately A.D. 200.

Reference Books That Help with Bible Study

J. Sidlow Baxter, *Explore the Book: A Survey and Study of Each Book from Genesis Through Revelation* (Grand Rapids: Zondervan, 1960). This book helped me in my first reading through the Bible about twenty-five years ago. Baxter's passion for the Bible is evident from his discussion of God's Word. His discussion of each book teaches us how to study the Bible for ourselves, and his passion is contagious.

J. D. Douglas, *New International Bible Dictionary* (Grand Rapids: Zondervan, 1999). Offers insight into the historical, chronological, archaeological, geographical, social, theological, and biographical aspects of the Bible. Based entirely on the NIV and cross-referenced to the King James Version.

Anson F. Rainey and R. Steven Notley, *The Sacred Bridge: Carta's Atlas of the Biblical World* (Jerusalem: CARTA Jerusalem, 2006). Describes the history of the Old and New Testaments, and includes three hundred maps, plans, illustrations, charts, and tables.

Deluxe Then and Now Bible Maps (Torrance, California: Rose Publishing, Inc., 2007). Contains maps of the lands of the Bible for several historic periods. Each map has a plastic overlay of the modern map of the region.

Edward W. Goodrick and John R. Kohlenberger III, *The Strongest NIV Exhaustive Concordance* (Grand Rapids: Zondervan, 2004). Lists every word of the Bible in alphabetical order, and below each word, gives the Bible verses in which the word appears. Includes numbers for each word, which can be used for cross-reference in the Hebrew, Greek, and Aramaic dictionaries at the back of the book. Also includes indexes that allow for easy cross-referencing to the Strong's numbering system, which is used in numerous reference materials.

W. E. Vine, *Vine's Expository Dictionary of Old and New Testament Words: Super Value Edition* (Nashville: Thomas Nelson Publishers, 2001). A great resource for better understanding the nuances of the original languages of the Bible.

PC Study Bible (http://www.biblesoft.com): Biblesoft offers a variety of excellent, PC-based Bible study materials, in a variety of price ranges, including collections that include several of the reference materials described above.

HOW TO READ THE BIBLE TO TRANSFORM YOUR LIFE

Sources to Consult	Steps to Take	Questions to Answer
		1. WHAT *WAS* THE BOOK ABOUT? [CONTEXT] a. Genre? (e.g., narrative, epistle, wisdom literature) b. Author/Recipients/Occasion? c. Time/Place? d. Structure/Organization? How is the content of the book organized to express its theme? e. Theme/Emphasis?
	1. Always pray for God's wisdom and guidance first.	
NIV Study Bible	2. Read study Bible introduction only to answer Questions 1.a.b.c.	
	3. First read: Read the book all the way through in one sitting. a. Mark changes of scene/time/audience/subject with hash marks to designate "segments" of text. b. Circle important terms or phrases that are repeated three or more times. c. Underline purpose-of-book statements and occasion statements.	
Bible Dictionary; Atlas	4. Deepen your understanding of context. a. Read about author and recipients. b. Read about places where author and recipients were. c. Look at atlas to orient setting and read about history.	

continued on next page…

HOW TO READ THE BIBLE TO TRANSFORM YOUR LIFE (*Continued*)

Sources to Consult	Steps to Take	Questions to Answer
		2. WHAT *DID* THE BOOK SAY IN DETAIL, AND HOW? [CONTENT]
	5. Second read: Read the book through a second time.	a. What are the meanings of key phrases/terms? b. Propositions: Focus on groups of related paragraphs ("segments"). What was God trying to convey through the author *to the original recipients* of the book?
Bible Dictionary; Concordance	6. Create an outline using change of scene/time/audience/subject hash marks. a. Look up key words ("terms"). What do they mean in this book, and other books of the Bible? b. Include key propositions and key terms in outline.	c Related Scripture: What do we know about the characters and situations in this book from other books of the Bible?
		3. DOES THE BOOK TALK ABOUT SITUATIONS/CONCEPTS THAT ARE TRULY COMPARABLE TO OUR LIVES TODAY?
	7. Compare the context of the book/segment with your society's current circumstances. Describe what circumstances are genuinely comparable, and what circumstances are significantly different.	a. Universal principles are handled consistently throughout the Bible, go beyond the surface of things, and still apply today. What universal principles of godliness do you find?

8. Describe how your behavior measures up to God's expectations, as revealed in the text being studied.	b. What are your life comparables? What is God trying to convey *to you* through the book, today?
	4. HOW DO YOU PLAN TO CHANGE WITH GOD'S HELP?
9. Ask the Holy Spirit to tell you how to respond to the Bible passage. Plan specific steps (e.g., times, actions). Schedule them on your calendar.	a. What specific changes will you make with God's help to follow the universal principles of godliness?
10. Share what you've learned with someone, and ask them to hold you accountable to your plan.	b. Who will you invite to hold you accountable to your plan for change?

NOTES

Chapter 1: Find Complete Joy

1. The Barna Group, "People's Faith Flavor Influences How They See Themselves," August 26, 2002, http://www.barna.org/FlexPage.aspx?Page=BarnaUpdate&BarnaUpdateID=119.

2. Gallup Poll News Service, "How Are American Christians Living Their Faith? Part II," Washington, D.C.: September 2, 2003, http://www.gallup.com/poll/9172/How-American-Christians-Living-Their-Faith-Part.aspx.

3. Ibid.

4. Ibid.

5. The Barna Group, "Surprisingly Few Adults Outside of Christianity Have Positive Views of Christians," December 3, 2002, http://www.barna.org/FlexPage.aspx?Page=BarnaUpdate&BarnaUpdateID=127.

6. David Kinnaman and Gabe Lyons, *UnChristian: What a New Generation Really Thinks About Christianity . . . and Why It Matters* (Grand Rapids: Baker, 2007), 27.

7. Dr. Bruce Wilkson puts it this way: "You see, God chooses to reward because it is an expression of His own generous nature. His plan to reward, like His provision to save, is a display of His amazing grace. And there's no other way to think about it. The Bible says if you want to please God, you *must* believe that 'He is,' but you also *must* believe something else. That your God 'is a rewarder.'" Bruce Wilkinson, *A Life God Rewards: Why Everything You Do Today Matters Forever* (Sisters, OR: Multnomah, 2002), 42–43.

Chapter 2: More Costly Than Gold

1. Some theologians have concluded that the Lost Commandment is essentially a restatement of the Golden Rule, in part based on their reading of John's epistles. In 1 John 2:7–8, the apostle wrote: "Dear friends, I am not writing you a new command but an old one, which you have had since the beginning. This old command is the message you have heard. Yet I am writing you a new command; its truth is seen in him and you, because the darkness is passing and the true light is already shining." (See also 2 John 5.) These theologians understand "new command" to refer to the Lost Commandment, and "old command" to refer to the Golden Rule. They believe that "the beginning" refers to the time of the giving of the Law to Israel.

I agree that John's reference to a "new command" is to the Lost Commandment, even though the command is not repeated word for word. The theme of 1 John is that under the new command, we must walk as Jesus did (1:6) by loving as Jesus did (3:23), because Jesus first loved us (4:19). But I also think that John was talking about the Lost Commandment when he referred to the "old command." Why do I think so?

First, concluding that the Lost Commandment essentially restates the Golden Rule flatly contradicts Jesus' statement that the command was new (John 13:34), as well as John's affirmation that John was writing a new command (1 John 2:8). Second, "the beginning," as used in 1 and 2 John, does not refer to the time of the giving of the Law, but rather the time when the apostles first followed Jesus. John begins 1 John by saying, "That which was from the beginning, *which we have heard, which we have seen with our eyes, which we have looked at and our hands have touched*—this we proclaim concerning the Word of life" (1:1, emphasis added). From the beginning of his earthly life, Jesus *demonstrated* the Lost Commandment to his disciples; he then *stated* it at the Last Supper.

So in what sense is the Lost Commandment old, according to John's epistles? In the sense that Jesus demonstrated and proclaimed the Lost Commandment long before John wrote his epistles. First John is difficult to date, but we can reasonably say it was written somewhere between A.D. 85 and 95—about sixty years after the Lost Commandment was given.

Today, we can still say that the Lost Commandment is both new and old. It was new when it was given at the Last Supper. It remains new to those of us who are just now realizing its significance. But it's also almost two thousand years old.

2. Walter Bauer, "χαινός," *A Greek-English Lexicon of the New Testament and Other Early Christian Literature*, ed. and rev. by Frederick William Danker, 3rd edition (Chicago: University of Chicago Press, 2000), 497. However, the lexicon defines the word translated *new* in John 13:34 as "pertaining to being not previously present, unknown, strange, remarkable." At a minimum, this definition indicates that the new commandment was noticeably different from the Golden Rule. For the reasons explained in chapter 2, I think the definition that I have quoted from Bauer more accurately defines "new" in John 13:34.

3. "This was the thick and gorgeously-worked veil which was hung between the 'holy place' and the 'holiest of all,' shutting out all access to the presence of God as manifested 'from above the mercy-seat and from between the cherubim:'—'the Holy Spirit this [*sic*] signifying, that the way into the holiest of all was not yet made manifest' (Heb. 9:8). Into this holiest of all none might enter, not even the high priest, except once a year, on the great day of atonement, and then only with the blood of atonement in his hands, which he sprinkled 'upon and before the mercy-seat seven times' (Lev. 16:14)—to signify that access for sinners to a holy God is only through atoning blood." Robert Jamieson, A. R. Faucet, and David Brown, *A Commentary: A Commentary Critical, Experimental, and Practical on the Old and New Testaments* (1877, 1993), in PC Study Bible, version V4.3C for Windows (Seattle: Biblesoft, Inc., 1988–2006), commentary on Matthew 27:51.

4. M. G. Easton, *Illustrated Bible Dictionary* (3rd ed., 1903), in PC Study Bible, version V4.3C for Windows (Seattle: Biblesoft, Inc., 1988–2006), s.v. *Salome*. This is a reasonable inference based on a comparison of the Gospel accounts. Matthew's gospel says that John's mother ("the mother of Zebedee's sons") was present at the crucifixion (Matt. 27:56). John's gospel says

that Mary's sister was at the crucifixion (John 19:25). Mark's gospel says that a woman named Salome was at the crucifixion (Mark 15:40) and brought spices to Jesus' tomb after his death so that he could be anointed (Mark 16:1). A reasonable inference can be drawn from these accounts that Salome was Mary's sister and John's mother.

We also know that Mary and Elizabeth, the mother of John the Baptist, were related (Luke 1:36). Mary was from the tribe of Judah, and Elizabeth was from the tribe of Levi, but Jewish law permitted Levites to intermarry with other tribes of Israel. Robert Jamieson, A. R. Faucet, and David Brown, *A Commentary Critical, Experimental, and Practical on the Old and New Testaments* (1877, 1993), in PC Study Bible, version V4.3C for Windows (Seattle: Biblesoft, Inc., 1988–2006), commentary on Luke 1:36.

5. Before Jesus' earthly ministry, Rabbi Hillel said, "Do not do to others what you would not want them to do to you; that is the entire Law, and all else is interpretation." *UBS New Testament Handbook Series.* Copyright © 1961–1997, by United Bible Societies, in PC Study Bible, version V4.3C for Windows (Seattle: Biblesoft, Inc., 1988–2006), commentary on Matthew 7:12.

6. Text note, Matthew 7:12, *NIV Study Bible* (Grand Rapids: Zondervan, 1985).

Chapter 3: RSVP

1. October 28, 1949, entry in the journals of P. James Elliot, Wheaton College, Billy Graham Center Archives, Collection 277, Box 1, Folder 8, Wheaton, Illinois. The entry can be viewed in Mr. Elliot's own handwriting at http://www.wheaton.edu/bgc/archives/faq/20.htm.

2. The significance and practice of baptism has been passionately debated within the Christian family. Some of us believe that baptism is a sacrament performed on infants, to signify God's covenant with his elect people. Some of us believe that baptism is required for eternal salvation. Some of us believe that it is merely symbolic of our profession of faith— though commanded—and as such must be performed after our decision to follow Jesus as Lord. In spite of these differences of opinion, I believe that God considers all of us to be members of his Christian family. For a good book on baptism, see Donald Bridge and David Phypers, *The Water That Divides: Two Views of Baptism Explored* (Fearn, Tain, Scotland, UK: Christian Focus Publications, 2008).

Chapter 4: Enjoy Your New Self

1. Jay McSwain, *Finding Your PLACE in Ministry: Participant Guide and Assessment Tool* (Alpharetta, GA: MDC Today, 2000), 1. Contact Place Ministries at http://www.placeministries.org.

Chapter 5: Shadow the Real VIP

1. *The West Wing*, created by Aaron Sorkin (Burbank, CA: John Wells Production, 1999–2006).

Chapter 6: No Mission Impossible

1. *Mission Impossible*, created by Bruce Geller (Los Angeles: Desilu Productions, 1966–1973).
2. *Pay It Forward*, DVD, directed by Mimi Leder (Burbank, CA: Warner Bros. Pictures and Bel Air Entertainment, 2000).
3. Scene 10, "That's the idea," ibid.
4. Scene 25, "Save *my* life," ibid.
5. Scene 30, "Forgiveness," ibid.

Chapter 8: No One Died and Made Us King!

1. "'Abba' is the word framed by the lips of infants, and betokens unreasoning trust; 'father' expresses an intelligent apprehension of the relationship. The two together express the love and intelligent confidence of the child." W. E. Vine, *Vine's Expository Dictionary of Biblical Words* (1985), in PC Study Bible, version V4.3C for Windows (Seattle: Biblesoft, Inc., 1988–2006), s.v. "*abba*" (Strong's word number 5).
2. Adam Clarke, *Clarke's Commentary* (1810–1826), in PC Study Bible, version V4.3C for Windows (Seattle: Biblesoft, Inc., 1988–2006), commentary on Mark 14:36.
3. W. E. Vine, *Vine's Expository Dictionary of Biblical Words* (1985), in PC Study Bible, version V4.3C for Windows (Seattle: Biblesoft, Inc., 1988–2006), s.v. "father" (*pater*, Strong's word number 3962).

Chapter 9: The Last Come First

1. W. E. Vine, *Vine's Expository Dictionary of Biblical Words* (1985), in PC Study Bible, version V4.3C for Windows (Seattle: Biblesoft, Inc., 1988–2006), s.v. "submit" (*hupotasso*, Strong's word number 5293).

Chapter 10: Love Letters from God

1. Gallup Poll News Service, "How Are American Christians Living Their Faith?" Washington, D.C., August 19, 2003, http://www.gallup.com/poll/9088/How-American-Christians-Living-Their-Faith.aspx.
2. The Barna Group, "Americans Are Most Likely to Base Truth on Feelings," February 12, 2002, http://www.barna.org/FlexPage.aspx?Page=BarnaUpdate&BarnaUpdateID=106.
3. Henry T. Blackaby and Claude V. King, *Experiencing God: Knowing and Doing the Will of God* (Nashville: LifeWay Press, 2004), 73.
4. Lewis described his conversion this way: "In the Trinity Term of 1929 I gave in, and admitted that God was God, and knelt and prayed: perhaps, that night, the most dejected and reluctant convert in all England. I did not

then see what is now the most shining and obvious thing; the Divine humility which will accept a convert even on such terms." C. S. Lewis, *Surprised by Joy* (Orlando: Harcourt Brace & Company, 1955), 221.

Chapter 11: Ask and It's Yours

1. W. E. Vine, *Vine's Expository Dictionary of Biblical Words* (1985), in PC Study Bible, version V4.3C for Windows (Seattle: Biblesoft, Inc., 1988–2006), s.v. "name" (*onoma*, Strong's word number 3686).

Chapter 12: Show Them How It's Done!

1. W. E. Vine, *Vine's Expository Dictionary of Biblical Words* (1985), in PC Study Bible, version V4.3C for Windows (Seattle: Biblesoft, Inc., 1988–2006), s.v. "apostle" (*apostolos*, Strong's word number 652).

2. Ibid., s.v. "disciple" (*mathetes*, Strong's word number 3101).

Chapter 13: Let It Go

1. Gallup Poll News Service, "How Are American Christians Living Their Faith? Part II," Washington, D.C.: September 2, 2003, http://www.gallup.com/poll/9172/How-American-Christians-Living-Their-Faith-Part.aspx.

2. W. E. Vine, *Vine's Expository Dictionary of Biblical Words* (1985), in PC Study Bible, version V4.3C for Windows (Seattle: Biblesoft, Inc., 1988–2006), s.v. "heart" (*kardia*, Strong's word number 2588).

3. Ibid., s.v. "forgive, forgave, forgiveness" (*aphiemi*, Strong's word number 863).

4. Ibid.

5. Ibid., s.v. "forgive, forgave, forgiveness" (*charizomai*, Strong's word number 5483).

6. Francis A. Schaeffer, *The Mark of the Christian* (Downer's Grove, IL: InterVarsity Press, 1970), 31–33.

7. Ibid., 32.

8. Ibid., 33.

Chapter 14: Get It Together

1. W. E. Vine, *Vine's Expository Dictionary of Biblical Words* (1985), in PC Study Bible, version V4.3C for Windows (Seattle: Biblesoft, Inc., 1988–2006), s.v. "reconcile, reconciliation" (*katallasso*, Strong's word number 2644).

2. William Barclay, *The Gospel of Matthew*, vol. 1, rev. ed. (Philadelphia: Westminster Press, 1975), 143.

3. Ibid.

4. Ibid.

Chapter 15: Shuttle Diplomacy

1. I am using the term "peacemaker" to mean someone who helps others to resolve *their* dispute, rather than someone who tries to resolve *his or her own* dispute. In either case, though, God obviously wants us all to work toward restoring peace within relationships.

Chapter 16: Feet and Hands

1. James Orr, *International Standard Bible Encyclopaedia* (1915, 1995–1996, and 2003), in PC Study Bible, version V4.3C for Windows (Seattle: Biblesoft, Inc., 1988–2006), s.v. "washing of feet."

2. Mother Teresa of Calcutta, *My Life for the Poor* (New York: Ballantine, 1987), 102.

Chapter 17: Dollars and Sense

1. Adam Clarke, *Clarke's Commentary* (1810–1826), in PC Study Bible, version V4.3C for Windows (Seattle: Biblesoft, Inc., 1988–2006), commentary on Matthew 19:24.

2. W. E. Vine, *Vine's Expository Dictionary of Biblical Words* (1985), in PC Study Bible, version V4.3C for Windows (Seattle: Biblesoft, Inc., 1988–2006), s.v. "compassion, compassionate" (*splanchnizomai*, Strong's word number 4697).

3. For example, here is the mission statement for the Evangelical Council for Financial Accountability: "ECFA is committed to helping Christ-centered organizations earn the public's trust through developing and maintaining standards of accountability that convey God-honoring ethical practices" (http://www.ecfa.org/Content.aspx?PageName=MissionStatement).